Protect Your Privacy on the Internet

Bryan Pfaffenberger

WILEY COMPUTER PUBLISHING

John Wiley & Sons, Inc.

New York ▲ Chichester ▲ Weinheim ▲ Brisbane ▲ Singapore ▲ Toronto

Executive Publisher: Katherine Schowalter
Editor: Tim Ryan
Assistant Editor: Pam Sobotka
Managing Editor: Erin Singletary
Electronic Products, Associate Editor: Mike Green
Composition: Impressions Book and Journal Services, Inc.
Text Design: Jane Tenenbaum Design

Library of Congress Cataloging-in-Publication Data:

Pfaffenberger, Bryan, 1949–
    Protect your privacy on the Internet / Bryan Pfaffenberger.
      p. cm.
    Includes index.
    ISBN 0-471-18143-9 (paper/CD)
    1. Internet (Computer network)—Security measures.   2. Computer
security.   I. Title.
TK5105.875.I57P4835   1997
005.8—dc21   96-30073
                                                       CIP

Printed in the United States of America
10 9 8 7 6 5 4 3 2 1

For Suzanne, always

Contents

Acknowledgments

Writing a book such as this one is never a solitary job, and I'd like to thank everyone who's helped to make this book a readable and useful tool, including Tim Ryan (Acquisitions Editor) and Pam Sobotka (Assistant Editor), Erin Singletary (Associate Editor) and Mike Green (Associate Editor). Very special thanks go to the shareware and freeware authors who provided software for this book's CD-ROM, which—as you'll find—is full of Windows programs that are indispensable for your privacy while you're using the Internet. Please be sure to register your programs when the evaluation period has expired—and help keep the shareware concept alive.

Your Digital DNA

You're a typical Internet user. According to CommerceNet and Nielsen Media Research, that means you spend about 5 hours and 28 minutes per week surfing the Web, exchanging e-mail with others, discussing important matters in mailing lists—and ranting and raving in Usenet newsgroups or mailing lists (Steinert-Threlkeld 1995). You're having a blast, and your TV and VCR just aren't getting the attention they used to get.

I'm sure you'd agree that the Internet is useful and fun. But what you might not realize is that you're leaving a trail behind you. It's a digital signature, a record of what you've done and said while you've been online—what you searched for in search engines, which sites you visited during late-night surf sessions, what you said in e-mail messages, which pages you looked at, which files you downloaded to your computer. This digital signature exists on backup tapes that might be kept for years, and in databases that are actively repackaged and sold.

Let's call it your *digital DNA.*

What's in Your Digital DNA

Find out for yourself.

If you have access to a Web browser, go to the Center for Democracy and Technology's Snoop Page (http://www.13x.com/cgi-bin/cdt/snoop.pl), shown in Figure I.1. Like many pages on the Web, this one is set up to

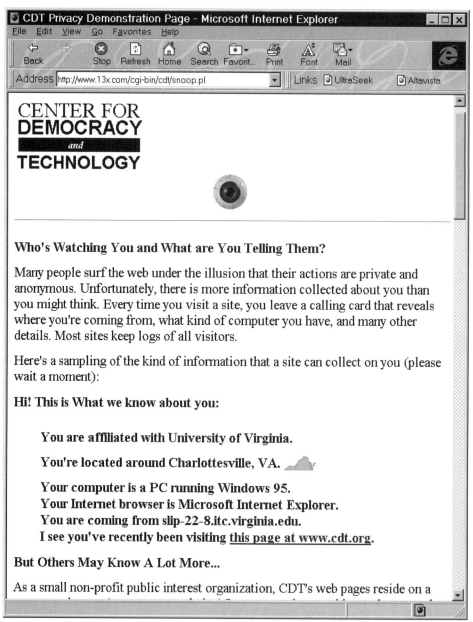

FIGURE I.1   The Center for Democracy and Technology's snoop page knows a lot about you.

snoop on you, but at least it tells you what it finds! The information obtained includes your organization, the Internet address of the computer you're using, the type of computer and the operating system you're running, and—potentially—your e-mail address.

Did you see your e-mail address on the Snoop Page? Good lesson, huh? Most people surfing the Web think that they're doing so in complete anonymity. But a number of tricks can be used to learn your identity while you're visiting a Web site.

One of the easiest works like this. There's a graphic on the page, and it looks like any other graphic. Unbeknownst to you, though, this graphic is set up so that your browser doesn't retrieve it using the normal Web methods. Instead, your browser is directed to retrieve the graphic using *anonymous FTP*, an Internet service that enables users to retrieve files from public data archives. Generally, you log on to anonymous FTP services by supplying the user name "anonymous," followed by your e-mail address as your password. Obligingly, browsers are set up to supply your e-mail address automatically when an anonymous FTP server demands it. (This isn't true of the latest Netscape and Microsoft browsers, however.) In this trick, the server demands your e-mail address before it will let the browser download the graphic, and a *script* (a miniprogram) sends it to the server's database. With a little subsequent work in e-mail databases such as Bigfoot (http://www.bigfoot.com), you can match the e-mail address with a name (see Figure I.2).

Let's find out some more about this Mr. Pfaffenberger, okay? Phone number and address, maybe? Switchboard (http://www3.switchboard.com/) can do the trick (see Figure I.3). And how about an author profile of his Usenet postings? Deja News's Author Profile (http://www.dejanews.com) (see Figure I.4) tells us that this individual posted 27 articles to Usenet between March, 1995 and June, 1996. (Dejanews has plans to archive Usenet newsgroups all the way back to the network's founding in 1979.) Judging from the newsgroups to which he contributed, it would appear that he likes Japanese animation (anime), is seriously into sailing, uses Adobe Photoshop, and has trouble with Microsoft Windows—and that he's worried about his privacy (I wonder why?).

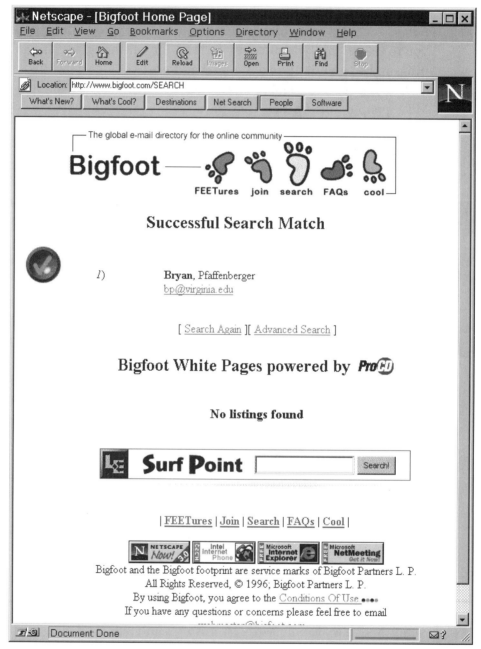

FIGURE I.2   Bigfoot is one of several Web databases that can give you the name of a person using an e-mail address.

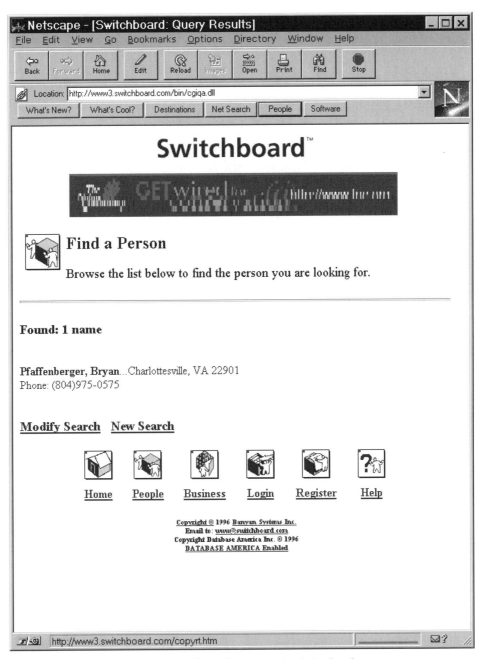

FIGURE I.3   If your number is listed, you're in this database.

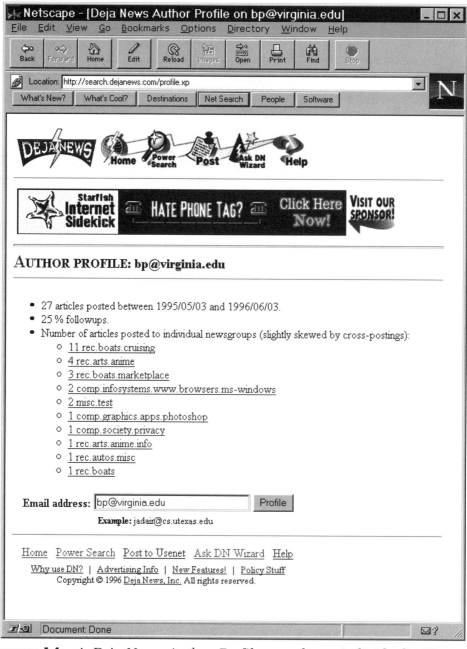

FIGURE I.4   A Deja News Author Profile reveals an individual's Usenet posting proclivities.

Have a Cookie, Mister?

What you've just seen is trivial from a technical angle. Driven by marketing firms and some pretty serious technology, Web programmers have figured out ways to learn much, much more about you.

A little-known capability of most Web browsers, called *cookies*, enables Web servers to deposit information on your own hard drive. This information can include a user ID that, when coupled with increasingly sophisticated backtracking capabilities, can link your Web surfing predilections with your e-mail address (and from there, as you've learned, it's pretty easy to learn your name, home address, and much more). Several companies are busily compiling this data into marketing databases. Without your consent and knowledge, they're compiling minutely detailed information about your Internet use, including the search terms you've typed into search engines, the Web sites you've visited, the pages you've viewed, and the files you've downloaded.

Is Your Boss Reading Your E-Mail?

Millions of business and professional computer users send e-mail messages every day—in fact, according to an article in the *New York Times* (February 5, 1995: p. 10), corporate usage of e-mail is experiencing exponential growth. But if you think you can expect privacy when you exchange e-mail with someone, you may be sadly mistaken. Most companies believe that, since they own the computers employees use, employees do not have a reasonable expectation that their communications are private. Nevertheless, fewer than one in five companies spell this out, and more than a few people have lost their jobs after making negative comments about their companies via e-mail—only to discover later that their bosses were snooping on their communications!

Think about it. Would you like everything you've said via e-mail to wind up on your boss's desk?

Maybe it has. According to a *MacWorld* survey of 301 businesses (Piller 1993), 22 percent searched the e-mail, voice mail, computer files, or other networking communications of their employees. The bigger the company, the more likely it is that snooping is practiced routinely, the survey disclosed.

If you've been using e-mail for awhile, your digital DNA is extensive. Why? In most organizations, backup tapes are routinely made for security purposes, and these may be retained for *years*. No law prevents your employer, or any other person armed with a subpoena, to obtain these tapes and ransack them for ill-considered remarks you may have made—remarks that you thought were private.

But I Have Nothing to Hide!

Yes, you do. Everyone does. Your personal affairs just aren't anyone else's business. Andre Bacard, author of *Computer Privacy Handbook* (1995a), puts it this way:

> Show me an e-mail user who has no financial, sexual, social, political, or professional secrets to keep from his family, his neighbors, or his colleagues, and I'll show you someone who is either an incredible exhibitionist or an incredible dullard. Show me a corporation that has no trade secrets or confidential records, and I'll show you a business that is not very successful (Bacard 1995b).

Not convinced? Consider this. According to 1994 statistics (cited in Privacy Rights Clearinghouse 1996a), over one million Americans have been stalked. And these aren't just celebrities. Most are women who are being stalked and threatened by ex-boyfriends and former husbands. Some stalkers are ex-employees who can't get over losing a job. From the Internet, a stalker could learn not only your current telephone number and address, but also intimate details about your life—perhaps enough to put together a profile of your daily activities.

Privacy is perhaps the most fundamental of all liberties. It's the right to be left undisturbed. The right to live and work without being constantly and unnecessarily monitored. The right not to have one's personal information exploited without consent.

To be sure, the U.S. government consistently maintains that Internet privacy must be curtailed so that government investigators can detect illegal activities, such as terrorism, drug dealing, and pornography-peddling. But this is a very dangerous argument. Suppose the government were to tell you that you cannot lock your home because there is very high possibility, as statistics attest, that illegal activities will occur within it! The simple truth is that this argument lays the foundation for totalitarianism—a state in which every citizen's private affairs are available for government scrutiny. When a peacetime government says that we must give up our basic liberties in order to deal with out-of-control crime problems, the solution is not to give in to this, but rather to replace the incompetent government with one that is better suited to dealing with the basic causes of criminal activity.

History teaches a very good lesson about liberty. If you don't defend it, you lose it.

Database America: Nowhere to Run, Nowhere to Hide

A mailing list company called Database America has embarked on an ambitious project: To collect the names, addresses, and telephone numbers of Americans from every possible source, including Internet postings, publicly available records, credit reports, returned warranty cards, software registration cards. And it's doing pretty well: Already, the company has 175 million records.

In 1996, Yahoo!, one of the Web's premiere search services, incorporated a link to Database America's People Finder service—but it wasn't received with universal praise. Many Yahoo! users were shocked to find that the service quickly retrieved their unlisted telephone numbers and addresses. Santa Clara County District Attorney George Kennedy was one of them. "A lot of people hate me and a lot of people would like to kill me, so of course I'm uncomfortable with that," Kennedy told a reporter (Anonymous 1996). The county's Sheriff, Charles Gillingham, concurred. "Now if you go to a bank or you go to Sears and ask them to fix your washer or dryer, [your unlisted telephone number and address] are going to be on the Internet" (cited in Rae-Dupree 1996).

A Database America spokesman insisted that the unlisted numbers had gotten into the database "by mistake." After a public outcry, Yahoo! insisted that Database America remove the unlisted numbers, reducing the size of the database from 175 million to 90 million records.

But the technology's there to create an all-knowing database. After the hue and cry dies down, chances are they'll be back—if not in Database America's People Finder, then in some other firm's database.

Snooping on a Budget

To be able to shield one's private affairs from prying eyes is one of the basic rights of civilized life. But the Internet is facilitating an unparalleled invasion into your personal affairs.

The Internet isn't the only way that snoops and stalkers can get information about you, to be sure; any competent private detective can put together a reasonably good profile of any U.S. or Canadian citizen for a fee of, say, $500.

What's new about the Internet is that it greatly reduces the cost of prying into other people's affairs. In fact, in many cases, it reduces the cost to zero (see the sidebar, "I'm very interested in you and the things that you've done").

But Isn't This Just Paranoia?

Not if you put it into perspective.

Much existing privacy legislation—what little there is—focuses on preventing governments from snooping on citizens. As University of Virginia sociologist Mark Shields observes, however, this legislation harkens back to a time when only the state possessed the resources and power required to pry into individuals' affairs. "The greatest threat to privacy right now isn't necessarily from the government," Shields observes, although one would do well to remember the Communist witchhunts during the 1950s. "It's from businesses and private citizens. Existing laws leave us practically helpless against private-sector snooping."

Still, there's a threat from government agencies—a very real one. Specifically, these cash-strapped agencies would love to package up information about you and sell it to the highest bidder (Anthes and Blodgett 1996). And who's buying? Your neighbors, your employer, your rivals at work, or maybe just somebody fascinated with your personal affairs.

As the cartoon character Pogo said, "We have met the enemy, and he is us."

A Historical Inevitability?

You may be amazed to hear this, but direct marketing zealots believe they have a right to collect information about you and sell it. They say it's their right to commercial free speech. They feel that any attempt to restrict or violate their snooping activities violates their First Amendment rights. If you

I'm Very Interested in You and the Things You've Done

It sounds innocent enough at first. John Kaufmann, a San Francisco-based writer, posted an ad on a local computer bulletin board for a program he wanted to sell. A woman called and later bought the program. The next day, the woman sent an e-mail message to Kaufmann, stating that she had done a search of Usenet and that she was very interested in Kaufmann and the things he had done. What really upset Kaufmann, however, was a three-page letter that he received subsequently—a letter that amounted to a nearly complete biography. "When this thing flashed on the screen," Kaufmann told a newspaper reporter (Weise 1996), "my mouth dropped open. . . . She's pieced together the puzzle of my life from Usenet," he concluded. "She knows my mother was a concert pianist. She knows what I wanted to be when I was growing up. . . . Here was a total stranger who knew my cat's name."

don't believe this, take a look at articles in *Direct Marketing*, the industry's trade journal. In a 1994 article in this journal, Robert Posch reflects that there's not much to be served by "pretending to placate the privacy forces with PR." Instead, he calls on direct marketers to assert their rights to commercial free speech, which have been much strengthened by recent decisions of the Supreme Court.

But in the end, Posch believes it won't matter, thanks to technology. "In two years," Posch argues, "technology will have moved beyond the recall of the privacy types. All privacy attacks will be upon an information industry too big to be defeated or thwarted from the historical inevitability of a new society built on this new economy. Our opponents' arguments will be so irrelevant that they will be ignored. . . . We are winning and we shall continue to do so."

What Can I Do?

This book is dedicated to proving Posch wrong, at least with respect to the Internet. There's one little thing he forgot: Ordinary people, like you and me, can learn to use technology to protect themselves from unwanted snooping. If the government won't help us—a government that is increasingly bought and sold by lobbyists working against the interests of ordinary people—we can darned well help ourselves.

But how? This book has the answers.

▶ **By following this book's step-by-step procedures, stop adding to your digital DNA**—This doesn't mean that you'll be out of the clickstream. It just means that you'll defend yourself against unwarranted snooping at each and every turn. In Part I, "Privacy Defense Strategies You Can Use Right Now," you learn how to stop adding to your digital DNA in just of couple of hours of work online, using the resources you've already got on your system.

▶ **Arm yourself with technology**—It's being used against you. Why not use it for you? In Part II, "Get Technology on Your Side," you learn how easy it is to use industrial-strength encryption tools to keep your affairs secret, the way they ought to be. Although this may conjure up images of difficult-to-use programs known only to hackers, the reality differs. On this book's CD-ROM disk (and also on the Internet), you'll find many easy-to-use Windows programs that can help you defend your right to privacy. This book discusses more than a dozen of them in detail.

▶ **Become part of the solution**—Several organizations are working hard on your behalf, as are a few civic-minded legislators (a rare species). In Appendix B, you learn how to help them.

From Here

Get started right now. Fire up your computer, log on to the Internet, and flip to Chapter 1, "Creating a Bulletproof Password." If someone can guess your password, they can read your e-mail, access your files, and do quite a bit of damage to your reputation!

A Word From the Author

The pages to follow introduce practical, easy-to-use strategies for protecting your privacy while using the Internet. But let me stress one important point. To use this book, you don't have to be a computer hacker or "cypher-punk" (a computer hacker who advocates and uses military-strength en-cryption for all online communication). This book is designed for *any* In-ternet user who would like to maintain a lower profile online—and, in so doing, gain some measure of protection from unwarranted snooping by the likes of abusive employers, envious co-workers, intrusive marketers, or stalkers. In Part I, you learn privacy-defense strategies that you can apply right now, just by using the Internet software that's already installed on your system. In Part II, you learn how to make full use of the Windows 95 software that's included on this book's CD-ROM. This software is easy to use, even if you're still an Internet or Windows novice.

References

Anonymous. 1996. "Privacy advocates didn't say 'Yahoo!'" *Web Review*, April 27–29. Online document: (http://webreview.com/96/04/29/news/index.html).

Anthes, Gary H., and Mindy Blodgett, 1996. "States eye online revenues: De-bate rages over who can see what and for how much." *Computerworld* 30 (August 19, 1996), p. 26.

Bacard, Andre. 1995a. *Computer Privacy Handbook: A Practical Guide to E-Mail Encryption, Data Protection, and PGP Privacy Software* (Berkeley, CA: Peachpit Press).

Bacard, Andre. 1995b. Frequently asked questions about e-mail privacy. On-line document: (http://www.rewi.hu-berlin-de/Datenschutz/EMail/MailPri-vacy-FAQ).

Piller, Charles. 1993. "Bosses with X-Ray Eyes: Your employer may be using computers to keep tabs on you." *Macworld* 10 (July 1993), pp. 118–124.

Posch, Robert. 1994. "Commercial Free Speech: Real Wins, Not PR." *Direct Marketing* 56 (January 1994), pp. 74–78.

Rae-Dupree, Janet. 1996. "Unlisted addresses removed from Net for privacy reasons." *San Jose Mercury News* (April 25, 1996). Online document: http://199.182.54.35/news/nation/priva424.htm.

Steinert-Threlkeld, Tom. 1995. "Internet usage begins to match VCR." *Interac-tive Week* (October 31, 1995). Online document: (http://www.zdnet.com/intweek/daily/951031g.html).

Weise, Elizabeth. 1996. "Powerful new search tools on Internet mean end to perceived privacy." Online document: (http://www.htimes.com/today/columns/private.html).

PART I

Privacy Defense Strategies You Can Use Right Now

Create a Bulletproof Password

Nothing's more valuable than your name and reputation. But using an Internet-linked computer might pose risks to both. Just ask Grady Blount, a professor of environmental science at Texas A&M. In October, 1994, an intruder guessed Blount's e-mail password and used Blount's account to send hideous, racist messages to some 20,000 Internet users in a four-state area. The response? Death threats and e-mail flames from more than 500 angry recipients. Blount was forced to cancel classes and move others to secret locations. "It was the digital equivalent of a drive-by shooting," Blount said.

If a computer criminal gets hold of your password, he can use it to gain access to your account, modify it for his own purposes, and use it as a launching pad for attacks on computer systems throughout the world. What's more, all these acts are committed in your name. You'll be getting plenty of e-mail, that's for sure!

Your first line of defense? A bulletproof *logon password* for your Internet and e-mail accounts. (A logon password is the password you supply to establish your connection to the Internet or to your e-mail account.) But it's a line of defense that too few employ. In an audit of British computer-using companies, a London-based consulting firm found that most users selected the names of spouses or pets, which are easy for colleagues to guess. Other favorites: "love," "sex," "genius," "hacker," and "God." According to a spokesperson for the consulting firm, "If a hacker [computer criminal] tries these, he will get through 20 percent of the time" (Cross 1986: 16).

In this chapter, you learn how to create a bulletproof password—and you'll also learn why doing so is absolutely necessary for Internet privacy.

Techniques for Creating a Bulletproof Password

First, learn what *not* to do. Then, you've got several good choices: The darned good manual method (which is actually fun, sort of), and space-age computer methods (including Web-based password generators and Random Password Generator, a Windows program that you'll find on this book's CD-ROM disc).

Don't ever use any of the following as your logon password:

► Your name or any close variation of your name—or any name at all, for that matter
► A password of fewer than eight characters
► A lazy keyboard sequence, such as QWERTY or dkdkdkdkd
► Your car make or serial number
► Your social security number
► Your medicare number
► Your user ID (login name)
► Your bank account numbers
► Any part of your address
► Your initials or any variation on them
► A date or time, however expressed
► A password you've used elsewhere or previously
► The names of spouses, friends, relatives, or pets
► A word found in an English or any other dictionary that has been converted to computer use (including legal, medical, and foreign-language dictionaries)
► A password that contains nothing but numbers or nothing but letters
► A word spelled backwards

The Darned Good Manual Method.   Think of a complete sentence, with eight words or more, that includes at least one number (or a word that sounds like a number, such as "too"). Make it sort of silly and unrelated to you personally. Don't make it something that coworkers could guess (such as, "I really love my wife Suzy.") Here are some examples (but please don't use one of these):

▶ I showed up too late for the third time in a row.
▶ Three large cats stared down the four puny dogs.
▶ Stupid computer, you take up too much room on my desk.

TIP **Don't use common phrases such as, "A stitch in time saves nine," or "A rolling stone gathers no moss."**

You're not done yet. Take the first letters of these sentences and transform anything you can into a number:

▶ isu2lft3tiar
▶ 3lcsdt4pd
▶ scytu2mromd

These are all great passwords. They'd be hard as heck to guess or predict.

Afraid you'll forget your phrase? Wait till you're alone. Then pick a phrase out of a favorite book, such as:

▶ " 'We have not a moment to lose,' said Aubrey to Maturin." Make a password out of it by taking the first letters and adding a number:
▶ whnamtlsa2m

Highlight the phrase, and *then put the book somewhere* very far away from your computer.

If you need to look it up again, you'll have no trouble finding it. But don't let anyone see you do this!

TIP **If your service provider's computer uses *case-sensitive* passwords, in which capitalization matters, you can add an additional level of security by capitalizing some of the letters (whnaMtLsa2M).**

Web-Based Password Generators.   You'll find a number of password generators on the Net. The best of them rely on randomization techniques to produce a truly uncrackable passphrase.

What's so great about randomization? Plenty. Computer criminals know that most people use a pattern of some sort to create a password—an English word, a commonly used phrase, a series of characters on the keyboard. By selecting letters and numbers randomly, a computer program can generate a truly bulletproof password. The best password-cracking programs now available would have to run for weeks to guess a truly random password.

Here's a list of sites that use randomization techniques to help you generate a good password:

▶ **Password Generator** (http://www.netone.com/cgi-bin/makepass)—This page generates five passwords that you can use. It's simple and straightforward.

▶ **Password Generator** (http://www.lilli.com/gpw.html)—This page uses a Java applet to create ten "pronounceable" passwords, using an algorithm originally developed by a Mitre Corporation computer scientist. (If you've turned off Java, as recommended elsewhere in this book, you'll need to turn it back on temporarily so you can run this program).

▶ **PassGen: A Password Generator Java Applet** (http://world.std.com/~reinhold/passgen.html)—This Java applet uses variations in your typing speed to generate a random passphrase (Williams 1996), a lengthy and virtually uncrackable password of up to 100 characters in length (see Figure 1.1).

▶ **The Diceware Passphrase Home Page** (http://world.std.com/~reinhold/diceware.html)—This page shows you how to get the ultimate in passphrase security. It uses a rather involved and time-consuming password-generation process that employs real dice. The result: You get a truly random passphrase. This is only for spies and the genuinely paranoid!

Random Password Generator.   You can also use the Random Password Generator, a program included on this book's CD-ROM. Created by Hirtle Software, this program enables you to select the permissible characters (lowercase letters, uppercase letters, punctuation, spaces, and numbers). Relying on a randomization technique, this program produces passwords that are truly random and therefore uncrackable by password-guessing

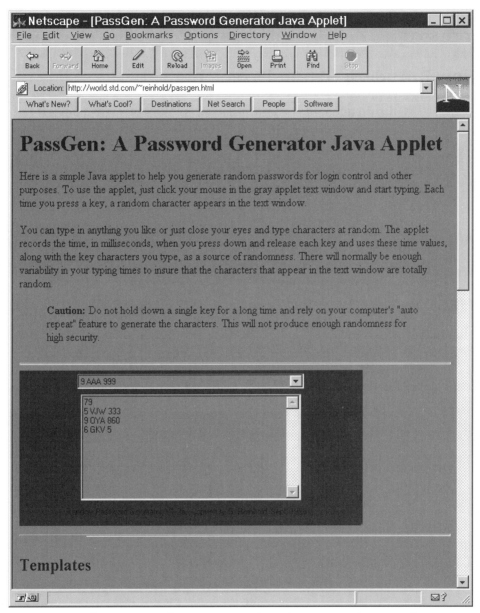

FIGURE 1.1 This Java applet uses variations in your typing speed to generate a random passphrase.

programs. For more information on Random Password Generator, see Chapter 9.

How Intruders Obtain Passwords

Why make such a fuss about passwords? Why torment yourself with entering a lengthy series of difficult-to-remember characters every time you log on to the Internet? Simple: Computer criminals are constantly trying to break into Internet-linked computer systems, and your password is the ticket they need.

Peeking and Stealing.   People do the dumbest things with their passwords—like writing them down on Post-It notes and sticking them on the wall next to their computer systems.

TIP Memorize your password—and don't write it down where it could be found by coworkers or friends!

Computer Security's SWAT Team

In 1988, a computer science graduate student unleashed an "experimental" program that got out of control. Wending its way throughout the Internet, it duplicated itself relentlessly, causing computer after computer to bog down and crash. Computer system administrators didn't know where to turn for help—and e-mail warnings about the program crashed along with the rest of the Net. Dubbed the "Internet worm," this rogue program convinced Internet administrators that some sort of central security agency was needed. In November, 1988, the Defense Advanced Research Projects Agency (DARPA) founded the Computer Emergency Response Team (CERT), which is housed at Carnegie-Mellon University. CERT serves as a central clearinghouse for information about computer security violations. It issues regular advisories and develops fixes for detected security shortcomings.

CERT's been busy. In 1995, the team logged 2,412 serious computer security incidents, most of which involved attempts at unauthorized com-

(continued)

Never give your password to anyone else; they might unthinkingly "lend" it to a third party, and then it's out of your control. Some of the worst security abuses in Net history stem from college students who unthinkingly lent their passwords to a "friend," who subsequently left it lying around in a computer lab (or, worse, posted it to Usenet). If you're using a computer in a public lab, make sure no one is watching when you type in your password.

Dumpster diving is a variation on the peeking-and-stealing theme. Computer criminals know that companies and individuals throw away all kinds of sensitive information, some of which might enable them to access computer systems (or to guess poorly crafted passwords). It's a wise organization that invests in a shredder—and uses it.

Password Sniffing.   As your Internet data makes its way from server to server, it passes through many computers. On a less-than-secure system, a computer criminal can set up a program called a *sniffer,* which examines the incoming data for passwords. Since most Internet service providers require you to send your user name and password as plain text, there's little

puter access. The means? Trying to guess someone's password, thus allowing an intruder to gain entry to the system.

What's especially scary about recent developments, according to Kathy Fithen, a CERT team leader, is that automated hacking tools are now widely available. "One of the stories we like to tell is of an intruder who used an automated tool to break into a UNIX system, gained root access, and then started issuing DOS commands because he didn't realize he had broken into a completely different kind of system," Fithen said (Duffy 1996: 1A1). This is a theme you'll see again and again throughout this book: The democratization of computer technology, and its worldwide dissemination by means of the Internet, has radically lowered the threshold of entry for a variety of computer crimes—including unauthorized computer access. Cracking computers used to be a test of prowess, a sort of rite of passage, in the hacking community. Now it doesn't take much more skill than obtaining a rogue program, finding a poorly secured system, and hitting the Enter key.

Hacker—Or Computer Criminal?

In the popular press, the term "computer criminal" conjures up images of a teenage genius who amuses himself by breaking into highly secured computer systems, and carrying out all kinds of mischief—including stealing credit-card numbers and erasing valuable data. This use of the term "computer criminal" violates long-standing traditions in the computer-using community. In this community, hacking is a problem-solving strategy that involves using clever or even devious programming tricks to solve a difficult problem.

One of the most famous hacks in the history of personal computing was Apple codesigner Stephen Wozniak's intuitively derived design for the first Apple disk controller. This design dramatically lowered the costs and complexity of the device. Computer criminals would sometimes test their skills against secure computer systems, but very much in the spirit of a game: Destroying data, or making the system unavailable for others, was strictly against the computer criminal's code of ethics (brilliantly described in Stephen Levy's *Computer Criminals* (1984)).

Those more civilized days are long gone, I'm sorry to say, and many computer intruders these days aren't after an intellectual challenge. They're after money. Here's an example: Suppose you're able to break into an insurance industry's database, and you access a list of unclaimed benefits. Probably what's happened is that someone has died but a distant relative didn't find out that he or she had been named as a beneficiary. You could then pose as a legitimate firm that would help this person obtain the benefit—for a hefty fee, of course. This isn't hacking—it's computer crime. It isn't done by computer hobbyists—it's done by computer criminals.

you can do to protect yourself from this form of attack, except to change your password regularly.

If you regularly log on to the Net by means of a telephone call directly to your service provider, you shouldn't worry too much about this particular form of privacy invasion. You should worry, however, if you're traveling and you use Telnet or a remote Internet connection to access your mail. For more information, see "More Ways to Safeguard Your Password," later in this chapter.

Password Guessing.   Using automated programs, computer criminals can search through password databases looking for a word or name—and to help them, they can make use of computerized dictionaries. These enable them to run through the entire English language, if necessary, in order to match the password of someone who used a word such as "innocuous" or "invertebrate"—words that the account owner thought no one would guess! Apparently, Grady Blount—the Texas A & M professor who was victimized by somebody posting racist mail using his password—had used an English word for his password, and that's how the imposter got into the system.

Peeking into Your System While You're Away from Your Desk.   If you're connected to the Internet at work, you're probably connected via a local area network (LAN)—and you've the luxury of staying connected all day. That's nice, but what if somebody comes into your office while you're away from your desk? Seeing that you're gone, and that you're still connected to the Internet, such a person could do all sorts of mischief—including getting your logon password.

TIP   **If you've installed Windows 95 with the Windows 95 Plus additions, you can set up a screen saver with password protection. When you're away from your computer and the screen saver kicks in, no one can access your system unless they supply the needed password.**

Here's how to turn on screen-saver password protection:

1. From the Start Menu, choose Settings, Control Panel. You'll see the Control Panel dialog box.
2. Double-click Display. You'll see the Display Properties dialog box.
3. Click the Screen Saver tab. You'll see the Screen Saver dialog box, shown in Figure 1.2.
4. Select Password Protected, and click the Change button. You'll see the Change Password dialog box, which enables you to type your screen-saver password (see Figure 1.3).
5. Click OK to save your password.
6. In the Wait area, choose the number of minutes of inactivity before the screen saver kicks in (I suggest 5 minutes).
7. Click OK to confirm your settings.

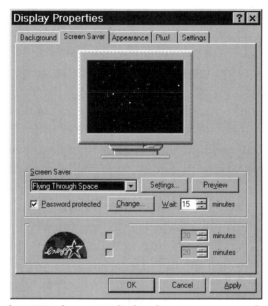

FIGURE 1.2   Use this Windows 95 dialog box to password-protect your system while you're away from your desk.

If you use a computer in a computer lab, be sure to log off before leaving the computer. A lot of damage is done when students unthinkingly leave the lab without logging off. A computer criminal or vandal lurking around the lab might just be waiting for this to happen!

Social Engineering.   It sounds official enough. You get a call from your service provider's system administrator. "Hi, this is Harry from the computer services department. While we were doing a routine system check, we found a problem with your account. We're afraid some data is corrupted. To keep you from losing files, we need to get into your account.

FIGURE 1.3   In this dialog box, you type your screen-saver password.

Can you please give me your password?" Without realizing you've done so, you're divulged your user name and password to an intruder.

"It's called *social engineering,* and it has a long tradition in the hacking community," explained computer criminal Susan Thunder at a recent DEF-CON conference (Berg 1995). Surely one of the most bizarre gatherings in computerdom, DEFCON is an annual convention that brings some of the most notorious computer criminals together face to face with "the enemy"—Secret Service agents, U.S. Customs Service representatives, FBI agents, and computer security. The objective? Learn as much as possible about each other's techniques. Apparently, both sides think it's to their advantage! "In brief," Thunder explained, "social engineering is a form of psychological subversion: You gain people's confidence, and they give you the information you need to get into an otherwise secure system."

Social engineering is common in interactive computer role-playing games, called MUDs and MOOs. While chatting with someone, you may be interrupted by an official-looking message that says something like, "Access terminated by disk read error. Please re-enter your logon name and password to continue." What you're seeing isn't an official system message; it's a scam.

TIP Don't use your logon password—the password you use to gain access to your Internet service provider's computer—as the password for a Web site. Some Web sites require you to register, and require a user name and password before you can log on (see Figure 1.4). Such sites may have very lax security—in fact, they may store user names and passwords in a text file that can be accessed and read by any moderately knowledgeable computer criminal. Pick a new logon name and password when you're registering for a Web-based service.

More Ways to Safeguard Your Password

To protect yourself from someone using your password to wreak havoc on the Internet, don't use automatic logon utilities, and change your password once per month.

Log On Manually.   Don't set up your computer to log on to the Internet without your intervention. To set up an automatic logon procedure, you

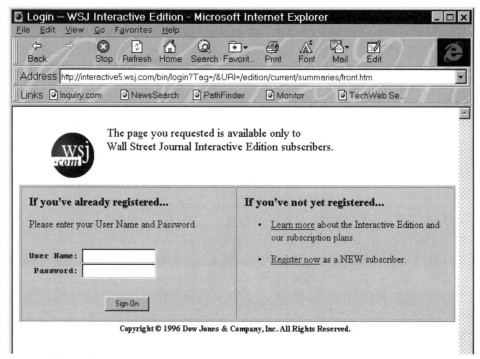

FIGURE 1.4   Don't use your logon password as the password for accessing secured Web sites.

would have to type your password somewhere in a *login script* (a mini-program that automatically handles the logon procedure by supplying your logon name and password). However, this information isn't secure from a knowledgeable intruder. Besides, someone could log on to the Net in your absence. It's a pain to type your password manually, but doing so ensures that it's present in one place only: Your head, and in the secured password file of your Internet service provider.

Change Your Password Once per Month.   Despite your best efforts to come up with an uncrackable password, you're still not quite safe. Every time you log on, you send this password in ASCII (plain) text via the network—and if someone's "listening in" using a sniffer, it could fall into the wrong hands. There's not much you can do to safeguard yourself from this type of intrusion, but you can at least change your password frequently

What You Should Do if You Forget Your Password

If you've forgotten your logon password, you'll need to call your service provider. They'll ask you lots of questions to make sure that you are actually the person you say you are. If they don't, consider changing service providers! You won't get your old password back. Instead, you'll get a new one, and this might be e-mailed to you—providing another line of protection against an imposter.

Are you the forgetful type? You might want to take a look at the demo version of Password Master, a Windows program that's on the CD-ROM disc packaged with this book. This program enables you to store your passwords in such a way that you can retrieve them with hints (for example, "stupid" would retrieve the password created from the phrase, "Stupid computer, you take up too much room on my desk" (scytu2mromd). There's just one rub, though—to safeguard your passwords, Password Master is itself password protected. And if you forget *that* password, you won't be able to access any of the other ones you've forgotten! Password Master is discussed in Chapter 9.

(say, once per month). That way, if someone's managed to get his hands on your password somehow, he'll come up short if he tries to use it.

Change Your Password Immediately after a Remote Logon.

You're walking down a street in London, not far from University College, and you run into an *Internet cafe*. "Cool," you say, and rent access to check your e-mail. You happily sip your espresso and read your e-mail. What you don't know is that, somewhere along the tenuous series of connections that link the cafe to your Internet service provider back in the States, someone's set up a sniffer—and got your password.

References

Berg, Al. "Cracking a Social Engineer: Enterprising Thieves Use a Variety of Common Techniques to Pilfer Information. *LAN Times* (November 6,

1995). Online document: (http://www.wcmh.com/lantimes/95nov/511a140a. html).

Cross, Michael. 1986. "How Fred Lets the Fraudsters In." *The Independent* (October 30, 1986), p. 16.

Duffy, Tom. 1996. "Tips to Minimize Vulnerability—Network Security: The Internet Factor." *Communications Week* (March 4, 1996), p. 1A1.

Williams, Randall T. 1996. "The passphrase FAQ" (June 16, 1996). Online document: (http://www.stack.urc.tue.nl/~galactus/remailers/passphrase-faq. html).

CHAPTER 2

Check Out Your Service Provider's Privacy Policy

Suppose you found out that the U.S. postal service routinely recorded the names and addresses of everyone to whom you sent first-class letters. Suppose, too, that they categorized these letters in a way that described your tastes—for instance, a letter to a gourmet coffee company would add the phrase "gourmet coffee" to your list of apparent interests. Then, they sold this information to direct-mail marketing firms. Finally, suppose that they kept copies of all your transactions for lengthy periods of time, enabling subpoena-armed attorneys and investigators to gain easy access to virtually all of your written communications (even those you thought you had destroyed by shredding them at home). Would you feel uncomfortable about using the postal service?

If so, you'd better think long and hard about using the Internet for anything other than casual or routine business communication, such as requesting information from a company. Here's why: The above fictitious scenario turns out to closely resemble *reality* in the world of Internet service providers. Worse, if you're connecting to the Internet via your employer's system, you had better get used to the following fact: You have no privacy at all. If you think otherwise, wake up and smell the coffee, baby.

This chapter shows you how to investigate your service provider's privacy policy. You'll learn how to get the information you need in order to evaluate this policy—and how to read it once you've gotten your hands on it. You'll also learn why every Internet user needs to take extraordinary steps, including encrypting your e-mail so that others cannot read it if you wish to prevent intruders from gaining ready access to your personal affairs.

Information about You: Up for Sale?

Advertising and marketing firms are intensely interested in what people are doing online. What sites are they visiting? How are they using the Web? Usenet? E-mail?

And who's in a better position to answer than your service provider? Your service provider's computer has a complete record of everything you've done while you've been online. The company's computers can analyze and repackage this information in an instant—and put it up for sale.

Let's imagine, for a moment, the Internet Service Provider from Hell. Let's call it "sleaze.com":

▶ This company uses information concerning your online transactions—which sites you've visited, to whom you've sent e-mail, which files you've downloaded—to construct marketing analyses of its membership. This information is sold to a third party.

▶ It collects far more information than necessary when you sign up for the service—including your income, age, gender, other consumer purchases, type of computer system owned, plans for buying additional equipment in the future, social security number, and much more. Subsequently, the company sells this information to a third party.

▶ You were never informed about this data collection activity, or given an opportunity to consent to this monitoring. You find out about it, though, because you start getting tons of junk e-mail.

▶ The service provider provides logon software "for your convenience." What you don't know is that, when you log on, this software uploads all your personal information, including income level and other personal details. This information is made available to information providers who are willing to pay fees to find out who's accessing them.

▶ Your name, e-mail address, and home telephone are available to other users of the same service provider. Even though you have an unlisted phone number, you start getting sales calls at dinner.

▶ The service provider actively monitors chat rooms. While you're "romancing" someone online, the late-night maintenance crew is watching the whole drama unfold on their monitors, laughing hysterically.

▶ The service provider indefinitely retains the contents of your e-mail even after you've downloaded and "deleted" it. You're not informed about this.

They've Got a Subpoena!

Your digital DNA—the electronic trail you've been leaving as you use the Internet—is open to anyone armed with a subpoena. Who's "anyone?" Potentially, lots of folks, including any party of a civil lawsuit; a police investigator; the Secret Service; the National Security Agency; the Drug Enforcement Agency; the Bureau of Alcohol, Tobacco, and Firearms; the FBI; a Congressional committee; and many more. Internet service providers know that they must provide this information, and they should inform you of this. Check out the small print. In MindSpring's user guide, for instance, you find the following: "In the event of a properly presented authority, MindSpring will coooperate with authorities to investigate claims of illegal activity including, but not limited to, illegal transfer or making copyrighted material available, posting e-mail containing threats of violence, or any other illegal activity."

The first e-mail bust? It's already happened. An engineer at AT&T Wireless Services discovered a CompuServe ad that offered to sell illegal cellular access devices. The Secret Service joined forces with the Drug Enforcement Agency (DEA) to tap the e-mail of the individuals who posted the ad. The result of the e-mail tap was the arrest of three persons, who were charged with conspiracy to manufacture and distribute the illegal devices. Concludes David Sobel, legal counsel of the Electronic Privacy Information Center (EPIC) in Washington, DC: "This case points out that as more and more communications are conducted through e-mail, law enforcement will have a greater interest in accessing that information" (Violino 1996).

During a divorce proceeding, your spouse's attorney finds out about your e-mail account, subpoenas your online mailbox, and discovers some correspondence with a friend—strictly Platonic—that included what you thought was some fairly innocent sexual banter. You thought those messages were long gone! You're shocked when your spouse's attorney walks into the courtroom with printouts of the document—and starts making the case that you're an adulterer and don't deserve custody of your kids.

Is your service provider like this one? You'd better find out.

Privacy Policies of the Major Online Services

To anyone who's been thinking about surveillance, the address is ironic—1634 Eye Street. But that's home ground for the Center for Democracy and Technology (CDT), a leader in raising public awareness concerning the implications of advanced technologies. Founded in December 1994, CDT is a nonprofit public interest organization that is supported by individuals, foundations, and a cross-section of the computer and communications industry.

One of CDT's most valuable online contributions is a Privacy Policy Chart for online service providers (CDT 1996). This chart explains the information practices of the major commercial online service providers, based on information available online and distributed to subscribers.

To access the Privacy Policy Chart, use the following URL:

www.cdt.org/privacy/online_services/chart.html

You can use this chart as a springboard for finding out just how your own current or prospective service provider handles privacy. Here are some of the questions you should ask:

▶ Does the service solicit unnecessary information on its application form?
▶ Does the service tell users how the collected subscription information will be used?
▶ Can you request that the service limit the internal use of subscription information for purposes other than billing and system administration?
▶ Does the service provider disclose subscription information to third parties (including direct marketers and content providers)?
▶ Can you limit the disclosure of subscription information to third parties?

▶ Does the service tell you what personally identifiable transaction data is being collected, and why?

▶ Does the service allow you to limit the *collection* of personally identifiable transaction data?

▶ Can you limit the *disclosure* to third parties of personally identifiable transaction data?

▶ Can you view the information that the service collects about you?

▶ Can you correct and update this information?

▶ Is your name and e-mail address automatically made available to other subscribers?

▶ Does the service retain the contents of your e-mail after you delete it?

Flap over AOL Privacy Policy Sparks Congressional Debate

AOL users were hopping mad. It turns out that the leading online service had taken out an advertisement in a direct-marketing magazine touting the value of its subscriber list, which included information on subscribers' names, genders, addresses, incomes, computer systems, and payment histories. The resulting fracas caused AOL Chairman Steve Case to post a letter to subscribers stating that the company would remove names from the lists at the customers' requests (Swartz 1994). Meanwhile, Rep. Edward Markey (D-MA), troubled by the lack of comprehensive privacy protections on the online services, launched an investigation. What Markey found troubled him: There were no industrywide guidelines dealing with the issue of subscriber data privacy, and there was also considerable variation in what was done with personal subscriber information: Some firms sold it, others "leased it," and still others refused to do either. Markey wrote legislation in an attempt to regulate the industry, but it was subsequently killed. If Markey's bill had made it through the Congress, service providers would be required to do the following (Meeks 1994):

▶ Inform subscribers whether information is being collected about them.

▶ Tell subscribers if collected information is sold to outside parties.

▶ Enable users to prohibit the sale of information about themselves.

Privacy on your Employer's System? Forget It!

Apparently, it's a common practice. In just one month, according to a recent study (reported in Swartz 1995), employees at three large corporations (IBM, Apple Computer, and AT&T) were found to have spent the equivalent of 1,631 work days visiting *Penthouse* magazine's Web site. Other companies report similar findings. In short, a lot of employees access sex sites at work.

But that doesn't mean it's smart. Everything you do on a company's computer can be tracked, and the information can be used against you. More than a dozen employees at Houston-based Compaq Computer Corporation lost their jobs when it was learned that they had scored more than 1,000 "hits" on sex-related sites while working.

E-Mail: It's Like Sending a Postcard.   From the point of view of most companies, the computer systems that employees use are the company's property (Sipior and Ward 1995). Electronic Frontier Foundation (EFF) spokesman John Barlow puts it this way: "There's this assumption that because the company you work for owns the computer system, it somehow owns or has the right to access the e-mail. But that's like saying that because the company owns the pen with which you wrote a letter, it owns the letter" (Bjerklie 1993: 14).

Most employees don't realize this. They think their e-mail is private (Weisband and Reinig 1995). But it isn't. Federal law simply does not protect

---

Factoids: The Internet at Work

▶ Peak hours of Internet usage: between 10 A.M. and 2 P.M.
▶ Percentage of Fortune 500 employees stating that they they spend at least four to five hours on the Internet at work: 70 percent
▶ Estimated number of U.S. companies with Internet access: 73,000
▶ Percentage of Internet sites access deemed "inappropriate" after audit at Boeing Co.: 10 percent

Source: Jon Swarz, "9-to-5 Internet Surfers Beware: Companies Tighten the Web on Workers," *San Francisco Chronicle* (October 14, 1996), p. A1.

employees against potentially abusive electronic monitoring, including the routine interception of e-mail, in the workplace (Samoriski, Huffman, and Trauth 1996).

Electronic Communications Privacy Act (ECPA): No Protection at Work.   In 1986, the U.S. Congress passed the Electronic Communications Privacy Act (ECPA), which was intended to deal with the question of government snooping on private electronic communications (including e-mail, cellular phones, and other electronic media). ECPA (Eckenwiler 1996) provides protection against e-mail snooping by any third party—the government, the police, or an individual—without a search warrant or subpoena. However, the law exempts communications service providers. Specifically, the ECPA allows an employer who provides e-mail for employees to engage in routine e-mail inspections, if such inspections are "necessary for business purposes," or to protect the employer's interests (Posch 1996). That's right: Your boss can legally snoop on your e-mail. Period.

As for government snooping, ECPA provides substantially less protection for e-mail than it does for telephone calls. To tap someone's phone line, for instance, the government must receive clearance from the U.S. Attorney General's office before submitting a request to a federal judge.

In contrast, any prosecutor who wishes to eavesdrop on electronic communications can obtain a warrant directly from a judge, without needing clearance from the Attorney General. All that's required is suspicion that the person has committed a felony. But these restrictions apply only to communications that are intercepted on the fly. Once the e-mail communications are stored on disk, much less stringent regulations apply.

Americans are turning to e-mail to take the place formerly occupied by first-class letters. But they are not aware that, in the transition to the new communication technology, they have lost the civic freedoms that have been enjoyed since the founding of the Republic. The lack of privacy protection for corporate e-mail has led many companies to adopt an Orwellian police state, in which the power of computers is used to perform sophisticated pattern-matching operations on all incoming and outgoing e-mail. To be sure, many companies believe that e-mail searches are justified in order to protect valuable trade secrets, prevent embezzlement, ensure a drug-free workplace, and discourage the use of corporate resources for nonbusiness purposes. In some companies, according to a security consultant, employees try to "sabotage coworkers by sending phony e-mail messages directing them to do unnecessary tasks, thereby diverting them from doing real work that might improve their standing with the boss" (Anonymous 1995: A1). But e-mail searching communicates a blatant mistrust of employees—at precisely the same time that, in many companies, management is talking up trust and empowerment as the keys to higher productivity.

You can't have it both ways (Bernstein 1991).

Companies claim that they need to search employee e-mail to protect their business, but this claim masks motives that are often more sinister. Scrutinizing employee e-mail provides an opportunity to identify and terminate potential whistleblowers, union organizers, or other dissidents within a firm or agency. Worse, it provides an open invitation to management to identify and terminate employees whose private lives meet management dissapproval. "Perhaps the person subscribes to left-wing periodicals, or has given money to pro-union causes, or once stayed at a hotel known to be favored by homosexuals, or has had financial problems. Perhaps the person has a family history of medical problems or bought antidepressive prescription drugs" (Miller 1996: 288). Such an employee could be easily terminated on trumped-up charges without any reference to the real reason for termination.

"We Can't Win It Anywhere."   In the absence of legislation protecting employee e-mail privacy, the courts have consistently sided with employers in court cases involving terminations connected with e-mail usage. Alana Shoars was the e-mail administrator for Epson, a Japanese-owned firm based in Torrance, CA. Shoars administered an e-mail system used by some 700 employees. Concerned about privacy issues, Shoars assured employees that the company respected privacy rights. However, Shoars discovered that her employer was reading employee e-mail. When she complained, she was promptly fired. Shoars subsequently sued Epson, but lost.

The defeat sent shock waves through the civil libertarian community. Lewis Maltby, of the American Civil Liberties Union's workplace rights project, commented, "We had the perfect set of circumstances: We had a wonderful plaintiff, we were in California of all places, and we had a great attorney. If we can't win that case in California, we can't win it anywhere" (Whalen 1996).

They Say They Respect Your Privacy? Don't Believe It.   To prevent misunderstandings and employee resentment, many companies inform employees concerning the privacy of their e-mail. At some firms, employees are assured that all e-mail communications will remain confidential and privileged. As a former Pillsbury Co. employee named Michael Smyth found out the hard way, you'd better take such statements with a grain of salt.

Smyth sent a number of e-mail letters over the company's e-mail system that included unprofessional remarks concerning other members of the firm. Although the company had repeatedly stated that employee e-mail privacy would be respected, Smyth's mail was intercepted and he was fired for unprofessional conduct. In a subsequent wrongful termination lawsuit, a United States District Court in Pennsylvania found that Mr. Smyth had no reasonable expectation of privacy in the use of his employer's computer system, even though the employer had promised not to intercept employee e-mail. "The company's interest in preventing inappropriate and unprofessional comments or even illegal activity over its e-mail system outweighs any privacy interest the employee may have in those comments" (cited in Brown 1996).

What Should You Do?

Use the Internet in general, and e-mail in particular, with extreme caution.

▶ At work, never say anything in an e-mail message that you would not want to see on your boss's desk. Do not use a corporate e-mail account for any personal purpose. On the Web, access only those sites that are clearly relevant to your job responsibilities. *Never* visit a sex-related site.

▶ At home, do not use e-mail for discussing anything that would prove embarrassing to you were it made public. Remember that any party to a lawsuit, or any investigating official, can subpoena your past e-mail—and Internet service providers are bound to provide it.

References

Anonymous. 1995. "Computer Crime Is an Inside Job." *Tampa Tribune* (October 25, 1995), p. A1.

Bernstein, Aaron. 1991. "How to Motivate Employees: Don't Watch 'Em. *Business Week* (April 29, 1991).

Bjerklie, David. 1993. "E-mail: The Boss Is Watching." *Technology Review* (April 1993), pp. 14–16.

Bowles, Scott. 1996. "Chat Lines Probed." *Washington Post* (January 26, 1996), p. 1.

Brown, Michael. 1996. "Are Employee E-Mail Messages Really Private?" Online document: (http://www3.monster.com/recruit/hr1/articles/email.htm).

Center for Democracy and Technology, "Privacy Policy Chart—Online Service Providers." Online document (http://www.cdt.org/privacy/online_services/chart.html).

clnet. 1996. "The Ultimate Guide to Internet Service Providers." Online document (http://www.cnet.com/Content/Reviews/Compare/ISP/).

Eckenwiler, Marck. 1996. "Net.Law." *NetGuide* (April 1, 1996).

Meeks, Brock N. 1994. "Markey vs. AOL et al.: Round Two." *InterActive Week* (November 7, 1994), p. 62.

Miller, Steven. 1988. *Civilizing Cyberspace.* New York: Addison-Wesley.

Posch, Robert. 1996. "E-Mail and Voice Mail: Basic Legal Issues for Corporate Management." *Direct Marketing* 58 (January 1996), pp. 54–57.

Samoriski, Jan H., John L. Huffman, and Denise M. Trauth. "Electronic Mail, Privacy, and the Electronic Communications Privacy Act of 1986: Technology in Search of Law." *Journal of Broadcasting and Broadcast Media* 40 (Winter), pp. 60–77.

Sipior, Janice C., and Burke T. Ward. 1995. "The Ethical and Legal Quandary of E-Mail Privacy." *Communications of the ACM,* Vol. 38 (December 1995), pp. 48–55.

Swartz, Jon. 1994. "AOL's Sale of Subscriber Lists Seen As Potential Privacy Threat." *MacWeek* (October 10, 1994), p. 37.

Violino, Bob. 1996. "Feds Tap E-Mail in Bust." *Information Week* (January 8, 1996), p. 16.

Weisband, Suzanne P. and Bruce A. Reinig. 1995. "Managing User Perceptions of E-Mail Privacy." *Communicatons of the ACM,* Vol. 38 (December 1995), pp. 40–48.

Whalen, Jon. 1995. "You're Not Paranoid—They Really *Are* Watching You." *Wired* 3.03 (March 1995). Online document (http://nswt.tuwien.ac.at:8000/bazar/being-watched.html.

CHAPTER 3

Get Your Name Out of the Databases

Just imagine yourself walking around with a video filming crew tracking your every move—and you don't know it. If they capture enough film, they'll know everything about you—what you do, what you buy, what you say. From all that data and some sophisticated analysis, they could extrapolate from this information to start making predictions about what a person *like* you might do—which car this person would buy, what kind of beer she'd drink, whether she prefers perfumed toilet paper. It's called *psychographics*—a way of knowing more about you than you even know about yourself (Fox 1994). And this is a very, very valuable product. A lot of people would like to know what you will do—whether you're likely to become pregnant soon, or abuse alcohol, or file for workers' compensation, or drive recklessly. These techniques can produce impressive results. At the O.J. Simpson trial, for example, "defense lawers . . . accumulated detailed profiles on potential jurors and used these profiles to predict which people were more likely to vote for conviction. These people were, of course, peremptorily challenged to prevent them being on the jury" (Wexelblat 1995).

The marketing industry isn't about to start filming your every move, but they're using computer technology to do much the same: gathering information about you like crazy, and without your consent or knowledge.

What's made this possible is technological advancement—specifically, rapid advances in computing power, the ubiquity of computers (including computerized point-of-sale systems), and the database technology needed to sift through millions or even billions of bits of information in seconds. And they're gathering data constantly. Every time you make a call, buy groceries, use your credit card, or fill out a product registration card, you're adding more information to the databases. The more information these companies can collect, the more valuable their product will be, and the more they'll gain. What's at stake here financially is a market currently bringing in $1.5 billion, and expected to grow to $7 billion by 1999 (Jacobs 1996).

With the rise of the Web, two new opportunities arise for the direct marketing industry. The first is the possibility of a new, potentially massive market for their products. Right now, database owners sell subscriptions to their products via clunky, text-based systems that use public data networks, such as Telenet. Virtually every one of them is planning to move their subscription operations to the Internet. The second opportunity is increased surveillance. Database marketers would love to record your digital DNA, your clickstream of Web accesses and file downloads, which could do wonders for filling out some of the missing points in your psychographic profile.

As you'll see in this chapter, there's a gold rush mentality in the direct marketing industry. Computers have enabled the collection and analysis of data on a scale unimaginable even a decade ago. There's a tremendous amount of money to be made by collecting, analyzing, and selling data— data about you. Admitting that some citizens will find all this monitoring intrusive, the marketing industry nevertheless believes that consumers will find it to be in their best interests.

After all, or so marketers believe, consumers will get better products (for a sharply dissenting view, see Larson 1993). What this self-serving picture doesn't recognize, though, is that people get badly hurt when their information falls into the wrong hands. It's getting easier and easier, and cheaper and cheaper, to get hold of this information. What's at stake? Every time you apply for a job, or for credit, or for just about anything, you'll be tried in absentia and convicted if the data don't look good, simply because you *might* get pregnant, smoke pot, or file for workers' compensation. And with databases migrating to the Web, the day is not far off when virtually any person will be able to put together an astonishingly accurate portrait of the initimate details of any other person's life, for whatever reason, be it discrimination, blackmail, or the denial of employment based on political or lifestyle preferences. If you're not comfortable with this, read this chapter carefully and follow the steps recommended to get your name out of as many of these databases as possible.

If you *are* comfortable about this, take a look at Stalker (http://www.attach.net/users/furvert/stalker.htm), one of several pages of its type on the Web. It's a page for people who are "obsessed" with someone who "stomped on your heart and left it in the gutter. . . . If only you could see their faces once again . . . and confront them . . . and release the turmoil of RAGE that has consumed you. . . ." There follows a list of links to e-mail and address databases on the Web.

"We Can't Control What Our Customers Do with This Information"

How do you make money in the direct-marketing database industry? Just start collecting information. You don't really have to have a defined purpose. You can adopt all sorts of policies that make it look as though you're serious about protecting privacy—for example, by insisting that you're careful about with whom you do business and whom you allow to have access to the stored information. But database publishers typically add, "Of course, we have no control over what our customers do with this information" (Foley 1996).

Does that satisfy you? Think again. A Fullerton, CA-based company sells lists of arrests that ended in acquittal, discharge, or no deposition; while a Gretna, LA-based firm tracks employees who have filed for workers' compensation. These companies will tell you the same thing that every database publisher does—that they have no control over how their customers use the data they provide. And what do they do with it? Just as Ernest Trent, a former Pennzoil Co. worker who was injured on an oil rig and filed for workers' compensation. Since that time, Trent has pursued nearly 200 jobs—without luck. Why? "I'm blacklisted," Trent told a reporter (Rothfeder 1990).

Are there any limits to what kind of information is collected? Apparently not, as Marc Klass found out. Klass, the father of murder victim Polly Klass, was deeply shocked to discover a Metromail database that listed the names and addresses of millions of children. The company that offered public computer access to this database, Lexis-Nexis, withdrew the database after charges that the information could have been used by pedophiles hoping to locate young children.

What are we to make of a world in which just about *anyone* can afford to access highly sensitive, personal information about just about anyone else?

The Not-So-Gentle Art of Database Merging

Right now, there are lots of databases here and there. Each of them seems innocent enough—the data's collected for a clear and limited purpose, with all kinds of talk about privacy safeguards. For example, it seems legitimate enough that the major credit reporting firms collect information about your bill-paying habits and make this available to lenders. And these firms try to make sure that they're selling their data to people with legitimate business interests. But what happens when somebody—perhaps somebody with fewer scruples—starts putting all the data together?

It's called *database merging*, and it's made possible by the nearly ubiquitous use of Social Security numbers as a universal identifier. Armed with a person's Social Security number, you can access several database services, incrementally building information about you. For a relatively modest expenditure of, say, $100 (Piller 1993), you'll have an astonishingly complex portrait of a person's private affairs: name, address, telephone numbers, credit history, sexual orientation, religion, race, voting record, medical record, names and ages of her children, whether the person's ever been a party to a lawsuit or filed for workers' compensation, consumption habits, and much more. And it's all available from online sources.

TIP **One way to stem the tide of database merging is to resist the illegal demand that you supply your Social Security number for identification purposes. For more information, read the Social Security FAQ (http://www.cpsr.org/dox/program/privacy/ssn/ssn.faq.html).**

What's involved here is intrusion—intrusion into your personal affairs, and on a scale that most people find repellant once they realize how much they know. Erik Larson, a *Wall Street Journal* feature writer, started to wonder what was going on when a free sample box of diapers arrived at his home—exactly one week after his second child was born (Larson 1992). But that's exactly what the marketing industry is after: one-to-one marketing. A firm pushing an antiaging cream put together a list of prospects, and mailed them ads with before-and-after pictures. Scrawled across the top of the note was a

Will the IRS Get into the Act?

Database merging enables marketers to put together an astonishingly accurate picture of your personal affairs, tastes, and actions. And guess who wants to join in? The IRS (Graves 1995). In a program called Compliance 2000, the IRS proposes to do a bit of data merging on its own, using commercial databases, DMV records, credit bureaus, state and local real estate records, commercial publications, newspapers, airplane and pilot information, U.S. Coast Guard vessel registration information, state fishing licensing records—in other words, everything they can get their hands on. And the purpose? According to the IRS, the purpose of this database is to gauge compliance trends in broad market segments. Sure— and if you believe that, I've got a very nice bridge I'd love to sell you. Does the IRS have sufficient internal controls to prevent an overzealous agent from accessing a potential audit target's records to determine whether that individual's consumption patterns testify to a greater income than this individual has reported on tax returns?

Even the direct marketers aren't happy with this. Says Jerry Cerasale, a spokesman for the Direct Marketing Association, "A belief that your purchases will put you on some government list could have a chilling effect on sales" (cited in Graves 1995).

personalized message, such as "Kathy—Try this. It works. R" (Carroll 1993). According to Larson (1992), a woman who received one of these notes thought it was from her ex-husband's new wife, and she shot them both.

The Many-Headed Hydra

In classical mythology, it's just the kind of monster you wouldn't want to run into. You chop off a head, but another one appears to take its place. The database industry has something in common with Hydra: A company tries to push too far, gets into the public relations doghouse, and is forced to withdraw. After the fuss dies down, though, somebody else makes the same product available, and nobody notices.

Take the case of Lotus Marketplace, a joint venture between Lotus Development Corporation (the publishers of Lotus 1-2-3) and the Equifax credit bureau. Marketplace was to be published on a CD-ROM, priced at only $700, and it would contain the names, estimated incomes, purchasing habits, marital status, and additional information concerning 120 million consumers (Carroll 1993). The resulting public outcry killed the project, and the major credit reporting firms decided to get out of the direct-marketing business.

But what about their customers? These firms are in the business of selling data. They claim to be selective, but this runs up against an incontrovertible economic fact: You don't make money by being too choosey. All the major credit reporting firms sell data to database repackagers, who may not have the credit bureau's scruples. Make no mistake about it: Something like Marketplace is going to be marketed again, once all the fuss dies down. Except next time, it's going to be on the Web. Is it here? Just take a look at SearchAmerica, Inc., a fee-based database of over 220 million surnames, businesses, and telephone numbers (http://www.searchamerica.com). The service doesn't retrieve Social Security numbers or addresses, but these are available to commercial customers. Just about every database publisher in the business, including credit reporting firms, is studying ways to make information available on the Web to paid subscribers—who could be, at the extreme, just about anyone with a credit card and a few extra bucks.

Here Come the Data Cowboys

In the direct marketing industry, scruples and ethical codes have a way of disappearing when there's money to be made. Consider the data cowboy. Because the big credit database firms charge as much as $100 for preemployment screening and other checks, there's a booming business for these freelance data entrepreneurs, who charge much less for their investigations. These freelancers "assemble raw, unchecked data from credit bureaus, motor vehicle departments, courthouses, and other [publicly available] sources," according to Thomas C. Lawson, the president of Apscreen, an established preemployment screening service (Rothfeder 1990). But the use of this data for preemployment screening may not be legal, Lawson says.

What's even more frightening is that the information very likely contains inaccuracies. It's well known that credit-reporting and other large databases of consumer-related information are riddled with errors; according to one study, 48 percent of credit reports requested from the three largest credit-reporting firms contained errors, and nearly one in five contained errors that could result in a denial of credit (Carroll 1993). And what can that do to your career? Just ask James Russell Wiggins, formerly an employee of District Cablevision in Washington, DC. After Wiggins was hired, District Cablevision hired Equifax, Inc., of Atlanta, GA, to perform a routine background check on Wiggins. The result? A James Wiggins had been convicted of cocaine possession. After only six weeks on the job, Wiggins's was fired. But it was all a mistake. James Russell Wiggins's records had been erroneously combined with another man named Wiggins. Equifax and District Cablevision both apologized for the blunder, but Wiggins hit both of them with a $10 million lawsuit, alleging defamation and invasion of privacy (Rothfeder 1995).

Equally frightening is that data records just don't go away. According to Alan Brill, an investigator for a large private investigation firm, an incriminating bit of data is likely to stay around for years—far beyond, for example, the statute of limitations that would require courts to expunge records of convictions for a minor offense. "It's like vampire data," Brill says. "It rises up from the dead to bite you" (Piller 1993).

Data cowboys have far fewer scruples than the big credit reporting firms, and much less to lose from reporting inaccurate or out-of-date information. They don't really have the resources to check out the validity of this data, anyway. And they don't really care, for the most part. You don't make money by correcting mistakes in the data you mine; you make money by selling the data.

As database companies seek to amortize their investments by increasing their user bases, more and more databases are becoming available online (and migrating to the Internet), and they're charging lower prices. Soon, anyone will be able to become a data cowboy.

The Rise of the Data Warehouse

Direct marketing firms try to collect information about you in every way they can: computerized point-of-sale terminals record how much beer and toothpaste you're buying, for example, and they're willing to pay some serious money for such information. Corporations, meanwhile, have been spending big money trying to create centralized storehouses (called *data warehouses)* of all the data they possess about their customers and other aspects of their business. And they're beginning to ask, Why not sell this information?

One Database to Rule Them All.   Back in the old days, companies had just one, big mainframe computer. And this computer contained all the data. Then something happened: distributed computing. Suddenly, there were dozens or even hundreds of databases scattered all over an enterprise, often using incompatible data formats. Put together, they'd be valuable as a strategic resource, and perhaps as a commercially marketable item.

Putting all these databases together—into a *data warehouse*—is becoming increasingly feasible, companies are finding. It isn't easy to define the term data warehouse, since the concept's so new, but in most corporations the term implies three things: humongous size (we're talking about trillions of bytes of data, not millions or billions), remarkably intelligent software that can reconcile the differences in varying database recording techniques, and—in many cases—sophisticated, statistically based analytical routines that can make behavioral predictions based on the accessed data (Foley 1996). Data warehousing projects are underway at an estimated 95 percent of Fortune 1,000 companies (Marshall 1996).

And the Payoff?   Enormous. At MCI, a three-terabyte data warehouse is cutting the cost of finding new customers. According to MCI Chief Information Officer Lance Boxer, in 1994 MCI spent 65 to 70 cents to generate new sales leads. Thanks to the data warehouse, this cost has been cut to 4.5 to 6 cents per lead. "This is one of the most important projects in the company," Boxer points out, "and it's being expanded" (Foley 1996b).

The proliferation of data warehousing has given rise to a new term, *data mining.* This is the exploratory querying of data warehouses just to see

---

How Big Is a Terabyte?

A terabyte of data is enough to hold:

▶ A 100-character record for every person on earth, or
▶ A graphic image of every square meter of land on earth, or
▶ The text of books that would take 150 miles of bookshelf space

Source: Foley 1996b

what conclusions can be drawn from the huge amount of collected data. At Holiday Inn Worldwide, for example, a new data warehouse houses data drawn from more than 2,000 hotels in 50 countries. Data mining is used to examine customer patterns: for example, whether they used a travel agent to book their room, and how long they stayed (DePompa 1996).

The VAR Opportunity.   Most companies are currently using their data warehouses for internal analytical purposes, like Holiday Inns Worldwide. But they increasingly recognize that the data that's so valuable to them might very well be valuable to others. It's an opportunity to transform what was formerly a collection of incompatible data sets into a value-added resource (VAR). In a way, it's like free money.

Even as you're reading this, companies everywhere are planning to make their data warehouses available on the Web—to paid subscribers, who are often close business partners. What makes a data warehouse so appealing to business partners is its sheer richness. Green Bay, WI-based ShopKo Stores Inc., for example, accumulates "market basket" data from its 130 stores, feeding it into a 400-GB data warehouse. It's a gold mine of information for suppliers. "We know what is in every shopping basket," according to Gene Klawikowski, ShopKo's Director of Information Services (Foley and Caldwell 1996). By accessing the data warehouse (for a fee, of course), suppliers will be able to find out just what's selling and what's not. They can also measure the effect of advertising.

Moving to the Web?   Most companies are still planning to use data warehouses internally, opening up the data only to company insiders by means of corporate intranets. Still, the possibilities for external marketing are very real—and potentially very lucrative. Michael Saylor, Chairman of a Vienna, VA-based database firm, believes the time has come to "consumerize" data warehouses by making them Web-accessible. Saylor says, "There's no reason you can't have 100 million people asking questions [of a data warehouse] every day on the Internet" (Foley and Caldwell 1996). Driving this market is the very real hope of amortizing the high costs of developing the warehouse by exponentially expanding the user base. Just make it available on the Web, or so this line of thinking goes, and the revenue's going to come rolling in.

So there's an economic law operating here. The greater the market you can create for your product, the more you can lower your prices—and the more you lower your prices, the greater the market. The only things standing in the way of this inexorable process are the scruples of well-established marketing firms, who don't feel entirely comfortable about making sensitive information available to just anyone browsing the Web and willing to fork over a small fee. They mainly distribute their products via proprietary database services, such as Lexis-Nexis or DIALOG, or by means of subscriber-based access via public data networks. Will they be pushed aside by newer, less ethical firms that don't share their scruples?

Maybe We Can Make a Little Money on the Side

Increasingly, federal agencies, as well as state and local governments, look on their own data resources—such as databases of driving records—as a marketable trove of information. After all, they reason, this information is supposed to be publicly available—so why not put it on the Internet, and make a little money? It turns out that major database vendors, such as West Publishing Company and Lexis-Nexis, would like to make public records available for fee-based searching—and, of course, they would pay a licensing fee to the cash-strapped government agency. For its massive geographical information system database, the City of Phoenix gets rates from commercial database vendors ranging from $25 for a single access, to $36,000 for a copy of the entire database (Anthes and Blodget 1996). Even public schools are getting into the act (Browning 1995).

What's available through these services? Lots: real estate records, corporate and limited partnership records, Social Security records, Uniform Commercial Code filings, liens and judgments, motor vehicle records, voter registration records, docket information, professional licensing information, OSHA inspection reports, and much more (Pritchard-Schoch 1995). This information isn't available on the Web—yet. You'll have to go through a private database search service, such as DIALOG, which charges hefty fees. The same economic law is operating, though, and you're bound to see database publishers move their products to the Web.

But sometimes it's all for free. Want to find out which of your neighbors has contributed to a presidential campaign, and how much? Access http://www.tray.com/cgi-win/zip.htm, and type in your zip code. You'll see the names, addresses, amounts of contributions, and political affiliations of the contributors. Very interesting!

The Mother of All Databases

From a direct marketer's viewpoint, the present situation is—well, *inefficient*. You have lots of different databases—thousands of them, in fact—with incompatible data formats and varying restrictions on use. Wouldn't it be nice to have just one, central database that contains everything you'd ever want to know? A database that would include credit data, nuggets from corporate data warehouses, revealing items from public sources, consumer purchasing information, psychographic profiles, the works?

Ideally—at least from the direct marketer's viewpoint—such a database would be truly comprehensive. It would include the most intimate details of your life—everything you've bought from retail vendors, your school records, your driving records, your health records, your credit records, and much more.

An Arkansas-based company called Acxiom Corp. is well on the way to creating such a synoptic database, according to a recent report. With data on an estimated 95 percent of U.S. households, Acxiom probably knows your name, addresses, phone numbers, estimated income, height, weight, credit-card usage patterns, and *psychographic* data such as hobbies and interests (Foley and Caldwell 1996). Right now, Acxiom makes its data available only to trusted customers, such as Wells Fargo Bank. But the firm is quick to point out, like all database publishers, that it can't control what its customers do with the information.

Into the Public Relations Doghouse

The direct marketing industry is walking a tightrope. On the one hand, it wants to intrude ever more aggressively into the details of your personal life. On the other hand, it's deathly frightened of a public relations fiasco that would renew dormant calls for federal regulation.

That's why direct marketing people cringe when there's a public outcry over a venture that goes too far. A Lexis-Nexis database called P-Trak, designed for attorneys who are trying to locate people named in lawsuits, offered online access to your Social Security number, maiden and assumed names, month and year of birth, current and former addresses, and phone numbers. (Because these phone numbers are compiled from direct marketing sources as well as phone books, they may include unlisted numbers.)

Consisting of more than 300 million records, access to P-Trak is available by means of subscription to the firm's proprietary online service, but this service is available without restriction to anyone with a credit card and the means to pay the search fees.

What's of concern here is the very real prospect of somebody appropriating your Social Security number, and then assuming your identity in applying for credit. This scam is increasingly common and has ruined many people's lives. In upholding a Virginia man's refusal to provide his Social Security number as a requirement to register to vote, a Federal court noted that "an unscrupulous individual, armed with one's SSN, could obtain a person's welfare benefits or Social Security benefits, order new checks at a new address on that person's checking account, obtain credit cards, or even obtain that person's paycheck" (cited in Aguilar 1996).

Lexis-Nexis withdrew access to Social Security numbers soon after the database was made available, but it soon found itself on the wrong end of a public relations debacle. A warning letter made its way into thousands of Internet mailing lists and Usenet newsgroups, and concerned Internet users forwarded this message to hundreds of thousands of e-mail addresses. The letter wasn't quite accurate—in response to an outcry soon after the database's release, Lexis-Nexis disabled the feature that enabled you to search for a person's Social Security number—but the letter set off a furor. Lexis-Nexis was besieged with thousands of telephone calls and faxes by people demanding to have their names removed from the database. Worse, the matter came up in Congress—a direct marketer's nightmare come true.

In a "preemptive strike" (Thyfault 1996), the American Association of Advertising Agencies (AAAA), the Association of National Advertisers, and the Direct Marketing Association (DMA) adopted the following recommendations:

▶ Consumers should be able to prevent online marketers from selling their names.
▶ Consumers should be able to obtain a summary of the information marketers have on them. In addition, most responsible Web-based marketing firms believe that users should have the option of removing their names from databases if they wish to do so.

But these measures will protect you only if you're proactive enough to contact these companies.

Table 3.1   **Removing Your Name from White Pages**

Database Name	Web Address	Notes
Bigfoot	http://www.bigfoot.com/	Bigfoot maintains a list of people who do not wish to receive unsoliticited e-mail. Although there is no assurance that direct marketers will consult this list, you may wish to add your name to it. To remove your name from Bigfoot's e-mail directory, access http://www.bigfoot. com/FAQS. HTM.
Database America	http://www.databaseamerica. com/html/gsupprs.htm	Type your phone number to remove it from the database.
Four11 Directory Services	http://www.four11.com/	Send e-mail to support@Four11.com and include your name and all your listed e-mail addresses.
Internet @ddress Finder	http://www.iaf.net/noframes/ faq.htm#remove_listing	You can remove your e-mail address from this database.
OKRA	http://okra.ucr.edu/okra/ removelisting.html	Enter your e-mail address to delete it from OKRA's database.
Switchboard	http://www.switchboard.com/	Send e-mail to www@switchboard.com, and enter Delete in the subject field, or write Switchboard Administrator, P.O. Box 1296, Westbro, MA 01581.
WhoWhere	http://www.whowhere.com/	Send e-mail to privacy@whowhere.com. You'll receive verification by return e-mail.
Yahoo! White Pages	http://www.yahoo.com/search/ people/suppress.html	Type your phone number to remove it from Yahoo!'s database.

> ## Getting Your Name Out of P-Trak
>
> Telephone 888-965-3947 or fax 800-470-4365. Include your Social Security number, full name, and current address for fastest processing.

How to Remove Your Name from Internet "White Pages" Databases

In response to P-Trak and other public relations fiascos, database marketers have learned that they may need to do something to buy off public discontent. The alternative? Government regulation. So some of them are making it possible for you to remove your name from databases—particularly the ones that provide Web access. These services know that Internet users are more sensitive about privacy than the typical consumer. (According to an Equifax/Harris survey, for example, 71 percent of Internet users did not want online service providers to track their Web surfing patterns for marketing purposes [cited in Edupage 1996]). If you don't care about strangers contacting you or possessing your personal information, fine—leave your name in these databases.

These databases, called *white pages,* use publicly available phone directories to make your listed telephone number and address available for free to anyone with a Web connection. To prevent Internet users from accessing your phone number or address, you may wish to remove your name from these databases. Table 3.1 shows you how.

References

Aguilar, Rose. 1996. "Research Service Raises Privacy Fears." Online document (http://www.news.com/News/Item/0,4,1527,00.html.

Anthes, Gary H., and Mindy Blodgett. 1996. "States Eye Online Revenues: Debate Rages Over Who Can See What for How Much." *ComputerWorld* (August 19, 1996), p. 26.

Barrett, Jennifer. 1996. "Databasing in the 1990s: Data and What We're Doing with It." Online document: http://www.acxiom.com/wp-03.htm.

Browning, Dan. 1995. "Schools with Data for Sale." *The IRE Journal* 18 (September-October 1995), pp. 3–6.

Carroll, Jon. 1993. Review of *The Naked Consumer: How Our Private Lives Become Public Commodities. Technology Review* (July 1993), p. 96.

DePompa, Barbara. 1996. "Data Mining—There's Gold in Databases—New Tools Will Help Companies Extract Valuable Information." *Information Week* (January 8, 1996), p. 52.

Foley, John. 1996a. "Data Dilemma: Data Warehousing and Mining Are Booming." *Information Week* (June 10, 1996).

Foley, John. 1996b. "Databases—Towering Terabytes—Fast Growing Data Warehouses Are Reaching Terabyte Size and Creating a New Elite among Corporations." *Information Week* (September 30, 1996).

Foley, John, and Bruce Caldwell. 1996. "Dangerous Data: Linking Data Warehouses to the Web Can Bring In Billions of Dollars—And Violate Your Customers' Privacy." *Information Week* (September 30, 1996).

Fox, Wade. 1994. Review of *The Naked Consumer: How Our Private Lives Become Public Commodities. Whole Earth Review* (Winter 1994), p. 97.

Gehl, John, and Suzanne Douglas, 1996. "Internet Users Value Their Privacy." *EDUPAGE* (October 13, 1996). Online document (http://www.educom.edu/).

Graves, Jacqueline. 1995. "Is Big Brother Backing Down?" *Fortune* (March 20, 1994), pp. 15–17.

Jacobs, Ian. 1996 "Building a Warehouse: More Data and More Disparate Systems Make It a Great VAR Market." *VAR Business* (January 1, 1996), p. 57.

Larson, Erik. 1992. *The Naked Consumer.* New York: Henry Holt.

Marshall, Martin. 1996. "Worries about Warehouses: Data Warehouses on the 'Net Elicit Security Concerns." *Communications Week* (June 24, 1996), p. 16.

Piller, Charles. 1993. "Privacy in Peril: How Computers Are Making Private Life a Thing of the Past." *MacWorld* (July 1993).

Pritchard-Schoch, Teresa. 1995. "Public Records 1995." *Database* (October 1995).

Rothfeder, Jeffrey. 1990. "Looking for a Job? You May Be out Before You Go in." *Business Week* (September 24, 1990).

Rothfeder, Jeff. 1995. "Nothing Personal—Privacy's Dead. Your Life's an Open File Online." *NetGuide* (July 1, 1995).

Thyfault, Mary E. 1996. "Internet Data Gathering Rules Sought—Chilling Effect Feared by Industry Groups." *Information Week* (June 10, 1996).

Wexelblat, Alan. 1995. "How Is the NII like a Prison?" Online document (http://lcs.www.media.mit.edu/people/wex/panoptic-paper.html).

4

Think Twice about Filling Out Site Registration Forms

Y̶ou've surely been through this drill. You want to access a "free" site on the Internet. In order to do so, however, you have to fill out a registration form. It asks for your name, address, sex, age, and lots more—at the extreme, your annual income, and even the ages of your children! What's going on?

Basically, Web sites can't attract advertising unless they can prove to potential advertisers that an ad will reach its intended market: "The value of the future of the Internet for advertisers is to eliminate waste by targeting both psychographically and demographically" (cited in Ward 1996).

As far as it goes, that's innocent enough. But what happens if the Web site turns around and sells this information? After all, many magazines find that selling their mailing list provides them with the revenue stream they need to stay in business. And if a Webmaster is short on cash and sells your name and personal information, this information is going to get into the same data stream with those snoopy user registration cards—and everything you say will eventually wind up in huge marketing databases.

You should think twice about filling out these forms—and if you do, you're not alone. According to a recent study, nearly 30 percent of Internet users intentionally falsify data on site registration forms. Why? In part, it's because these forms are too pushy and manipulative: You can't move on to the next page without filling in all the required forms. And increasingly, people are getting concerned about what's going to be done with this information. In this chapter, you'll find out why you should be concerned, too.

Aren't We Getting a Little Personal Here?

Consider the Site Registration Form from Hell. You'll be asked to supply all of the following:

- Name
- E-mail address
- Birthdate
- Mother's maiden name
- Age
- Sex
- Marital status
- Spouse's name
- Number of children
- Children's names
- Address
- Phone number
- Fax number
- Occupation
- Method of Internet access
- Annual income level
- Type of computer
- Amount of RAM of computer
- Size of computer's hard drive
- Internet connection speed
- Business use of computer

Intrusive, isn't it? What's worse, the site doesn't say anything about what's going to be done with this information.

Web marketers are beginning to understand that Internet users are sensitive about such things, so most of the registration forms you'll encounter aren't quite so intrusive. The *Los Angeles Times* Web site assures you that the information you supply will remain confidential—but what does this mean? Does this mean it won't be sold or rented to others? You can't really tell. You're given the opportunity to supply sensitive information, such as the number of children in your household and your annual income, but you can skip these if you want (see Figure 4.1). That's not true of the basic demographic information—they want that, and you don't register without it. Period.

Driving Away Customers?

What's driving the push for intrusive site registrations is the traditional mentality of advertisers, who want to see glittering demographics before

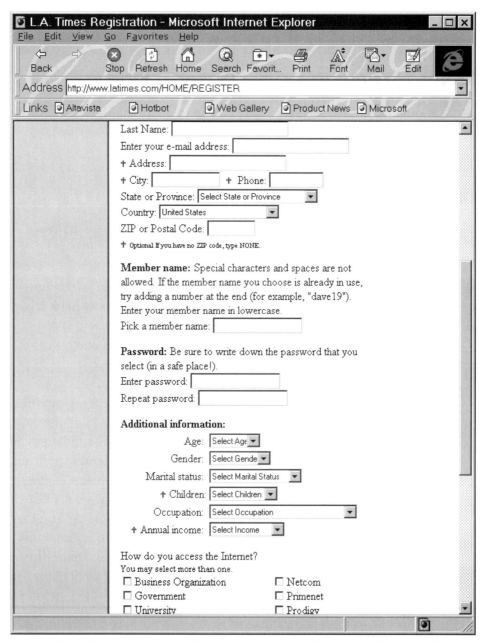

FIGURE 4.1   The *Los Angeles Times* registration form asks for lots of information, but lets you omit your address, number of children, and annual income.

they'll foot the bill for a banner advertisement (Goldman 1996). A key factor: a relatively affluent audience and big hit counts. The top ten most popular Web sites drew more than 60 percent of the advertising revenue (Anonymous 1996a), with the rest distributed among more than 600 sites trying to sell space for banners (Goldman 1996).

Pushy site registration tactics might be responsible for the slow progress of Web commerce, according to some commentators. To be sure, the main reason for sluggish growth lies in the lack of a completely worked-out security scheme for Internet credit-card ordering. But one study revealed that concerns about loss of privacy are driving down sales on the Internet (Marjanovic 1996). If advertisers don't understand and respect Internet culture, including Internet users' sharp concerns about privacy, their efforts may backfire (Robbins 1994).

Economist Frank Fukayama argues that trust and transaction costs are directly related—the higher the trust, the lower the costs. If so, transaction costs must be going up on the Web, because it's clear that trust is declining. Intrusive site registration forms are partly to blame.

Getting You to Divulge Your Demographics

Having grasped that Internet users aren't very happy about coughing up sensitive personal information, there's a new wrinkle on the site registration scene: Offering prizes (Figure 4.2). At Riddler.com, you win prizes by registering and then competing in a series of free games. The prizes currently offered include a Ford Explorer lease, a nine-day tour of Alaska, a Casio digital camera, and more.

Do It Once and Get It over With

Here's a variation on the prize theme. Since Internet users obviously hate to fill out registration forms, why not have them do it just once on a centralized registration site? Then they can access participating sites without having to go through all the registration hassles for participating sites. And you can win free prizes!

That's the idea behind I/CODE (http:/icode.ipro.com/icode_description. html), a service of Internet Profiles Corporation, which is sensitive to privacy issues. The service promises not to sell your registration information to

FIGURE 4.2   Riddler.com offers incentives for site registration.

anyone. In addition, participating sites receive your demographic information, but not your name or contact information—at least, that's what the site's privacy page says. According to Internet Profile Corporation's president, Ariel Poler, the contact information isn't necessary: "ESPN doesn't need the name of each of its visitors to sell ad space if it can get a very good breakdown of their characteristics" (Ubois 1996).

But it's reasonable to exercise some caution here—particularly in view of the fact that Internet Profiles Corporation and similar companies are for-profit firms. "I think the centralized registration systems managed by a for-profit company are the biggest threat to personal privacy the world's ever seen," says Terry Myerson, president of a company that makes a Web site management tool. "You are letting a company know everything about you. The current management may be nice guys, but then they retire and they've got cash flow problems and they have the most valuable database in the world. What do you think they're going to do with it?" (Carl 1996.)

Let's Not Be So Intrusive

Another approach: Don't demand so much information. Instead, use reverse matching techniques to round it out.

NetCount (http://www.netcount.com) is currently developing a Web access measurement system called HeadCount that doesn't use an intrusive, annoying, and suspicion generating registration questionnaire; instead, users are asked to provide only their addresses. Through a backwards matching process, this information is matched with demographic data, and then supplied to the Web sites that have contracted with this service.

The advantage of this approach, according to Robin Richards, NetCount's CEO, is that user privacy is protected. The address and ZIP code are matched to demographic census data on the fly, and only when reports are generated for Web site subscribers. There's no question about storing or selling the information—NetCount doesn't have it. According to a media executive at a San Francisco firm, the data NetCount provides is on a par with what other services provide (O'Loughlin 1996).

HeadCount isn't available yet, and it would seem to offer some advantages to users concerned with privacy. Still, these firms are for-profit companies, and you have to wonder what's going to happen if they get into

> ## Questions to Ask before Filling Out a Site Registration Form
>
> **B**efore filling out a Web site registration form, you should ask the following questions—and get answers:
>
> ▶ Will this information be sold to a third party?
> ▶ Will this information result in my receiving junk e-mail or junk snail mail?
> ▶ Can I choose to prevent you from selling this information?
> ▶ Can I trust you not to sell my information if I ask you not to do so?
>
> Web sites that are conscious of users' privacy concerns won't demand unnecessary information. They'll promise not to divulge information to others, and they won't add your name to e-mail or any other mailing lists without your express consent.

cash-flow trouble. HeadCount's technology seems to be designed so that selling names isn't an option, but it's debatable whether increasingly cynical and suspicious Internet users will believe this.

A Better Way: Community Casting

Technical fixes like HeadCount might not be necessary. According to critics of current Web advertising practices, such as Philippe Boutié (1996), the whole notion of Web advertising is wrong-headed and will wither and die. The point isn't to hang your advertising banner on Web sites that have high hit rates and the right demographics, as shown by more or less intrusive measurements. According to Boutié, that's just like putting up a tiny billboard on a frantic, busy interstate highway.

"The most effective way to get your message across on the Web is to concentrate on building community and constituencies," Boutié says. Tom DiScipio, president of a media group whose clients do a good deal of Web advertising, concurs. "I don't know that demographics have a role in online media. The medium allows you to push past them and focus directly on user characteristics" (Goldman 1996).

Future Web advertisers might do better to refrain from pushing Webmasters into intrusive demographics monitoring, and focus instead on choosing sites that attract users with their desired profiles. Most successful Web sites appeal to a narrowly defined community, such as seniors, ethnic groups, teens, sailors, joggers, and many more. Just by choosing a successful site that successfully addresses a narrowly defined audience, an advertiser can achieve the "dream" goal of all direct marketers: directing your message to an audience with a defined psychographic profile, interest, demographic profile, gender, and even sexual orientation (Yamamoto 1996). Simple enough, isn't it? Daniel H. Rimer, an Internet analyst with Hambrecth & Quist, calls it *community casting*: directing your message to "specific groups or persons dictated by tastes and affinities" (Yamamoto 1996). An example: LatinoLink (shown in Figure 4.3), which is directed toward Latino users.

Look for the eTRUST Logo

Because Internet users have become increasingly cynical about trusting Web sites to keep personal information in confidence, there's a need for an independent, authoritative privacy rating service. And that's just what eTRUST is for (Comaford 1996).

eTRUST (http://www.etrust.org) is short for Electronic Transaction Ratings Using Secure Technology, and it's a joint project of the Electronic Frontier Foundation (http://www.eff.org) and a consortium of industry practitioners. eTRUST proposes to rate and label Web sites with three levels of privacy:

▶ **Level One**—This site gives the greatest level of privacy and protects the user's anonymity. It's designed for sites that have no need for, or legitimate interest in, collecting personal information. No specific identifying information is kept. Log files are regularly deleted, and no information is sold to any third party.

▶ **Level Two**—This site gives midlevel privacy. It's designed for sites where consumers want to establish a personal relationship with an online vendor. Consumers authorize how much information is collected, and they're told what's going to be done with it.

▶ **Level Three**—This site may resell the data users supply, but they're told what's going to be done with it and they have an opportunity to stop the transaction before the information is collected.

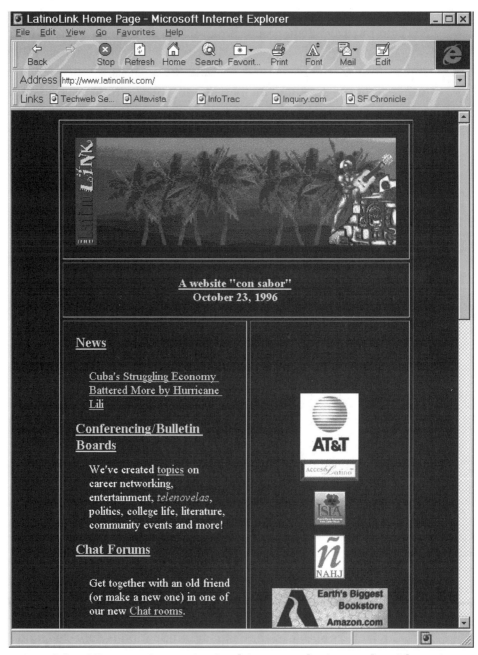

FIGURE 4.3 "Community casting" achieves marketing goals without intrusive measures.

Currently, eTRUST is planning a global rollout in early 1997. Look for the eTRUST logos!

References

Anonymous. 1996. "Percentage of Respondents Who Have Falsified Online Registration." *Electronic Buyer's News* (July 1, 1996).

Anonymous. 1996. "Web Ad Revenue Jumps 83 Percent in Second Quarter." *PR Newswire* (September 3, 1996), p. 903.

Boutié, Philippe. 1996. "Will This Kill That?" *Commmunication World* (April 1996).

Carl, Jeremy. 1996. "Flexibility Is the Aim of Intersé's Next-Generation Tracking Tool. *Web Week* (March 1996).

Comaford, Christine. 1996. "Toward Mutual Electronic R-E-S-P-E-C-T." *PC Week* (July 15, 1996), p. 50.

Goldman, Debra. 1996. "A Banner Business." *ADWEEK Eastern Edition* (July 8, 1996), p. 25.

Marjonovic, Steven. 1996. "Fear of Fraud and Loss of Privacy Crimp Online Sales, Study Finds." *American Banker* (October 16, 1996), p. 13.

O'Laughlin, Marty. 1996. "NetCount Offers Deeper User Data." *Inside Media* (November 29, 1996).

Robbins, Max. 1994. "Internet Advertising Must Reflect Network 'Culture.'" *Business Marketing* (January 1994), p. 10.

Ubois, Jeff. 1995. "The Art of the Audit." *Internet World* (December 1995).

Ujlfelder, Steve. 1996. "Online Snoop." *ComputerWorld* (August 12, 1996), pp. 82–83.

Walz, Gary. 1996. "The Ad Game." *Internet World* (July 1996).

Yamada, Ken. 1996. "Tracking a Silent Threat." *Computer Reseller News* (June 19, 1995), p. 45.

Yamamoto, Mike. 1996 "Marketing the Medium." *c | net Business* (September 27, 1996). Online document (http://www.news.com/SpecialFeatures/0,5,3915.html).

CHAPTER 5

Think Twice before Publishing Your Home Page

At last count—using the Alta Vista search engine—there were more than one million home pages on the Web. Many of these are corporate or organizational home pages, but several hundred thousand surely are *personal home pages*. What's a personal home page? Writing in *MacWorld*, Matthew Hawn sees fit to quote Whitman: "An attempt, from first to last, to publish a Person, a human being . . . freely, fully, and truly on record." Hawn concludes, "I can't think of a better guideline for creating personal Web pages."

Put your whole life online? Maybe you'd better think twice. Do you really want to publish personal details about your life, in a medium that enables anyone in the world to perform a highly precise key-word search? Although there are valid reasons to put a home page on the Internet—for example, making your résumé available—you aren't able to control who sees what you've written about yourself. This could have adverse consequences if a prospective employer doesn't like something about your politics or your lifestyle.

This chapter explores the privacy issues connected with home-page publishing, beginning with an exploration of the urge for self-revelation. It continues by discussing the risks of home-page publishing, which include e-mail harassment, job discrimination, and even job loss. You'll learn how

---

Why Snoop? I'll Tell You Everything . . .

► A college student, majoring in electrical engineering, includes his resume on his home page—as well as a list of his favorite Scotch whiskeys.

► A woman, married with two school-aged children, reveals that she is bisexual and includes a love poem addressed to another woman.

► A librarian reveals that she has a potentially fatal genetic disorder.

► A blue-collar collar worker reveals that he is an ardent unionist and includes many links to union activist pages and resources on the Web.

---

easy it is to use Web search tools, such as Alta Vista, to locate people's home pages and learn a great deal about the people who published them.

Valid reasons exist for publishing a home page—not the least of which is that doing so opens up the possiblity of meaningful, positive contacts as well as intrusive ones. For this reason, this chapter doesn't argue *against* publishing your home page, nor indeed against taking a well-considered stand when you feel that you must—instead, it counsels you to think twice about the plusses and minuses of publishing personal information about yourself. If you decide to publish your page, you'll find guidelines for home-page publishing at the end of the chapter.

Where Does the Urge for Self-Revelation Come From?

The Internet builds communities, reunites friends, and enables people to connect in myriad ways. That's why people are so willing to divulge very personal information about themselves. The following list contains some common reasons for publishing home pages:

► **To link with other people of similar interests**—If you've just discovered that you have a serious disease, making this public may enable you to get in touch with others who have the same condition. Some medical practitioners believe that children suffering from Down syndrome may be experiencing better care and increased longevity precisely because there is such an active information-sharing community on the Internet.

▶ **To provide information about yourself to people you meet in MUDs or IRC**—A common means of introducing yourself in multiuser Dungeons & Dragons games (MUDs) or Internet Relay Chat (IRC) is to give online friends the URL of your home page.

▶ **To reshape one's identity in a more favorable light**—It's tempting— you can emphasize the things about yourself that you would like others to perceive and appreciate.

▶ **To reestablish old friendships**—In our increasingly mobile society, it's hard to keep up with old friends. Yet reestablishing those relationships can do wonders for self-esteem and general psychological health (Brown 1996). By publishing your home page, you increase the chance that someone might find you.

▶ **To find a mate**—People can learn more about your hobbies and interests, and judge whether you're compatible.

▶ **To find a job**—One of the most common reasons for publishing a home page is to include a resume. You can make contact with potential employers via e-mail, and tell them your home page's location. If they're intersted in you, they can obtain your resume right away. Many job seekers have found employment this way.

In sum, many valid reasons exist to publish your home page. What you need to consider is whether they're worth the risks.

But What Are the Risks?

Many positive contacts can emerge from publishing your home page. But you're making your personal information public. You could find yourself on the wrong end of harassing e-mail. If your boss doesn't like your politics, lifestyle, or links, you could get passed over for promotions—or even lose your job.

Unwanted E-Mail.   If you're female, you'd best be aware that publishing your home page will bring unwanted e-mail. As one online chatter put it, "Chicks on the Internet are considered to be chicks first and human beings second (if at all)" (Herz 1996). It's a fact of life online, some say. One woman, who complained of getting "hit on" almost daily, finally started using "Auntie" as her online moniker. "There are not too many guys out there who want to talk dirty to their auntie" (cited in Anonymous 1996). The ruse worked.

Sometimes online contacts lead to worthwhile relationships. But be forewarned. If you feel tempted to meet somebody who contacts you online, you'll need to take special precautions. Stephanie C. Crawford, a Missouri-based computer science major who publishes her home page, offers the following advice: "If you end up going on a date with someone you've met on the Internet, always meet in a public place, such as a restaurant, preferably with a group of friends. Gut feelings tend to be correct here. . . . If you don't like the vibes you're getting, get out."

Online Harassment.   There's a world of difference, though, between an occasional expression of interest and online harassment. E-mail harassment is a "methodical, deliberate, and persistent communication that disturbs the recipient," according to Catherine Buzzell, who has published a Web presentation on the subject (Buzzell 1996).

In Michigan, sending such mail is a crime, thanks to a stalking law that includes unwanted e-mail. The possible sentence? A year in jail and fines of up to $1,000. The law has already resulted in at least one conviction. A Michigan man met a woman through a video dating service. After she spurned him, he sent her 20 unwanted e-mail messages and several letters and packages. The man was arrested and charged with "electronic stalking" (Lewis 1994). The man reportedly pleaded no contest, and received a year of probation and an order to submit to a psychiatric examination.

"Conservatives Are Smarter."   There's another risk of publishing your home page. What if your boss reads it and doesn't like what's found there?

If you're a Democrat, you'd best be aware of the statistics: According to a *USA Today*/CNN/Gallup Poll (cited in Jones 1996), 65 percent of senior executives described themselves as conservative, while only 37 percent of all likely voters described themselves the same way. In other words, there's a pretty good chance that your boss is more conservative than you are.

For some bosses, this isn't just an honest difference of opinion. It's not uncommon for conservatives to believe that liberals are fuzzy thinkers. For this reason, there's a temptation to work political prejudice into performance evaluations. A Columbia, SC, logistics management specialist didn't

What to Do if You're Victimized by Online Harassment

A Web developer and author, Catherine Buzzell offers the following advice to any woman plagued by repeated, unwanted e-mail:

1. **Archive every piece of mail relating to the situation**—Save every piece of communication you get from this person. Save all of the header information you can if it's an e-mail or newsgroup posting. If you're getting talk requests, IRC messages, or any other type of communication, take a screenshot, print it out, and write notes on it. Send copies of each harassing communication to your postmaster and the harasser's. Don't forget to save communications to postmasters, system administrators, police, supervisors at work, and security specialists.

2. **Start a log**—In addition to your archive of communications, start a log that explains the situation in more detail. Document how the harassment is affecting your life, and document what steps you're taking to stop it.

3. **Tell your harasser to cease and desist**—It's important that you contact your harasser directly, telling him or her in simple, strong, and formal terms to stop contacting you. You must state that the communications are unwanted and inappropriate and that you will take further action if it does not stop. Don't worry about whether your letter sounds too harsh—make sure it's professional and to the point. CC: your postmaster and your harasser's. Archive the mail you've sent, and note in your log that you sent it. After you send this mail, your communication to this person must stop. Any further communication can feed the situation. The harasser's behavior will be rewarded by your attention, so it

mince words in telling a *USA Today* reporter that "a Republican working for me might get a better job report" (Jones 1996). The politics could certainly work the other way. Would a conservative Republican get a fair shake from a manager devoted to extremist environmental politics? It's illegal to fire employees based on political convictions expressed outside the workplace (Anonymous 1994), but you're well advised to stay below the political radar screen if you care about your chances for promotion.

will continue. Also, if the case goes to court, your harasser can report that the communication was going both ways, and it could damage your case. It's best to keep quiet no matter how tempted you are to defend yourself. It's important that you tell your friends not to communicate with the harasser in your defense for the same reasons.

4. **Tell the right people**—Report the situation to your system administrator(s), your friends, family, and coworkers. Tell your supervisor and work security personnel. Tell your apartment building's security people. Report the situation to your local police. The FBI will also take down a complaint, and they'll follow up on it if they have the manpower.

5. **Take police action**—Many states have modified their stalking laws to include electronic communications. Many states will let you file for a restraining order in cases like this, and the courts will often let you ask that your harasser pay for any filing fees. You'll need the person's address if you want to serve them with a restraining order or press charges against them. The police can get this information from the harasser's postmaster if they need to.

6. **Protect your online space**—Change your password frequently. Pay attention to your files, directories, and last logout information. Monitor information about yourself on the Net with Alta Vista and other search engines. You might want to lay low for a while if the person is haunting you in Usenet or on IRC.

7. **Protect your offline space**—Take all the precautions you would if an old boyfriend were acting crazy, especially if you think the person can find you at home or at work.

Source: http://www.phantom.com/~barton. Used with permission.

Could Your Home Page Put You at Risk of Losing Your Job?

On November 7, 1995, Kmart Corporation fired Rob Fournier, a programmer/analyst who was responsible for the firm's Web page. Fournier's home page allegedly contained links to sites with sexually explicit graphics.

Fournier did not go quietly. To tell his side of the story, Fournier created a "Kmart SUCKS Page"—now retitled Mart SUCKS Page (http://www.

concentric.net/~rodf/mart.htm) after the firm's attorneys demanded that Fournier stop using Kmart's copyrighted logo.

Finding Someone's Home Page: A No-Brainer

How hard is it for somebody to locate your home page—somebody like your boss, a competing coworker, or somebody who holds a grudge against you? Very easy.

Searching by Sex, Marital Status, Age, and More.   A Web-based search service called Housernet (http://www.housernet. com/) enables Internet users to search for home pages by sex, marital status, age, birth date, and entry date (see Figure 5.1). In short order you can produce a list of divorced females aged 30 to 39—or boys aged birth to 9.

But Housernet doesn't search the whole Web. In order for your page to be retreived by a Housernet search, you must register your page with the service. This is fair enough—if you judge that the risks are worth making your home page available, you can register.

Searching All of Cyberspace.   You can use any Internet search engine to search for personal home pages. In Alta Vista, a search for "+home page" followed by the person's name will bring up the page in short order, as long as the person has used the word "home page" somewhere on the page. Other services create indexes of home pages that enable you to search for the home pages of people who meet specified demographic criteria, and another enables searches for any key word.

WhoWhere, one of several Web-based e-mail directories, offers a Personal Home Page search service (http://homepages.whowhere.com), which is apparently based on automated search routines as well as individual submissions.

Chicks First and Human Beings Second: The "Babes on the Web" Page.   Your home page might attract unwanted attention—for example, it might wind up on Mirsky's Worst of the Web page (http://mirsky.com/wow/), which is something of a reverse compliment, actually, since it does bring lots of visitors to your site. But there are ways to list sites that aren't so easy to write off with good humor.

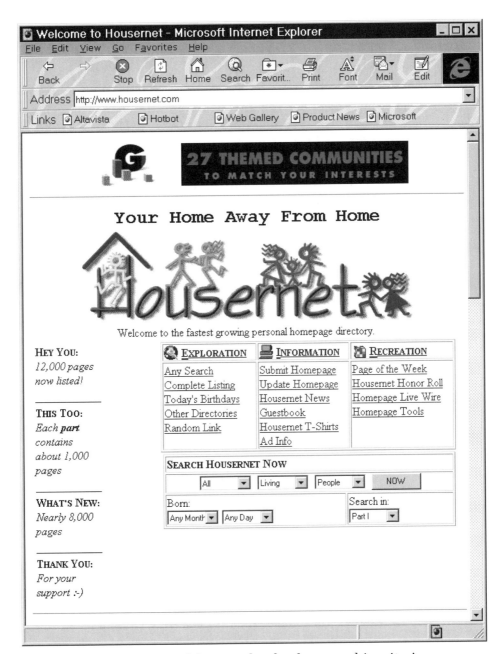

FIGURE 5.1   Housernet enables searches by demographic criteria.

Protecting Your Children from Online Predators

The ability of any Internet user to search for children's home pages is sure to give children's advocates pause. Pedophiles are using the Internet to make contact with kids who establish home pages and join chat groups, say children's advocates. To be sure, the risk is almost certainly exaggerated by a press bent on fueling public hysteria, and politicians looking for votes (Carroll 1995). But a cautious parent should think long and hard about any risk to children, no matter how much it might be exaggerated.

Here's what troubles many parents about the Net: It enables child predators to establish e-mail friendships that parents don't know about. It's one thing when your kids get a string of letters through the mail—something you're almost certain to notice. Unless you're monitoring your kids' e-mail, though, you won't know if they've made contact with an adult online. If your child wants to publish a home page, make absolutely sure that it contains no information that would enable an online predator to locate your child—no e-mail address, no location information, no school name.

Robert Toups, a self-described male chauvinist pig, created a page called "Babes on the Web" (now withdrawn) that listed the URLs of women who had placed home pages on the Web. Based on their personal pictures, Toups rated them with a scoring system of Toupsies, four Toupsies being the highest rating a page could earn.

One of the listed women, an MIT student, wrote to Toups and requested that he remove her name and URL from Toups's page. According to this woman, Toups refused, stating that he had done nothing illegal. In defending his creation of the page, he argued that it was his *right* to do so because it was *possible* to do so. Toups added—provocatively—that criticism of his page only made its author happy (Kantor 1996). In other accounts, Toups seems to have responded favorably to such requests.

What was Toups's motive? Publicity, apparently. Toups hoped to parlay his Web site skills into a career in Web site design (Gunn 1995). The same motive led more than a few women to submit their URLs to Toups for inclusion.

Toups has withdrawn his page from the Web—but the links still work. They take you to a Toups-designed Web site that has nothing to do with women's home pages. Apparently, Toups has gotten all the publicity he can handle!

Guidelines for Publishing Your Page

Still committed to publishing your home page on the Web? Keep the following in mind:

▶ Recognize that information about yourself could become an issue for an employer, insurer, or credit agency.

▶ If you're female, be mindful of online harassers. Don't disclose your address or telephone numbers. Consider using a sex-neutral pseudonym. Don't respond to harassing e-mail, but carefully log and save such messages.

▶ If you're helping a child publish a page, don't include specific information regarding the child's age, school, home town location, or any other information that might enable a predator to find the child. Include *your* e-mail address—and if you receive any messages that offer pornography or solicit unsupervised meetings, don't hesitate to call the police.

▶ Don't include telephone or fax numbers. If someone's interested in contacting you, let this person open communication with an e-mail message, which you can check out to see how you feel about it. Try replying to make sure the return address is valid, and ask for identifying information.

▶ Imagine your home page on your boss's desk—and revise it until you think it will pass muster.

▶ Don't link to anything that might prove controversial to an employer. To develop Web material concerning a controversial subject, don't use your employer's system. Get a personal Internet account and keep your name off the page.

References

Anonymous. 1994. "When the Politics Get Personal." *Supervisory Management* (October 1994), p. 3.

Anonymous. 1996. "Female Users Take Measures to Avoid Online Harassment." *Salt Lake Tribune* (May 14, 1996). Online document (http://www.nando.net/newsroom/ntn/info/051496/info894.html).

Brown, Edwin W. 1996. "A Great Boost to Emotional Health: Reestablishing Old Relationships." *Medical Update* 19 (March 1996), p. 2.

Buzzell, Catherine. 1996. "Online Harassment Resources." Online document (http://www.io.com/~barton/harassment.html).

Cantor, Lorrie Faith. 1996. "It Shouldn't Be Allowed!" *ACM Crossroads.* Online document (http://www.acm.org/crossroads/xrds2-2/lorrie.html).

Carroll, Jim. 1995. "Internet Hysteria Is Silly." *Toronto Globe and Mail* (March 21, 1995). Online document (http://www.e-commerc.com/JACC/articles/22.htm).

Gunn, Angela. 1995. "Judge for Yourself." *Web Week* (July 1995). Online document (http://www.webweek.com/95July/op-ed/editrial.html).

Hawn, Matthew. 19096. "Song of Myself: Personal Publishing on the Net." *MacWorld* (August 1996), pp. 131–132.

Herz, J.C. 1994. "Even Console Cowgirls Get the Blues." *Time Warner Electronic Publishing.* Online document (accessible through PathFinder at http://www.pathfinder.com).

Lewis, Peter. 1996. "Persistent E-Mail: Electronic Stalking or Innocent Courtship?" *New York Times* (September 16, 1994). p. B11.

Spertus, Ellen. 1995. "Thoughts on Web Pages Listing Women." Online document: (http://www.ai.mit.edu/people/ellens/Gender/webwomen.html).

CHAPTER 6

Consider Disabling Cookies

Suppose you visit a supermarket. Unbeknownst to you, an employee sticks a tiny electronic gizmo into your coat pocket, where it will stay, unnoticed by you (even after you leave the store). While you're shopping, this device keeps track of everywhere you go in the store. Unseen, it notes which products you looked at, how long you looked at them, and what you bought. All this is done without your knowledge or consent. And the next time you visit the store, you find everything rearranged in accordance with your preferences. Finally, the anchovy paste and Italian tomatoes are right there where they're easy to find! Meanwhile, the supermarket makes $1 by selling information about you to a marketing firm.

That's impossible with a physical store, but it's more than practicable on the Web. And in fact, that's just what hundreds of Web sites are doing right now. Not only that, but some of them also have joined monitoring networks that are busily assembling huge databases that contain information on your online meanderings. They've got ten million records already. Think that's scary? Read on.

What makes all this possible are *cookies*—and I don't mean the chocolate-chip kind. Cookies are text files that Web servers write to your hard disk "transparently"—as technical people like to say—that is, without your knowing. These files are used to store information, such as preference choices, your user ID and password, or a list of the advertisements you have viewed. The next time you access the site, your browser uploads any cookies that this Web site might have left behind previously. When the cookie is sent, the server reads it and uses the information to provide you with customized services of some kind (Barr 1996, Byczkowski 1996, Kingston 1996, Kristol and Montulli 1996).

Is there a good side to cookies? Yes. As this chapter explains, cookies can be used for your benefit. They enable you to choose configuration options so that your choices are visible the next time you access the site. They also enable other convenient features, such as logging on to a subscription site automatically, without your having to type your user name and password.

Are cookies a threat to your privacy? Right now, it's debatable. If you're sensitive about Internet sites gathering data about you without your knowledge, you're not going to like what you read in this chapter. And if you don't like Web sites using your hard disk for data storage without your permission, you'll like it even less. The companies busily assembling databases of people's clickstreams claim that this is being done anonymously by means of numerical identification numbers that aren't linked to personal names or e-mail addresses, but who's to know what some ultra-aggressive marketing firm will try next? It's technically possible to create a central clickstream database that links those numerical IDs with a name, e-mail address, and much more. You may wish to seriously consider whether it's worth sacrificing some of the Web's interactive features to gain a measure of anonymity while you surf.

What makes cookies so galling is that you're faced with a rather cruel choice. If you don't disable them, you get more interactive Web features—but you won't know whether there's something more sinister going on. If you do disable them, you can prevent sites from using cookies in ways you dislike—but you have to give up on many convenient features of the Web.

You'll find, too, that browser publishers, such as Netscape and Microsoft, find themselves walking a tightrope where cookies are concerned. It's clear that Web developers and advertisers want them, for reasons you'll fully understand after reading this chapter. Yet it's also clear that users fear that cookies will violate their privacy. In an attempt to work this side of the street, too, both companies include provisions that ostensibly "disable" cookies in their latest browser versions (3.0). As you'll see, though, this was done in such a way that it imposes intolerable burdens on the user, who has to click away literally hundreds of intrusive dialog boxes in the course of an evening's surf.

Face it, folks, they don't *want* you to disable cookies. In this chapter, you'll find out why.

How Do Cookies Work?

The best way to understand cookies is to see them in action. Fire up your browser and access http://www.jasmin.com/kidinfo/. You'll see the "Just-for-You" Kids Page, shown in Figure 6.1. Make some selections, and display the custom page. Nothing special, yet. But quit the Internet and log on again. You'll find that the page recognizes you and displays your choices.

What's going on? The "Just-for-You" Kids Page has written a cookie to your hard drive. If you're using Netscape, you'll find it in the file called cookies.txt, located in the Netscape directory. In this file, you'll find a line of text from the "Just-for-You" Kids Page server (jasmin.com) that includes your page configuration choices.

Take a Cookie Tour

Robert Brooks's Cookie Taste Test (www.geocities.com/SoHo/4535/cookie.html) enables you to browse a number of sites that use cookies for a variety of reasons. Examples include Biography.com, AT&T World-Net, DigiCrime, Inc., Disney.com, InfoSeek Guide, Illuminati Online, and many more.

So what's wrong with this? What makes Internet users nervous about cookies is the sense of violation—somebody has written something to your hard drive without your knowledge. This conjures up a number of scary scenarios, but take heart—most of them aren't true, as the next section explains.

What Cookies Can't Do

When Microsoft Windows 95 was released, the Internet grapevine was working overtime with rumors about Microsoft's installation software. According to the rumors, the software scanned your hard drive and your network to see

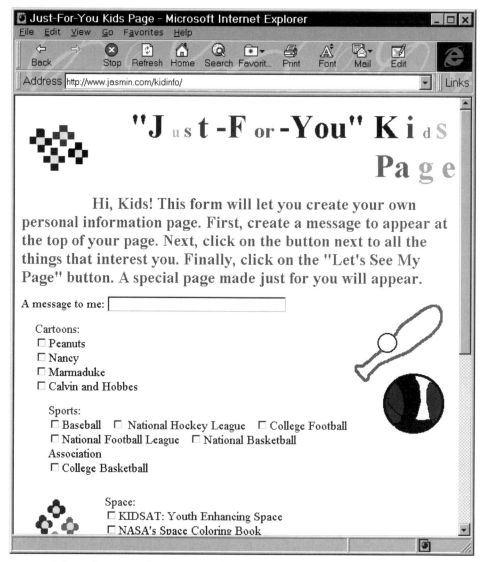

FIGURE 6.1   The "Just-for-You" Kids Page uses cookies to enable children to create their own customized Web pages. The next time you log on to this site, you'll see your custom choices.

whether any competitors' products were installed. Allegedly, this information was then uploaded to Microsoft when you used the online registration program.

Can cookies do something like this? No. Cookies are just text files, up to 255 characters in length. They aren't programs. Cookies can't scan your entire hard drive to see what programs or files you have. They can't figure out your e-mail address. Because cookies are domain-specific, it's not possible—or at least not convenient—for one server to read another server's cookies. And, cookies can't search your hard drive for sensitive personal information, such as your Social Security number.

That is, they can't do these things now, but security bugs enabled clever programmers to come up with some chillingly invasive hacks with previous versions of Netscape. When combined with insecure, early versions of JavaScript and Netscape (see Chapter 8), cookies could be used to obtain your e-mail address—one particularly insidious hack forced your browser to send an e-mail message from you to the intruder's e-mail account without your knowledge, thus disclosing your e-mail address! But this and other security holes have been plugged (Kington 1996) in a more recent version of the program.

TIP *Don't use early versions of Netscape.* **Even if you're reluctant to upgrade, you should do so in order to protect yourself from the many security holes in early versions of the program, such as 2.0. Always use the latest version of Netscape—incremental releases (those numbered in the tenths or hundredths) are commonly motivated by the discovery of security holes or other potentially dangerous bugs.**

So now you know what cookies can't do. Before examining what they *can* do, let's consider why cookies were invented in the first place.

Why Do Web Authors Consider Cookies Necessary?

Given Internet users' paranoia about programs writing things to your hard disk without your knowledge or permission, why would Web authors risk their sites' reputation by using cookies? "It's simple," says Dan Ancona of the University of Virginia's Center for Advanced Technology in the Humanities. "They're too useful to give up."

Here's why. The key is to understand that HTTP, the standard (protocol) underlying the Web, is *stateless*. No, this doesn't mean that it's a standard without a country—although that's true, too (the Internet standards *are* international). It means that the interaction between your browser and a Web server is a one-shot deal. When you click a hyperlink, your Web browser initiates contact with the server, obtains the desired page (along with any associated graphics)—and closes the connection. Zap. That's it. There's no *retrievable* recollection of what you did, what you chose, what you viewed. Nothing. Apart from an entry in the server's access log, which might only indicate the *domain* (network) from which you accessed the site, it's as if the connection never existed. The next time you log on to the site, it's as if you had never visited it before.

The motivation behind cookies was to create a way for Web pages to leave behind some kind of *trace of their passage*, in such a way that this information could be recovered in a future session. This would greatly benefit the user, in that you wouldn't have to reenter passwords, resupply your Visa or MasterCard number, or make configuration choices repeatedly. This happens automatically, without your knowledge or consent—for convenience, of course. But the upshot of cookies is that a Web page can "remember" you from your last visit. As one Web developer put it, "It's as if a marketer could [surreptitiously] tattoo customers once they entered a store so that upon returning they can be recognized as repeat customers" (Raisch 1996).

In principle, then, cookies enable a *stateful session* (Kristol and Montulli 1996), in which a Web server can set up a dialog with a Web browser. The state that's created persists as long as the cookie persists. (That's why Netscape's documentation refers to them as "*persistent* client state HTTP cookies." They reside on your client—that is, your browser—and define a persistent state, or relationship between a specific browser and specific server.) Since cookies are stored on disk, they can persist for weeks, months, or even years. (In practice, though, cookies rarely persist for longer than a few months, for reasons to be explained subsequently.)

So what's in this message that the server leaves on your drive? For the technical details, see the sidebar, "What's in a Cookie?" However, it's enough to know that every cookie establishes a unique user identification, usually expressed as a code number of some sort. Note that this doesn't *necessarily* mean that the server knows your name or e-mail address. As far as the server is concerned, you're just a code number. But you're a *unique* code number. "Even though I don't know it's you," says Jonathan Nelson, CEO of Organic Online, "here's a heavy user whom I've seen before." And here's where some real possibilities open up. "Maybe I'll tailor some more content, give it to you in greater depth, maybe give you some offers," Nelson says (cited in Andrews 1996). That's the basic motivation behind the invention of cookies: to make things more convenient for the user. What was it somebody said about the road to hell being paved with good intentions?

What's in a Cookie?

Each cookie consists of a *name* (the cookie's name) and a *value* (the data contained in a cookie). The value includes the following:

- **Expiration date**—If this isn't specified, the cookie expires when the current session ends. Cookies are often set to expire in a matter of weeks or months; sometimes they're set to persist for years.
- **Domain**—This is the Internet address of the server that originates a cookie. Browsers upload only those cookies that come from the same domain as the page you're viewing. In other words, if you're viewing www.nice.com, your browser won't upload any cookies from www. naughty_pictures.com.
- **Secure**—If this value is set to True, the cookie is transmitted only if the user has established a secure (encrypted) channel with the server.

In addition, a Web author can set up a server to store and retrieve additional information, up to a maximum of 4K per cookie and 20 cookies per server. This information can include the user's ID number, user name, real name, login password, previous configuration choices, and much more.

To see your Netscape cookies, access the file cookies.txt, which you'll find in the Netscape folder. All your Netscape cookies are stored in this file. To see your Internet Explorer cookies, open the Windows folder, and open the Cookies folder. As you'll see, Internet Explorer stores your cookies as separate, individual files—and some of the information is coded so that you can't read it.

When you listen to technical people talk about cookies, they always mention the anonymity of numerical user IDs and the many useful things cookies can do. As you'll see in the next section, cookies are indeed very useful—and you may be as unwilling as Web authors to give them up.

But you'll also see that cookies can be quite easily paired with individual identities. When you agree to use cookies and supply personal information, you're trusting Web authors to refrain from developing personalized marketing databases based on your clickstream—databases that could prove to be so valuable that they could keep a company on the healthy side of the balance sheet.

Just what is the risk here? Let's look more closely at the interactive features that cookies can provide.

Cookie Applications That Benefit Users

Cookies provide the foundation for much of the interactivity that makes the Web an entertaining and commercially viable medium. As you'll learn in this section, many of the most interesting Web sites—the ones that pop up in Best of the Web rankings—make extensive use of cookies to provide interactive services that are clearly beneficial to the user.

Providing Page Customization.   Throughout the Web, you'll find many services that enable you to customize a Web page with your own choices so that you see these choices the next time you log on. One of the most impressive of these pages is My Yahoo! (my.yahoo.com), a service offered by the popular Yahoo! subject directory (www.yahoo.com).

To configure your page with My Yahoo!, access my.yahoo.com. You'll see the screen shown in Figure 6.2 (or a more recent version of it). You can start creating your own My Yahoo! page by clicking the new user hyperlink. After you do, you'll see the page shown in Figure 6.3. In this page, you use forms to create a login name and password. In addition, the site demands that you supply your age—ostensibly for enabling you to recover your password in case you lose it (but we know better than that, don't we?)—and your sex. You're also asked to suply your e-mail address—which, of course, makes it quite possible to determine your identity. Although you're not asked to divulge your name, you're doing so, for all practical purposes. If you fail to supply any of the demanded demographics, you'll see a page insisting that you do so before registration can be completed.

After you've supplied the needed registration information, you're asked to select the topics in which you're interested (Figure 6.4). Ostensibly, what you're doing here is choosing the items that you would like to see on your customized My Yahoo! page. But what you're also doing is filling out a very nicely detailed marketing profile. From this submission, marketers could learn that a particular person—quite identifiable from her e-mail address— is interested in health, tennis, movies, television, lesbian/gay issues, rock and roll, automobiles, books, and WWW authoring.

Just what is this information to be used for? In the "It's personal" section of the registration page, you're told that it won't be given to anyone else—

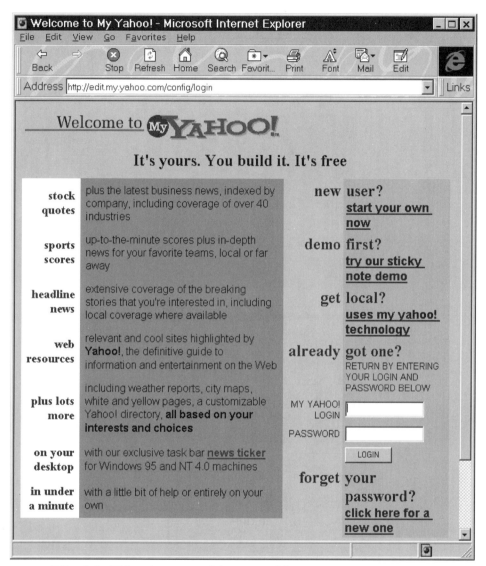

FIGURE 6.2   My Yahoo! uses cookies to enable you to create a custom news page, complete with the news stories, sports scores, and stock quotes that you want to see.

that it's used only by Yahoo! and "our content providers" (such as Firefly) to develop personalized services. On the Firefly registration page, there's a similar message—but it says only that Yahoo! promises to never release your e-mail address to a third party without your consent. This page says nothing about keeping your demographics confidential!

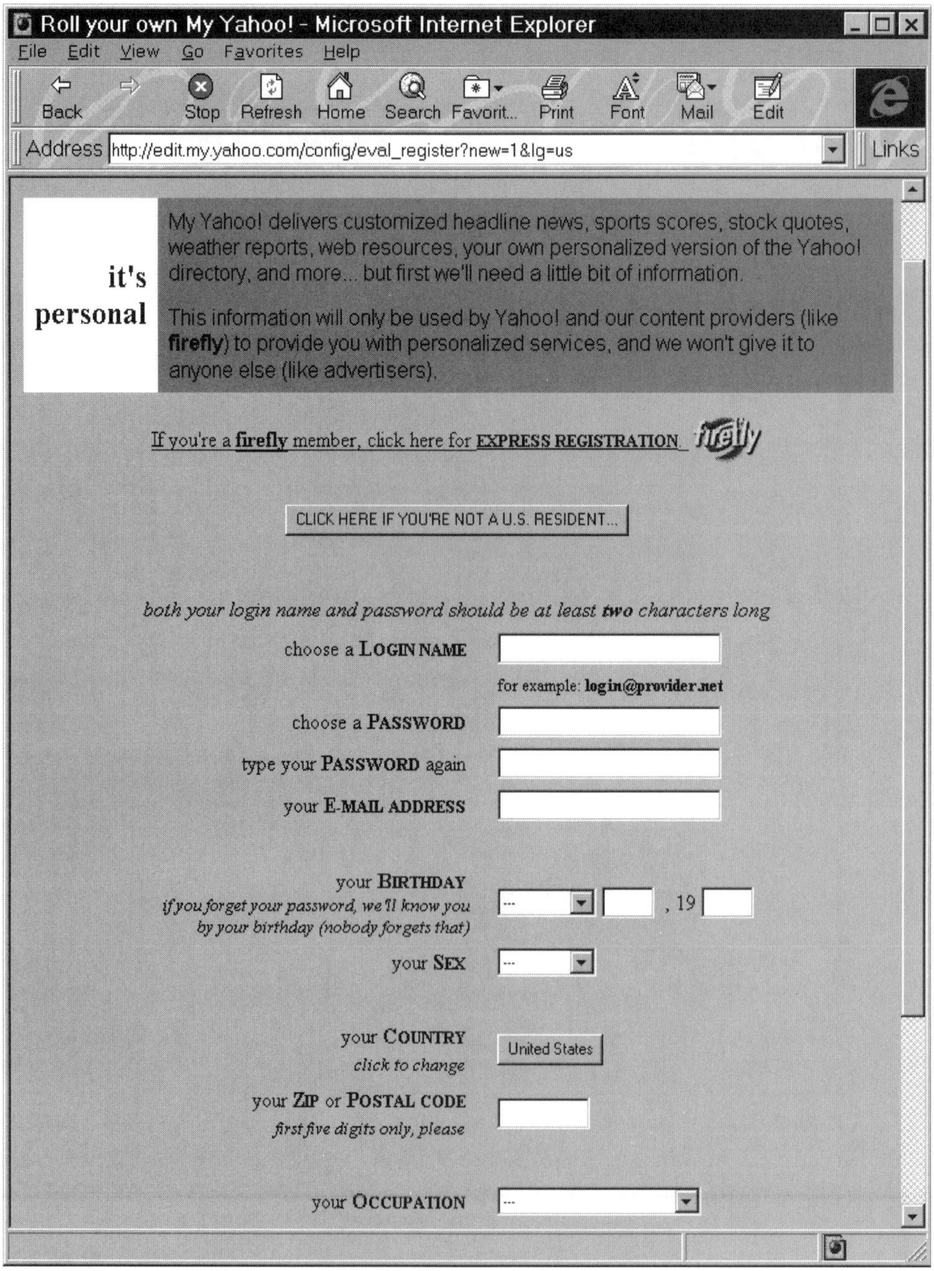

FIGURE 6.3 My Yahoo! demands demographic information as the price of registration.

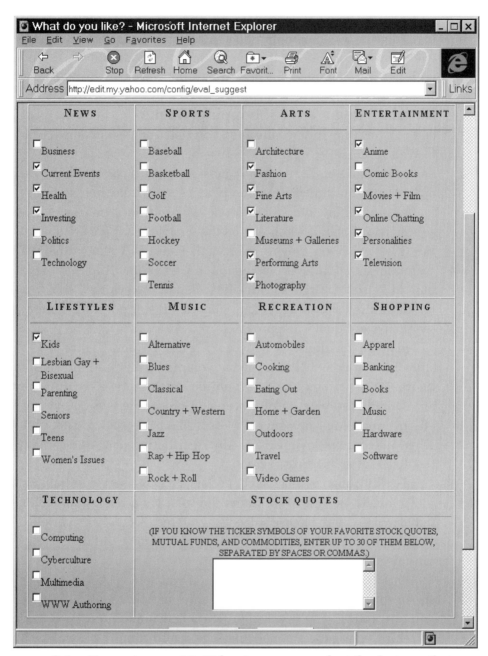

FIGURE 6.4   To create your My Yahoo! page, you select the features that you would like to see.

Basically, this boils down to a question of trust. Do you trust Yahoo! not to divulge your demographics to a third party—information that could very well prove lucrative? I sent an e-mail message to Yahoo! asking what's done with this information—I received no reply. Were they just too busy?

Keeping Items in a Shopping Basket.   Cookies raise privacy qualms, but they're virtually indispensable for Web commerce, according to Web authors. Let's explore the use of cookies at amazon.com, an online bookstore that's one of the Web's most successful commercial enterprises. I order from Amazon.com frequently and I really like their service.

Boasting an inventory of over one million titles, Amazon.com features a supple and capable search engine that enables shoppers to quickly choose the titles in which they're interested. Figure 6.5 shows the results of a search for an audio cassette version of *The Yellow Admiral*, the latest volume in Patrick O'Brian's critically acclaimed sea stories. To add this book to your online shopping basket, you click the appropriate button and you see the page shown in Figure 6.6.

Note the relationship between Figure 6.5 and Figure 6.6—the page shown in Figure 6.6 "knows" what you did in the page shown in the other figure. Without cookies, this would be much more difficult to implement and would involve a lot of server-side processing—which would eventually overload Amazon.com's servers. (This is another reason, incidentally, why Web authors love cookies—by distributing data storage, they reduce the demand on overtaxed servers.)

Like My Yahoo!, Amazon.com offers a custom service—but this one employs e-mail, not the Web. Called Editors, it's a book notification service that enables you to choose subjects of interest. Once every couple of weeks, you'll get an e-mail message informing you of new and interesting books in the categories you've selected.

What's the privacy risk here? Zilch if you believe Amazon.com's privacy statement: "We do not sell or rent information about our customers." If you're skeptical, you're asked to send blank e-mail to never@amazon.com; in return, you get an e-mail message reaffirming the company's privacy pledge. Apparently, this is supposed to inspire confidence by giving you what appears to be a binding contract; after all, an exchange of first-class letters does establish such a contract. However, the question of whether an

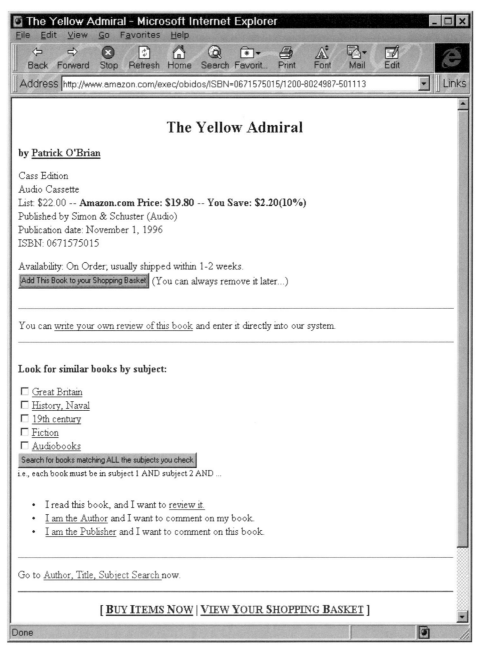

FIGURE 6.5   Choosing an item to place in your shopping basket generates a cookie.

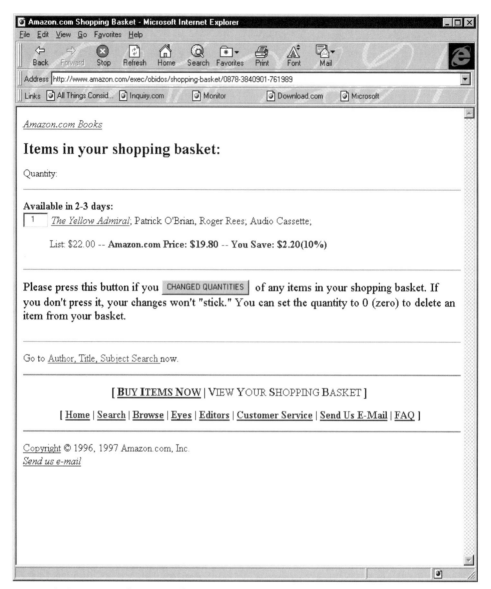

Amazon.com Books

Items in your shopping basket:

Quantity:

Available in 2-3 days:

[1]   *The Yellow Admiral*; Patrick O'Brian; Roger Rees; Audio Cassette;

List: $22.00 -- **Amazon.com Price: $19.80** -- **You Save: $2.20(10%)**

Please press this button if you [CHANGED QUANTITIES] of any items in your shopping basket. If you don't press it, your changes won't "stick." You can set the quantity to 0 (zero) to delete an item from your basket.

Go to Author, Title, Subject Search now.

[**BUY ITEMS NOW** | VIEW YOUR SHOPPING BASKET]

[Home | Search | Browse | Eyes | Editors | Customer Service | Send Us E-Mail | FAQ]

Copyright © 1996, 1997 Amazon.com, Inc.
Send us e-mail

FIGURE 6.6   Your shopping list.

exchange of e-mail constitutes a binding contract has never come before the courts, and it's far from certain that it does. E-mail doesn't currently have the Constitutional protections given to first-class mail. I don't mean to suggest that Amazon.com is being duplicitous here—doubtless, this is a sincere gesture—it's just that it's probably meaningless, from a legal point of view. Once again, you're back to the basic point: If you do business with Amazon.com and subscribe to Editors, you're going to have to trust them to resist the temptation to sell the valuable information they've collected.

Showing You Fresh Content.   Another way users benefit from cookies: When you reaccess certain sites, you don't see the same static page that some sites display. Instead, you see fresh content, based on the retrieval of a cookie that tells the server which content you've already seen.

Here's an example of this technology in action. When you first access LookSmart, the *Reader's Digest* Web site (www.looksmart.com), you see the page shown in Figure 6.7. This page enables you to choose which version of the site you want to view. After you make your choice, you see the version of the site you've selected. Figure 6.8 shows the Java version of the site—which is very interesting. It disables your browser's toolbar, and substitutes its own. Included are customization features that are based on cookies and Java (see Chapter 7).

Logging You In Automatically.   Web sites that require registration or subscription sometimes use cookies to enable you to log in (supply your user name and password) automatically. The first time you log in, you'll be asked to type your user name and password manually. Subsequently, you'll see a page (such as the one shown in Figure 6.9) that enables you to choose an automatic login option. If you choose this option, you won't have to log in manually the next time you visit the site. This is a welcome convenience.

TIP Is your computer used by more than one person? If so, think twice before choosing an automatic login option. Doing so enables anyone using your computer to access a registration-based or subscription-based site. If the site has a chat room or message board, this person could leave messages that would appear in your name.

FIGURE 6.7 LookSmart's initial screen never appears again, thanks to cookies.

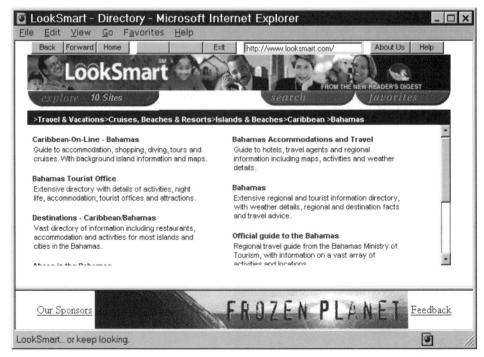

FIGURE 6.8 LookSmart's appearance after choosing your preferred format.

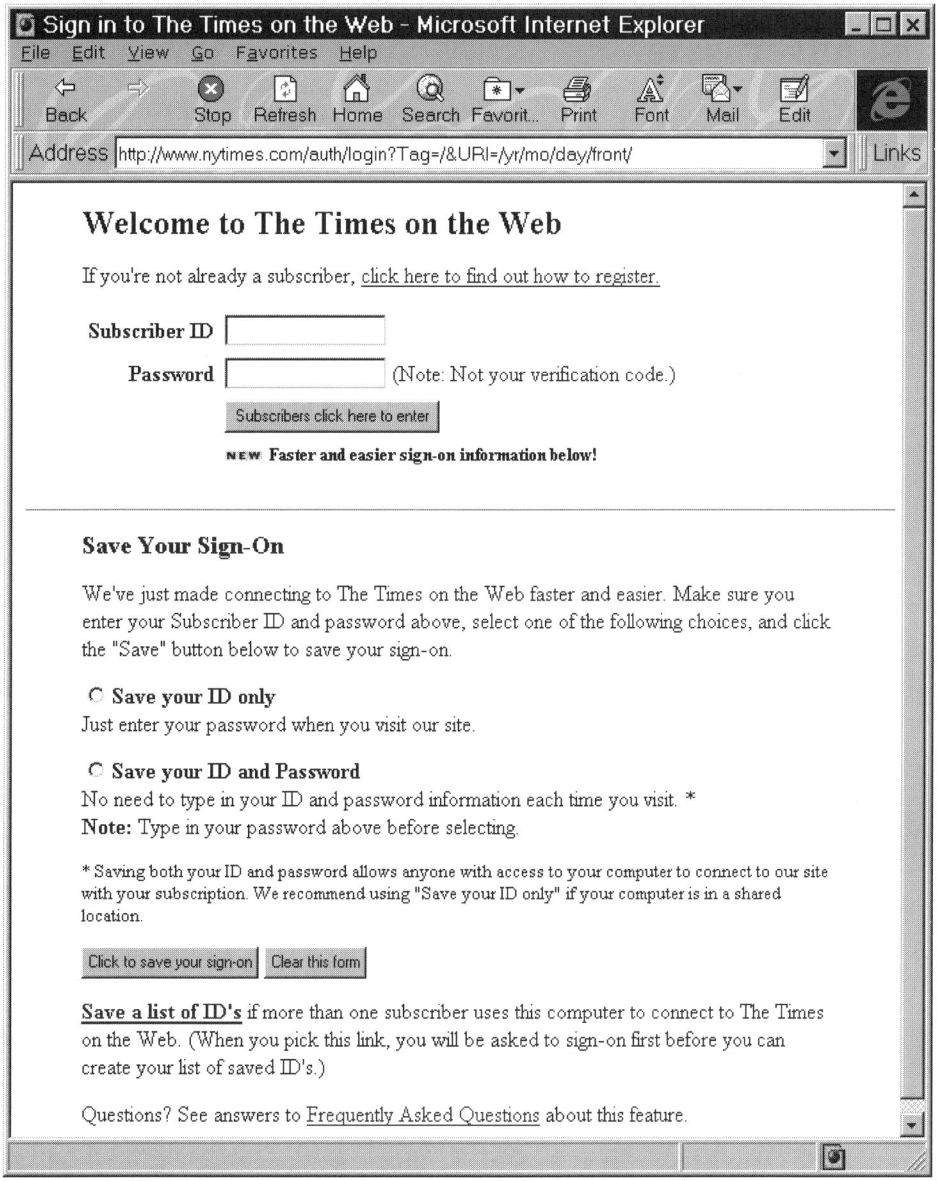

FIGURE 6.9 Cookies enable you to save your sign-in information.

Cookie Applications that Benefit Web Site Developers and Advertisers

The cookie applications discussed previously benefit the user. But there are other applications that work in the background, unseen, while you're visiting a site. These chiefly benefit Web site developers by providing them with detailed information concerning what you're doing online.

Monitoring Your Usage of a Web Site.   At many sites, cookies are used to track everything you do—which pages you looked at, for how long, which links you clicked. It's like you're in a supermarket, and some assistant manager is following you around, watching everything you do. "Don't mind me," the manager says.

Why? The data attracts advertisers. As one Web site developer put it, "The kind of thing that really gets [advertisers'] eyes open is when you hit the stats feature that shows here's where your traffic is coming from. That's where they begin to see the power of the Web" (cited in Byczkowski 1996).

Overcoming the Domain-Specific Limitations of Cookies. Cookies are domain-specific. This means, essentially, that a Web server can read only those cookies originating from its own domain (Internet address). For example, suppose your server is www.pushy-ad.com. You would be able to retrieve only those cookies that originated from www.pushy-ad.com. In practice, this would be easy to surmount—all you'd have to do is instruct the server to look for cookies originating from some other domain (such as www.arm-twist.com or www.in-your-face.com). However, you would have difficulty predicting whether such cookies would be present. It would be a hit-or-miss operation, at best.

But several marketing firms have figured out how to surmount this shortcoming. Here's how it works. The server leaves a cookie that doesn't refer to the server's domain. Instead, it refers to the domain of some centralized advertising firm (such as www.central-ad.com). This cookie contains a unique ID number that identifies you. The ID number doesn't contain your name, necessarily, or any other personal identifying information, but it does identify your computer. Any server subscribing to the centralized firm's services will know to look for www.central-ad.com's cookie—and when it finds this cookie, the server knows that you've visited another site on the network.

Information about which sites you've accessed (and what you did while you browsed there) can be relayed back to www.central-ad.com, which can put all this information into—you guessed it—a huge database.

Doubleclick.com.   That's the theory. And it's already been implemented in practice, most notably by Doubleclick.com, an Internet advertising agency that *Fortune Magazine* recently picked as one of its "cool companies" for 1996.

DoubleClick, Inc., is one of several advertising networks on the Web that offer advertisers the ability to distribute their ads to dozens of popular Web sites. DoubleClick's cookie-based technology enables the firm to target ads to users who are most appropriate for the advertised goods or services. An ad for a $10,000 high-end multimedia projector, for example, would go to people who might have sufficiently deep pockets—and the presentation needs—to fork over five figures for a projection device (Moukheiber 1996).

How does DoubleClick know who you are? The firm doesn't, actually. According to David Henderson of DoubleClick, "What we do is we tag [users] with a cookie just to identify them as unique, and then build a profile based on what we can derive; data we can derive off the Internet." No effort is made to obtain the individual's e-mail address or name.

Current subscribers include Quicken Financial Network, Investor's Edge, NETworth, PC Quote, Computer Currents, MapQuest, Doonesbury, Internet Movie Database, and USA Online.

Here's how it works. When you access a Web site that's contracting with DoubleClick, the DoubleClick server assigns you an ID number and stores that number on your computer via a cookie. Subsequently, when you visit any of the sites in the DoubleClick network, the server looks for your ID number and recognizes you. Based on a proprietary algorithm, the firm's software analyzes your browsing habits and other readily available information, such as the known demographics of the domain from which you're accessing the Internet, and chooses an ad that's likely to prove of interest to you. What you see on the Web page you're viewing, then, isn't a static advertisement that's a fixed part of the page design. On the contrary, it's an ad that DoubleClick thinks is especially likely to resonate with your interests.

Gradually, the server builds up a dossier on you and your browsing habits. Note, though, that this database doesn't include all your activities online—it includes only the several dozen sites that are currently paying for DoubleClick's services. It's pretty innocuous stuff, really—which sport you prefer, which type of computer you like. Currently, DoubleClick has amassed some 10 million user profiles.

Is This a Privacy Risk?   What many Internet users fear about services such as DoubleClick is that their marketing databases could be sold for lots of money, were they to change their approach and start matching the profiles with names. DoubleClick's CEO, Kevin O'Conner, states that DoubleClick would "never" do such a thing—or if it did, "it would be voluntary on the user's part" (Moukheiber 1996). But who's to say what might happen if DoubleClick got into serious financial trouble, and realized that it could sell its valuable demographic profiles for some serious money?

It's certainly possible to use site registrations in order to match an "anonymous" user ID with a person's name, address, and e-mail number. In fact, this is done routinely by Web sites that require registration or enable you to log in automatically. It's not done by DoubleClick, though—but they or any similar firm could. All it would take is for one of the subscribing sites to link your user ID to a site registration form, and upload the information to the centralized database. Bingo! Now we know who you are.

And here's a theme that's been repeated several times in this chapter: trust. The present management of DoubleClick seems to be strongly committed to preserving users' anonymity. But what if the firm were acquired by a third party that wasn't so scrupulous? There's nothing you'd be able to do about it. "Once your information is disclosed to a third party, your ability to control and limit its use evaporates," says Ann Cavoukian, an Assistant Commissioner for Ontario's Information and Privacy Commission (cited in Garfinkel 1996).

There's no doubt: Cookies represent the leading edge of a concerted effort to monitor your online viewing habits. According to *Privacy Times* editor Evan Hendricks, "Cookies represent a coming effort by organizations to monitor people's interest in their products and services through the covert gathering of personal data without their knowledge" (cited in Kurkowski 1996).

Should You Disable Cookies?

It's a difficult choice:

▶ If you *do* disable cookies, you can't take advantage of many cool interactive features that use cookies in a harmless way. You'll give up some of the features that make the Web so cool.
▶ If you *don't* disable cookies, you won't know what's going on when you access a site. You won't be told what kind of monitoring is taking place, what use is going to be made of this information, or what's being stored on your hard disk.

***Can* You Disable Cookies?**   Basically, no. The current versions of Internet Explorer and Netscape Navigator don't really enable you to disable cookies. On the contrary, they give you an option that lets you selectively approve the downloading of new cookies. This feature is implemented in such a way that you will quickly grow tired of the dialog box appearing (see Figure 6.10) that asks you to confirm or reject the cookie; at some sites, you'll have to do this a dozen times or more to deal with each downloaded cookie, one by one.

What's Going On Here?   I don't mean to sound paranoid, but it's almost as if this "cookie-disabling" feature were designed with the knowledge that you'd quickly tire of it, and turn it off! Try it, and you'll see what I mean.

If you're not suspicious yet, read on. The "cookie-disabling" features of both programs work only when a server attempts to *download* a cookie. But they do nothing to stop the browser from *uploading* an existing cookie from your hard drive—there's no notification of this event, and no way to turn it off!

Want some more evidence that neither of these firms really wants you to disable cookies? Try this:

▶ In Netscape, cookies are stored in a file called cookies.txt, in Netscape's directory. If you delete this file, Netscape will just write a new one.
▶ In Internet Explorer, cookies are stored in a folder called Cookies (it's within the Windows folder). If you delete this entire folder, Windows will just create a new one for you, without so much as a by-your-leave.

Isn't that nice?

FIGURE 6.10   If you disable cookies, you get this dialog box dozens of times in an average search session.

Disabling Cookies with Microsoft Internet Explorer 3.0.   If
you'd like to try disabling cookies with Microsoft Internet Explorer version
3.0, do the following:

1.   Choose View Options, and select the Advanced tab.
2.   Click Warn before accepting "cookies."
3.   Click OK.

Disabling Cookies with Netscape Navigator 3.0.   To disable
cookies with Netscape Navigator version 3.0, do the following:

1.   Choose Options Network Preferences, and click the Protocols tab.
2.   In the Show an Alert Before area, click Accepting a Cookie.
3.   Click OK.

What Browsers *Should* Do.   According to Frank Chen, Security
Product Manager at Netscape, cookies are necessary but browsers need to
do more to inform users what's going on (Staten 1996). Recently, Netscape
has joined with other Internet firms to propose an Internet standard (Kristol
and Montulli 1996) concerning cookies. To conform to this standard, a
browser should enable the user to:

▶ Disable the sending and saving of cookies.
▶ Determine whether a stateful session is in progress.
▶ Control the saving of a cookie on the basis of the cookie's domain at-
  tribute.

In addition, the browser should:

▶ Notify the user when the browser is about to send a cookie to the server.
▶ Let the user decide which cookies, if any, should be saved when the user
  closes a window or exits the browser.
▶ Enable the user to examine the contents of a cookie at any time.

The current versions of Netscape Navigator and Internet Explorer fall
very short of the mark with respect to these criteria.

What Should *You* Do?

You need to decide whether you believe that cookies pose a genuine threat to your privacy. Currently, I don't think they do—but who knows whether some pushy, unscrupulous firm might enter the centralized advertising business and start collecting personal data on your clickstream? With current technology, you have absolutely no way of knowing whether a given cookie is being used for or against you. Worse, the two most popular browsers really don't give you a meaningful way to avoid cookies. Still, you can take certain steps to counter the cookie trail, as described in Chapter 14.

TIP If you would like to avoid cookies altogether, there is a way—but it means consigning the two leading browsers to the digital equivalent of the garbage dump. You can use a cookieless browser, such as Ariadna. This very capable browser, which can handle tables, frames, and Java, is included on the CD-ROM disc packaged with this book. For more information on cookieless browsing with Ariadna, see Chapter 15.

References

Andrews, Whit. 1996. "Sites Dip into Cookies to Track User Info." *WebWeek* (June 3, 1996).

Barr, Christopher. 1996. "The Truth about Cookies." Online document (http://www.cnet.com/Content/Voices/Barr042996/).

Bunger, Stan. 1996. "Internet Privacy." *Leading Off.* Online document (http://www.newmedianews.com/92196/lo4ip.html).

Burning Door Networked Media. "Cookies: Design, Implementation, and Appropriate Use." Online document (http://www.burningdoor.com/sandbox/javascrp/cookies.htm).

Byczkowski, John. 1996. "'Cookies' Track You on the Web." *Cincinnati Enquirer* (March 3, 1996).

Kington, Andy. 1996. "Andy's Netscape HTTP Cookie Notes." Online document (http://www.illuminatus.com/cookie.fcgi).

Kristol, David M., and Lou Montulli. 1996. "HTTP State Mangement Mechanism." Internet Engineering Task Force Internet Draft (HTTP Working

Group), (November 4, 1996). Online document (http://portal.research.bell-labs.com/~dmk/cookie.txt).

Kurkowski, Cynthia. 1996. "Cookie Reviews." *The Spider's Web.* Online document (http://www.incontext.ca/spidweb/archives/news/may15/cookie8.htm).

Moukheiber, Zina. 1996. "DoubleClick Is Watching You." *Forbes* (November 4, 1996).

Negrino, Tom. 1996. "Cookies: A MacWorld Online Special Report." Online document (htttp://www.macworld.com/netsxmart/cookiestory.html).

Netscape Communications. N.d. "Persistent Client State HTTP Cookies: Preliminary Specifications." Online document (http://www.netscape.com/newsref/std/cookie_spec.html).

Raisch, Robert. 1996. "True Names Have Power: User Identity and the Web." Advertising and Marketing Report. Online document (http://netday.iworld.com/business/ad-mkt/am960723.html).

Rejonis, Charles. 1996. "Opening the HTTP Cookies Jar." *Netscape World* (July, 1996). Online document (http://www.netscapeworld.colm/netscape-world/ nw-07-cookies.html).

Staten, Frank. 1996. "Netsape Tricks Raise Security Concerns." *MacWEEK Gateways* (March 13, 1996).

CHAPTER 7

Consider Disabling Java, JavaScript, and ActiveX

It's the latest rage. Throughout the Web, you'll find Web pages that contain something much more exciting than garden-variety HTML. They also contain programs, written in languages such as Sun Microsystem's Java, Netscape's JavaScript, or Microsoft's ActiveX. The latest versions of Netscape Navigator and Microsoft Internet Explorer act as *interpreters* for these languages. (An interpreter carries out, or *executes*, the program's instructions.)

What's cool about these programs is that they add live content to Web presentations, enabling Web pages to take on many of the characteristics of desktop applications. For many site developers, such as w3media's Michael Mehrle, Java holds the key to providing real interactivity for the Web: "It allows a lot of [browser-based] activity that you just can't do" with existing Web tools, such as HTML (Levin 1996).

When your browser is running a Java or JavaScript program, it comes alive with active content, going far beyond the animations and other tricks you've seen within your browser's window. After accessing a page with an embedded Java program, for example, a Web page takes on added functionality. In Figure 7.1, for example, you see WallStreetWeb, a Java applet designed for investors. This impressive application tracks your investments throughout the trading day using real-time stock quotes.

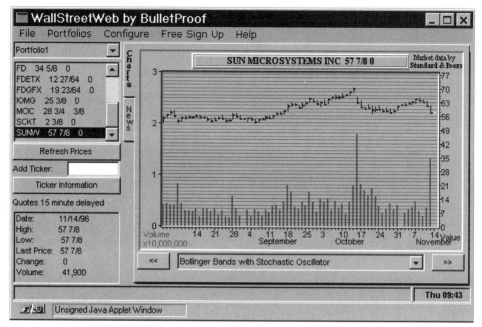

FIGURE 7.1   WallStreetWeb is a Java applet designed for investors.

What's not so cool about these programs, as Web users are discovering, is that they introduce new possibilities for attack and intrusion. To be sure, there's no evidence—as yet—that anyone has suffered serious losses of data or damaging privacy invasions as a result of these features. As you'll learn in this chapter, though, a prudent Internet user will do well to consider disabling Java, JavaScript, and ActiveX. You'll lose the cool, interactive features these languages enable. But this isn't a total loss; you can still selectively enable Java, JavaScript, or ActiveX, should you encounter a trustworthy site that employs them.

This chapter introduces Java, JavaScript, and ActiveX, explaining what's at risk, from both the security and privacy angles. You'll learn what's going on behind the scenes in this very competitive (and hype-filled) arena—and why you should remain skeptical about the claims made by Sun, Netscape, and Microsoft that these languages pose no threat to the security of your computer system or your personal privacy.

Introducing Java

Java has been hailed by some as a revolutionary new programming language that will forever change the face of computing, by others as merely an interesting footnote in programming history, and by still others as little more than an organized computer virus. Where's the truth?

Programming the Old Way.   To understand Java, it's best to begin by looking at how programmers created computer programs before Java came along. To extract the maximum speed from the programs they wrote, programmers used versions of programming languages that were specific to a certain type of computer, such as a Macintosh or an IBM PC. They tended to write big, complex programs, and they sold them to you in shrink-wrapped boxes that had to be transported all over the world and sold in stores. And this added significantly to the cost of software.

Then the Internet exploded in popularity. Many software publishers immediately grasped that the Internet could be used as a new, low-cost channel for distributing software. They started selling the same old, machine-specific programs in a new way. This new distribution method has many advantages—not the least of which is that you can quickly distribute a new version when bugs are discovered. Many software companies send out most of their software over the Web, such as Nico Mak Computing, the makers of the respected WinZip compression/decompression software for Windows computers. There isn't much to worry about here from a security angle—you're downloading trustworthy software from the Web site of a trusted company. You'd be wise to think twice, though, about downloading and running software from less trustworthy sources—you could find yourself saddled with a computer virus.

The Network Is the Computer.   The Internet provides a convenient, low-cost medium for distributing application programs. But the Internet visionaries at Sun Microsystems started thinking in ways that went beyond merely using the Internet as a new distribution channel. They knew that the Internet's popularity is partly linked to its ability to network many different types of computers. Why not use the Internet as the vehicle for distributing a new *platform-independent* programming language, one that could be distributed over the Internet and run on virtually any machine out there? (A platform-independent language is written in code sufficiently general that it can be made to run on any computer.)

For programmers, platform independence holds out the very appealing promise that you can "write it once, run it anywhere" (Levin 1996). The only drawback to this idea is that you'd need to distribute *interpreters*—programs capable of reading the programs' instructions and executing them on a specific type of computer. Why not include the interpreter in a Web browser?

That's the brilliant idea underlying Java—and it's the perfect way of fulfilling Sun's oft repeated prophecy that "the network is the computer" (Hof 1996). Instead of trying to stuff your PC full of the software needed to give you functionality, you go to the network to get software as needed. You download snippets of Java code, called *applets*, which perform the tasks you need performed at the moment. Think of it as just-in-time software delivery!

To demonstrate the concept, Sun developed and distributed a Web browser called HotJava (Karpinski 1995). Subsequently, Netscape and Microsoft, as well as any other browser publisher that wanted to stay in the game, developed Java-capable browsers. Chances are, you're using one today.

Whether Java will fulfill its promise remains unclear. For one thing, interpreted languages such as Java run much slower than languages that can speak directly to the kind of hardware you're using—if you're skeptical, try accessing the Java version of LookSmart (www.looksmart.com), and see how your computer slows down. More efficient interpreters might reduce this problem in the future, though. In the long run, what's going to determine Java's success—or ensure its demise—is whether computer users are going to be comfortable downloading executable code from the Internet, and running this code on their computers.

Java: Will It Stay in Its Sandbox?

Developed by Sun Microsystems, Java is a full-fledged programming language designed for use by professional programmers. It is very similar to C++, the most widely used programming language for software development. However, it was specifically designed to omit several features of the C++ programming language that could be exploited to create highly destructive programs. Whether this and other security measures are sufficient to safeguard Internet users is still very much in debate.

How Java Works.   Java programs download from a server just the way a Web page does. When they're received by your computer, your browser starts a *byte-code interpreter* that executes the Java program one byte at a time. In theory, the Java interpreter should safeguard your system against intrusive or destructive attacks: Attempts to access your computer's file system are stopped dead in their tracks before the code can execute. In particular, Sun has designed Java to prevent the following:

▶ Inspecting or changing files on a client file system.
▶ Using network connections to circumvent file protections or people's expectations of privacy (JavaSoft 1996).

To ensure that untrusted applets will behave nicely, Java restricts them to a *sandbox*. In essence, this means that applets can use only the screen and computer power of your computer. They can't get to your files, or to other computers on your network. Java runs in a "virtual computer," which is created inside your computer's memory. Every line of code is scrutinized as it executes to make sure that it does nothing destructive.

Is this a complete solution to the dangers of downloading untrusted code? As experience has shown, the answer is plainly No. Merely restricting Java to it sandbox is an unsatisfactory solution to the Web's security and privacy problems. To find out why, read on.

What Are the Risks of Using Java?   The Internet is complicated. The underlying technology isn't well understood by most of the people using it. But experienced Internet security people will frankly tell you that existing Internet system software is riddled with flaws that attackers and intruders exploit in various ways. Adding Java to the mix creates many new opportunities.

Although there's no evidence that anyone has lost data or suffered system intrusions due to Java, several researchers have discovered ways that "rogue" Java applets can monopolize or exploit your system's resources in an annoying, inappropriate, or destructive manner (LaDue 1996b), largely by consuming your computer's system resources. But rogue applets can also be used to bring about major system security violations and privacy intrusions. An example: It's theoretically possible to write a program that can insert or delete data on the page of a "secured" Web site.

Java Mischief.   Fortunately, much of the risk posed by Java falls into the malicious prank category (see LaDue 1996a for a variety of rogue applets). In a *denial-of-service attack*, a hostile Web page—a page that may masquerade as a benign, attractive Web site—forces your browser to launch Java applets that consume all of the available system resources or memory in your system. In one such attack, an applet paints huge black windows on your screen so that you can't see what you're doing.

Some of these pranks, though, have disturbing implications for privacy. One rogue applet prompts you to enter your user name and password—a blatant attempt, obviously, to obtain this information so that a hacker can make an unauthorized intrusion into your Web service provider's system.

Exploiting a well-known bug in the UNIX sendmail program, a rogue Java applet has been written that enables a hacker to send forged e-mail by gaining access to another person's account (without authorization, of course). The forged e-mail cannot be traced to its source (LaDue 1996b).

Potentially the most serious security bug to date was recently discovered by a Princeton security team (Dean, Felton, and Wallach 1996). In this flaw, the researchers discovered, a rogue applet can manipulate your browser to execute any command that you can carry out on your computer. For example, a hostile applet can read, modify, and delete your files. Never mind that this isn't supposed to happen with all of Java's sandbox safeguards!

Don't Worry—It's Fixed.   As each new revelation of serious Java security and privacy flaws hits the newsstand, there's a fix. According to Java-Soft's home page, when bugs are discovered, fixes are promptly developed and transferred to all licensees (JavaSoft 1996). The flaws discussed in the previous section have all been addressed by new versions of Java. And according to some experts, the number of serious flaws is decreasing over time.

But this process — finding bugs and then releasing new versions—testifies to a fact that software developers don't want you to know. There's no technology or procedure in existence that can fully test programs for flaws prior to their public release. That's why software publishers are increasingly amenable to releasing "free" prerelease versions of their programs to the public at large. There's nothing like having a million people testing your program!

TIP   **Don't be the first on the block to download and try prerelease (beta) versions of Web browsers, such as Netscape Navigator and Microsoft Internet**

Explorer. Besides the obvious risk that these programs might contain bugs that might crash your system, causing you to lose unsaved work in other applications, they might also contain flaws that enable attackers to violate your privacy.

You can be sure that new flaws will be discovered as software companies attempt to add new features to their products. And that's what makes using Internet-distributed software such as Java so unsettling. According to Stephen Cobb, director of Special Projects for the National Computer Security Association (NCSA), "The situation is scary. Software companies are releasing products on the Internet without even considering the hacker perspective. . . . There is a real danger allowing users to freely access the WWW" (Home Page Press 1996).

Out of the Sandbox—And into Your File System?   And there's ample evidence that the sandbox approach just isn't working, as a Sun security expert candidly admitted, according to a recent report. "Trying to build a secure sandbox paradigm for running untrusted downloaded applets on the web is hard," she said (Home Page Press 1996b). Echoing this point at a recent security conference was Paul Kruger of IBM's Thomas Watson Research Center, who stated that it wasn't just hard to secure Web program code—it's "rocket science" (Leopold 1996). It's not surprising, then, that JavaSoft's documentation plainly states that, despite all the measures taken to safeguard users, they "must be wary of executing any code that comes from untrusted sources" (cited in Wolfe 1996).

Toward Authentication.   To resolve public uncertainty regarding Java's safety, Netscape Communications reportedly plans to include a *code authentication* feature in the next version of its Navigator software, version 4.0. Code authentication provides a way for software developers to sign a program digitally—attesting, in effect, that it comes from a trusted source.

You'll be warned before a Java applet attempts to do something potentially destructive, and you'll have an opportunity to inspect the code's digitally signed certificate of authenticity, which tells you—presumably—that the code is benign.

But Netscape is planning to pair digital certificates with less rigorous restrictions on Java's access to your computer. You'll be able to choose which features of your computer Java will be able to use, including your hard disk, says Netscape spokesman Eric Greenberg, who adds: "We broke a wall in the side of the sandbox" (quoted in Balderson 1996).

JavaScript: An Incredibly Insecure Scripting Language

JavaScript is a scripting language designed for use by nonprogrammers. A creation of Netscape, JavaScript is essentially a subset of the Java programming language. Unlike Java, which requires a compiler that produces an executable program, JavaScript is written in text that remains on your Web page. It's hidden from view, but it executes when someone accesses your page with a JavaScript-capable browser. (Both Netscape Navigator and the most recent version of Internet Explorer can interpret JavaScript.)

One of the motivations underlying JavaScript was to give nonprogrammers part of the power of Java. Using JavaScript, Web amateurs could easily create Web pages with lots of active content, such as form fields that produced calculation results, animations, and much more. Perhaps this would help to ward off what many Internet users saw as an undesirable trend—a growing gulf in sophistication between amateur and professional Web sites.

Isn't This a Good Thing?   What concerns security and privacy experts regarding JavaScript is that the language simply isn't as well thought through as Java—which, as you've seen, has its own share of problems. There is also evidence that it wasn't well tested. Several potentially serious JavaScript security bugs were discovered by a 15-year-old Berkeley high school student, named Eric Perlman (Taft 1996). His testing techniques were hardly scientific. "I came across the bugs by accident. I stumbled upon them and said, Wait a minute, this isn't supposed to work. Then I wrote some code that did the rest of it" (Taft and Dunlop 1996).

Although both Netscape and Sun heatedly deny it, there are rumors of a rift between the two companies concerning JavaScript (Karpinski 1996, Taft and Dunlop 1996). According to a *Computer Reseller* article, a Sun insider said, "About a month before we were going to make Java available, Netscape came to us and said, 'By the way, we have this scripting language that we want to call JavaScript. Is that okay?' We said no." (Taft and Dunlop

This Is War, Folks

It's no secret that Microsoft and Intel have a lock-tight grip on the desktop computing market. But the meteoric rise of the Internet, and the arrival of Java, might just change all that.

There's plenty to like about the "Wintel" model. You get a relatively stable operating system and lots of great applications, such as Microsoft Word and Microsoft Excel. But all this is achieved at the expense of stuffing your desktop computer full of complex, expensive software—and what's more, you'll need plenty of computing horsepower to run these programs. Corporations find that Wintel PCs are very expensive to support and maintain.

Thanks to the Internet and Java, there's possibly another way: Transfer the complexity to the network. Tomorrow's desktop PC might be a relatively simple device, one that looks like today's PCs, perhaps, but, much simpler and easier to maintain. Instead of Microsoft Windows, you'll be running a Java operating system, and you'll be linked more or less permanently to the Internet, or a corporate intranet. When you need software, your Java box will obtain it from a network source.

Bill Gates knows that this is a serious threat to the Wintel platform's dominance. According to Steve Ballmer, Microsoft's Executive VP, "Job one for [Microsoft] right now is the Internet and defeating Netscape. . . . They're simply our smartest competitor." That's why Microsoft performed such a stunning maneuver, suddenly making the Internet the center of its development strategy. For the time being, Internet users can count on finding themselves in the middle of a huge, no-holds-barred battle, as Goliath (Microsoft) battles a whole slew of Davids, made up of all the firms who are hoping to get Java onto the desktop. "In many ways it's like World War III," says Eric Greenberg, a Netscape project manager. "It's very intense" (Wolfe 1996).

What all this means is that you're going to be seeing a lot of snazzy new technology pushed at you very fast, and very often—perhaps before it's ready for prime time.

1996). Reportedly, one reason for the rift is that Sun wanted Netscape to adopt Sun's Tcl/Tk, a Sun-developed Internet scripting language that had already been through two years of development (Gage 1996).

The reason had to do not only with the name. Sun had spent the equivalent of four to five years of effort to develop Java and ensure its safety. JavaScript took only a few months to develop. According to the rumors, the Java people weren't happy that Netscape had thrown JavaScript together in a few months, in an attempt to gain some market advantage over Microsoft. The move was understandable—it isn't fun to have Microsoft breathing down your neck—but JavaScript posed a threat to Java's credibility. Pressed to get as far in front of Microsoft as possible, Netscape is believed by some to have felt that it's better to release slightly imperfect software and deal with the bugs later—ironically, a strategy that Microsoft is often accused of following. For example, an executive at a Houston-based Internet services firm told a reporter, "Netscape follows the Microsoft model—get it out there and fix it later" (Taft and Dunlop 1996).

DigiCrime—Crime 'R' Us?

It's a joke, folks, so don't get worked up. But the Internet's sufficiently crazy that it might take a moment or two before you realize that it's a put-on. It's DigiCrime (www.digicrime.com), a site (see Figure 7.2) that purports to offer a "full-service criminal hacking organization."

You know you're in for something of an unsettling time the minute you arrive at the site. At the top of the page, you see the URL of the site from which you accessed DigiCrime. Appended to the message: "So much for privacy." How does this work? DigiCrime is exploiting a little known feature of HTTP that includes the referring page's URL in any HTTP request. In other words, it's a very trivial thing for a Webmaster to figure out just where you came from. But you already know that, don't you?

DigiCrime offers a full suite of criminal hacking services, including "Web site redesign services" (site spoofing), political dirty tricks, computer infection services, and custom pornographic blackmailing services.

DigiCrime's stock in trade is the new generation of cross-platform programming languages (Java, JavaScript, and especially ActiveX). As an illustration, DigiCrime includes an ActiveX control called Exploder, which performs a clean shutdown of Windows 95. Exploder (McLain 1996) is relatively well mannered—in a clean shutdown, you're prompted to save any unsaved work—but the possibilities give one pause.   *(continued)*

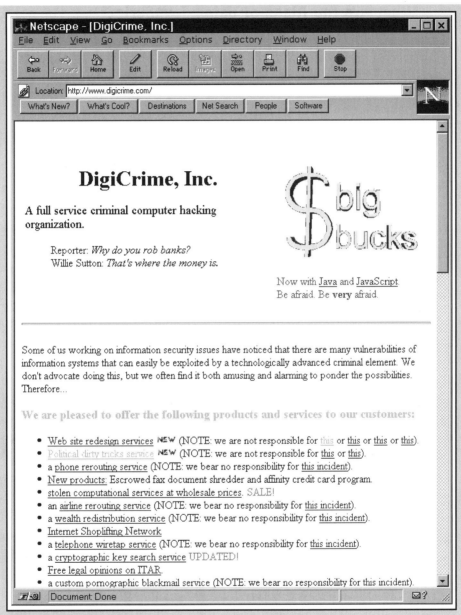

FIGURE 7.2   DigiCrime.

DigiCrime's amusing page is the work of its "Thief Scientist," Kevin S. McCurley, a computer scientist who teaches at the University of New Mexico, and his gang of accomplices.

What Are the Risks of Using JavaScript?   In contrast to hostile Java applets, which do much of their harm by consuming your system's computational resources, rogue JavaScript code frequently poses a threat to your privacy. Malicious JavaScripts have been created that do the following:

▶ Track the history of your Web surfing sessions
▶ Read your files and file directory listings
▶ Send file information back to a Web server
▶ Detect your e-mail address surreptitiously
▶ Originate e-mail messages without your knowledge (thus revealing your e-mail address)

Let's look more closely at some of these holes.

Who Are You?   The first release of JavaScript occurred with Netscape Navigator 2.0—and it wasn't long before JavaScript programmers discovered a clever trick. By means of a very simple script, one could discover the e-mail address of someone accessing your page.

This was accomplished by means of a very simple JavaScript program that made use of the Mailto: URL in HTML. The unsuspecting user would click a button on the page—and without realizing what was happening, the user would originate an e-mail message that would enable the user to determine the e-mail address of anyone browsing the page in which this script was embedded.

Why would someone do this? There are a range of motivations, not the least of which is to create a mailing list for junk-mail purposes. Suppose, for example, you set up a page called "Hot Naked Babes," and put up a couple of *Playboy* GIFs. You'll get thousands of hits per day. When you access the site, you see an R-rated picture, and a button that says, "Click here to see more of me!"

You click it and—without knowing—add your e-mail address to a growing junk-mail database. Netscape fixed this flaw in version 2.0.1 of Netscape Navigator.

TIP **Even though release 2.0.1 of Netscape Navigator addressed some of the security holes in JavaScript, it left others open—and what's worse, you can't turn off JavaScript. If you're using any version of 2.0, trash it and up-**

grade to 3.0 immediately. See the end of this chapter for information on turning off JavaScript in Netscape Navigator 3.0.

Where Have You Been?   One of the most serious breaches of Java-Script security was discovered by John Robert LoVerso (LoVerso 1996a), who discovered that the JavaScript implemented in Netscape version 2.0 could be used to track a user's browsing actions. The tracking occurs in real time, with the user's browser obediently sending its results back to a remote Web server—all without the user's knowledge or consent, of course. This serious privacy breach has also been fixed in recent versions of Netscape Navigator.

JavaScript Today.   When researchers and hobbyists discover a security or privacy flaw in JavaScript, Netscape—to its credit—responds quickly with a new version of Netscape Navigator that repairs the flaw. For example, Netscape released version 2.0.1 of Netscape Navigator in response to reports concerning privacy-related bugs in the 2.0 release of its browser.

But don't take it on faith that these problems have been permanently solved. Earlier in this chapter, you read about a flaw in version 2.0 of Netscape's JavaScript that enabled a rogue Web site to gather e-mail addresses. Version 3.0 of Netscape Navigator introduced a new JavaScript feature that unintentionally reintroduces this capability (McComb 1996).

TIP If you're using Netscape 3.0, immediately choose Options Security Preferences, click the General tab, and enable the Submitting a Form Insecurely option. This will ensure that Netscape displays a confirmation box before sending e-mail without your knowledge. This will prevent a rogue JavaScript program from instructing your browser to initiate an e-mail message without your knowledge.

In sum, JavaScript remains "an incredibly insecure scripting language" despite code fixes, according to Perlman (Taft and Dunlop 1996).

ActiveX: Open Season on Your File System?

With the release of Microsoft Internet Explorer 3.0, Microsoft launched its reply to Java and JavaScript. While supporting both languages in its browsers, Microsoft also created a new standard for distributing code snippets via the Internet. It's called ActiveX.

ActiveX differs from Java in many ways. First, it's not a programming language. Rather, it's best thought of as a way of encapsulating programs written in virtually *any* language so that they can be conveyed via the Internet. Second, ActiveX doesn't take Java's sandbox approach. On the contrary, ActiveX programs have full access to your computer's file system. That's right—full access. And that's precisely what scares the dickens out of security experts. According to Stephen Cobb, Director of Special Projects for the National Computer Security Association (NCSA), "OLE technology from Microsoft has even deeper access to a computer than Java does" (Home Page Press 1996b), and this fact alone means that you'd better think long and hard before using it.

What could an ActiveX control do? It's a trivial matter to write an ActiveX control that would scan your entire hard drive for all the GIF or JPEG graphics you've downloaded, and then mail them to the FBI—or your boss. You could then display a message such as, "You're toast, baby," and reformat the user's entire hard drive.

Whatever You Do, Don't Click This.   ActiveX's nefarious possibilities were immediately apparent to programmers—such as Fred McLain, a computer consultant in Bothell, Washington. McLain is the author of Exploder, an ActiveX control that will do a clean shutdown of Windows if you bypass Internet Explorer's warnings. McLain's site (shown in Figure 7.3) formerly enabled you to download Exploder. You can still see what it does—just make sure you've saved all your work before clicking the Exploder link!

McLain presented his control to Microsoft as evidence of ActiveX's security shortcomings. As you'll see in the next section, though, Microsoft didn't buy McLain's argument that Exploder represents a serious problem.

Will Code Authentication Solve the Problem?   Microsoft recognized that users would balk at downloading programs that could erase their hard drives. At this juncture, programmers are coming to a consensus regarding Internet-distributed programs: Users aren't going to feel safe using them—and in fact aren't going to *be* safe using them—unless they're distributed using some kind of security-encrypted certification system, which testifies to the authenticity and safety of the downloaded program. This is the approach (called Authenticode) that Microsoft is using for its ActiveX controls.

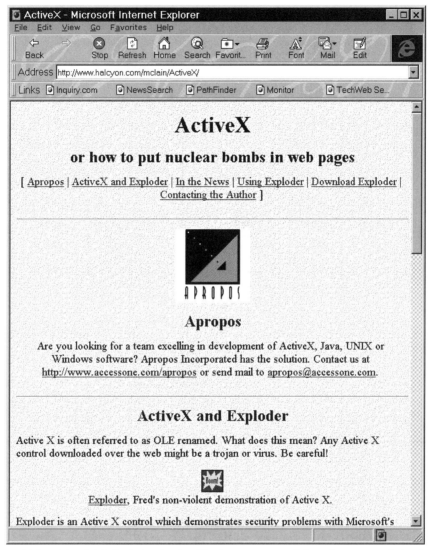

FIGURE 7.3   Fred McLain's ActiveX site warns of the dangers of ActiveX technology.

Authenticode works in the following way. When a software company wishes to develop an ActiveX control, it purchases a digital certificate from VeriSign, Inc., which provides secure, encrypted certificates for Internet use. When you're about to download an ActiveX control, Internet Explorer displays a warning and shows you the certificate (see Figure 7.4). If the control has no certificate, you see a warning message (Figure 7.5).

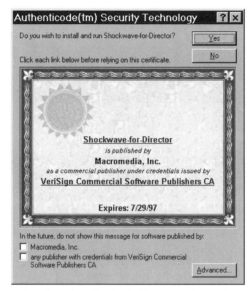

FIGURE 7.4   Authenticode certificate tells you that the software is from a trusted source.

When you install Microsoft Internet Explorer, the default security level is set at High, which means that the program won't download any ActiveX controls without warning you and giving you a chance to inspect the code's certificate. According to Microsoft Internet security manager Keith Szot, "What we're doing with ActiveX controls with the Authenticode technology is providing for consumer confidence" (Wolfe 1996).

In response to McLain, a Microsoft spokesman insisted that Authenticode protected users from the likes of Exploder. "If code is not signed [with a digital certificate], Internet Explorer 3.0 by default will not download it. The end user . . . must explicitly change this default behavior through Internet Explorer's safety settings" (cited in Gage 1996).

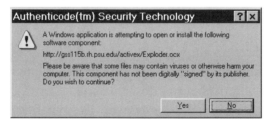

FIGURE 7.5   If there's no certificate, you see this warning message.

The McLain Gambit.   But what happens if the author of a rogue program obtains a VeriSign certificate? That's just what Fred McLain did. McLain, the author of Exploder, contacted VeriSign and received a certificate for Exploder! Because Exploder had a signed digital certificate, Microsoft Internet Explorer would present the control to a user as if it came from a trusted source. "This effectively addresses Microsoft's rebuttal to my claims of a security hole in their implementation of ActiveX," McLain told a reporter (Gage 1996b).

VeriSign and Microsoft quickly realized that they had a potential public relations disaster on their hands. VeriSign asked McClain to remove his program from the Web and withdrew the certificate, naturally, and pointed out to a reporter that "If a control does anything that damages users, the users [thanks to the certificate] have recourse to find out who did it, so they can take action" (Gage 1996b). As you can well imagine, neither VeriSign nor Microsoft are particularly pleased with McLain.

For his part, McClain believes that Microsoft should redesign ActiveX so that it runs in a virtual machine within your computer, the way Java does, so that file system calls can be scrutinized one by one to see if they might do something destructive. For now, you should be aware that ActiveX controls pose a significant security risk, and a potential privacy risk, if you're using Microsoft Internet Explorer. That's the conclusion many companies are reaching after examining the issues surrounding ActiveX. Richard Smith, CEO of Phar-Lap Software, in Cambridge, MA, tells his employees to turn off ActiveX support in Internet Explorer. "We will let other folks be beta testers for Microsoft's ActiveX security measures," Smith says (cited in Mardesich and Gage 1996).

TIP If you're using Microsoft Internet Explorer 3.0, be sure to set the security level to High. This will ensure that no active content is downloaded without your being able to inspect and approve the Authenticode certificate. To set the safety level to High:

1. Choose View Options, and click the Security tab.
2. In the Active Content area, click the Safety Level button.
3. Click High.
4. Click OK until you see Internet Explorer again.

What's Wrong with the Authentication Approach?   Plenty, according to researcher Steve Bellovin, of AT&T's Bell Laboratories. "All these requests for authentication every time somebody downloads an applet are going to bog down the Internet," he says (Leopold 1996). "Worse," adds McLain, "digital signatures are really just encrypted graphics files—they can't check for viruses or perform any other tests to see whether the downloaded code is destructive" (Gage 1996b). Moreover, authentication services don't really check out the programs. The certificate isn't saying that the program is safe; it's just saying that it comes from such-and-such a company. Ultimately, you're still left with the trust issue.

What Should You Do?

Should you disable Java and JavaScript? There are two areas of concern: security and privacy. Let's start with security. If your hard disk is full of valuable data, this one's a no-brainer. Do what many smart corporations are instructing their employees to do: Disable Java, JavaScript, and ActiveX until the security concerns are sufficiently addressed. That's going to take at least a year, and perhaps two.

What about privacy? If you're not too worried about security, but very concerned about privacy, you'll be wise to consider disabling these languages. There's still a risk that somebody could figure out a way to grab your e-mail address while you're browsing. The risk isn't huge, but it's there. You'll have to decide whether it's worth giving up all the fun content that you'll see if you leave these feature enabled.

Disabling Java and JavaScript in Netscape Navigator 3.0.   If you've decided to disable Java, JavaScript, or both, follow these instructions:

1. From the Options menu, choose Network Preferences.
2. Click the Languages tab. You'll see the Languages page, shown in Figure 7.6.
3. Deselect the Enable Java and Enable JavaScript check boxes.
4. Click OK.

Disabling Java, JavaScript, and ActiveX in Internet Explorer 3.0.   To disable Java, JavaScript, and ActiveX in Internet Explorer 3.0, follow these instructions:

1. Choose View Options.
2. Click the Security tab. You'll see the Security page, shown in Figure 7.7.
3. In the Active content area, deselect all the options. This will turn off ActiveX, Java, and JavaScript.
4. Click OK.

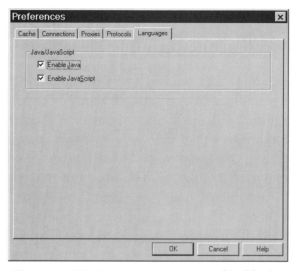

FIGURE 7.6   In Netscape Navigator 3.0, you can disable Java and JavaScript in this dialog box.

Selectively Enabling Active Content.   If you've turned off Java, JavaScript, and ActiveX, you may be in for a disappointment if you access a trusted page, such as the Reader's Digest page (www.looksmart.com), which makes extensive use of Java. However, you can selectively enable these languages if you wish. At present, there's no convenient way of doing this—you

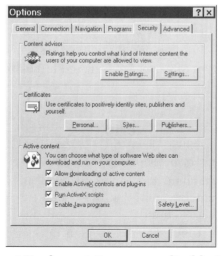

FIGURE 7.7   In Internet Explorer 3.0, you can disable Java, JavaScript, and ActiveX active content in this dialog box.

Using Internet Explorer?
Upgrade to the Latest Version Now!

Researchers at Princeton University (Banfanz and Felton 1996) have discovered a very serious security flaw in the first release of Microsoft's Internet Explorer 3.0. Exploiting this flaw, an attacker could put a rogue page on the Web, which would enable the attacker to run any DOS command on your computer. This would enable the attacker to read, modify, or delete any file on your computer, or to insert a virus into your system.

What's particularly insidious about this flaw is that it bypasses Internet Explorer's usual warnings about downloading untrusted code. Unless you turn off this feature, Internet Explorer displays a dialog box when you access a downloadable program. However, this flaw enables the attacker to bypass this dialog box. In addition, no action is required on the user's part, such as responding to a bogus dialog box or clicking a button on the rogue page—just accessing the page is enough.

The researchers alerted Microsoft concerning this flaw. It has been fixed in Internet Explorer release 3.0.1, and the researchers have verified that the new release fixes the flaw.

Choose Help Microsoft Internet Explorer to verify which version you're using. If you're still using 3.0, access home.microsoft.com and download the latest version of this program.

have to undo the steps you just took to disable active content, and then reload the page—but you might wish to do so on occasion. Just be sure to turn active content off after you've finished browsing the trusted site!

References

Balderson, Jim. 1996. "Java to Get New Jolt: Object Signing Extends Applet Reach." *InfoWorld* (September 16, 1996).

Dean, Drew, Ed Felten, and Dan Wallach. 1996. "Java Security; From HotJava to Netscape and Beyond." Online document (http://www.cs.princeton.edu/sip/pub/secure96.html).

Gage, Deborah. 1996a. "Netscape, Sun in Spat over Net Tool." *Computer Reseller News* (July 8, 1996), p. 3.

Gage, Deborah. 1996b. "McLain's Crusade: Consultant Sets Out to Prove Technology's Faults." *Computer Reseller News* (September 16, 1996).

Hof, Robert D. 1996. "Scott McNealy's Rising Sun." *Business Week* (January 22, 1996).

Home Page Press 1996b. "Java Black Widows—Sun Declares War." Online document (http://www.hppp.com/javablackwidow2.html).

Home Page Press. 1996. "Deadly Black Widow on the Web: Her Name Is Java." Online document (http://www.ninet.nf.ca/warning.html).

JavaSoft, 1996. "Frequently Asked Questions—Applet Security." Online document (http://java.sun.com/sfaq/).

Karpinski, Richard. 1995. "Hot Java Arrives—Sun Aims to Revolutionize the Web." *Interactive Age* (May 22, 1995), p. 1.

Karpinski, Richard. 1996. "Debate Sparks over Interactive Tools." *Communications Week* (November 13, 1995), p. 1.

Ladue, Mark. 1996a "A Collection of Increasingly Hostile Applets." Online document (http://www.math.gatech.edu/~mladue/HostileApplets.html).

Ladue, Mark. 1996b. "Hostile Applets on the Horizon." Online document (http://www.match.gatech.edu/~mladue/HostileArticle.html).

Leopold, George. 1996. "Web Security Threat Grows." *Electrical Engineering Times* (November 4, 1996).

Levin, Rich. "Java 1.0 Brewed Up Fresh—JavaSoft Ships the First Programming Language Developed for the Web." *Information Week* (February 12, 1996), p. 6A.

LoVerso, John Robert. 1996. "Netscape Navigator 2.0 Exposes User's Browsing History." *Risks Digest,* 17:79 (February 23, 1996). Online document (http://catless.ncl.ac.uk/Risks/17.79.html).

Mardesich, Jodi, and Deborah Gage. 1996. "Security Fears Dog Explorer." *Computer Reseller News* (September 16, 1996).

McComb, Gordon. 1996. "Netscape Introduces New 'Privacy' Bug." *JavaWorld* (October 1996).

McLain, Fred. 1996. "Exploder—Or, How to Put Nuclear Bombs in Web Pages." Online document (http://www.halcyon.com/mclain/ActiveX/welcome.html).

Taft, Darryl K. 1996. "Netscape's Navigator—Teenager Responsible for Hacking Out Bugs in Popular Netscape Browser." *Computer Reseller News* (April 29, 1996).

Taft, Darryl K., and Charlotte Dunlop. 1996. "Sun, Netscape Sing Different Tunes on the Net—Dispute over Use of JavaScript, Security Gaffe." *Computer Reseller News* (March 25, 1996), p. 1.

Wolfe, Alexander. 1996. "Web-Browser Battle Brews over Security." *Electrical Engineering Times* (August 19, 1996).

CHAPTER 8

Supervise Your Children's Surf Sessions

No, we're not talking about porn here—although any parent should know that there's material on the Net that's just not healthy for youthful eyes. We're talking about *privacy*. You'll find dozens of well-funded corporate sites on the Web that are designed to attract kids—and after you look at what they're doing, you'll understand why children's advocates and privacy groups are calling for Federal regulation.

This chapter visits a few of the sites that have been singled out for criticism, so that you can become familiar with the more egregious patterns. Next, we'll look at the specific criticisms of these sites offered by children's advocacy groups and the Center for Media Education (CME), which has taken leadership in this area. Finally, we'll examine the efforts by these regulatory groups to bring the Federal Trade Commission (FTC) and Congressional legislation into the picture.

The Lucrative Cybertot

Currently, about one million kids are surfing the Web—and this number is expected to rise to a whopping 16 million by the year 2000. And they've got money. In 1995, the under-14 set spent $14 billion, while teenagers forked over a whopping $67 billion (Paulson 1996). That's big money, and corporations want a slice of it. So what are they doing? They're going after kids online—and they're doing it in a way that's sure to give you pause.

There's another reason why corporations are investing so heavily in Internet advertising. They've seen figures showing that kids are doing the same thing that adult Internet users are doing: They're watching TV less (Nielsen Media Research 1996). This could pose a disaster for corporations if they don't get hold of kids at the earliest possible age in an attempt to build brand loyalty—and the earlier, the better. The basic goal of advertising is to get customers to buy as many products as possible over a lifetime (Perkins 1966). That's why many of these sites target kids as young as four years of age (Center for Media Education 1996a).

Goal 1: Microtargeting.   The basic strategy? Lure kids with prizes and games, and get them to reveal personal information about themselves—and even about their parents. After all, children are expected to influence parents' buying decisions regarding household consumer items, to the tune of $155 billion annually. By demanding that children fill out an extensive registration form before playing for valuable prizes, these sites can extract the following information from a child:

▶ Name
▶ Age
▶ Address
▶ City
▶ State
▶ School
▶ Grade

▶ Number of siblings
▶ Names of siblings
▶ Ages of siblings
▶ Number of people living in your house
▶ Favorite TV shows
▶ Favorite hobbies

At some sites, registration is optional—but there's often some arm twisting to make sure that kids supply the desired information. At Batman Forever, for example, kids see a message that says, "Good citizens for the Web, help Commissioner Gordon with the Gotham Census" (Center for Media Education 1996b).

A case in point is KidsCom (www.kidscom.com), a children's site developed by SpectraCom, Inc., a Milwaukee-based marketing firm. Kids logging on to the site are asked to fill out an extensive questionnaire if they wish to take full advantage of the site's fun resources for kids. According to a complaint filed against KidsCom by the Center for Media Education, the fun and games are really secondary to the information gathering; KidsCom masquerades as a children's entertainment site, when in fact it is a marketing tool. In the CME's view, the real purpose of the site is to collect personal data, conduct market research, and advertise certain products. While they are in the site, the complaint claims, children are questioned not only about their own product preferences, TV viewing habits, hobbies, and ambitions, but also about the composition and interests of their families. The complaint describes a Graffiti Wall, where children are lured into the area with the promise of interacting with other children in their age group from all over the world. But SpectraCom uses this area to gather personal information about children's tastes and preferences (Center for Media Education 1996c).

Once this information has been divulged and the cookies have been deposited on the kids' disk drives, a marketing site can follow and document children's every move. From this marketers get two goodies: the ability to microtarget advertisements to the kid's demographic profile, and a marketable commodity that you can sell to direct-advertising firms.

Marc Rotenberg, Director of the Electronic Privacy Information Center, offers this view of the dangers of this kind of direct marketing to kids:

> Now you're targeting a particular boy, who has a particular interest in a particular program, who lives in a house, whose parents have a certain income. And at that level of targeting, I think the opportunity for manipulation becomes much greater, really almost overwhelming for parents who are trying to control the upbringing of their kids. Because we've never really existed before in an information environment where the TV could reach out to your child and say, Bob, wouldn't you like to have this new action figure, just like in the movie you saw last week? Little Bob, needless to say, will be flattered and intrigued by this new TV that talks back, a device that magically remembers his last visit and tailors the next one to correspond to his special interests. . . . Bob and millions of children like him will be transformed. They won't simply be children any more, but something much more valuable to the corporations investing vast sums to develop the World Wide Web: They'll be customers (cited in Center for Media Education 1996b).

Goal 2: Break the Link between Content and Advertising.

In other advertising media, rules require that advertisers clearly distinguish between entertainment content and advertising. But these rules don't apply to the Internet. Taking advantage of this, marketers have created huge, complex environments in which children spend hours interacting with product logos, character spokesfigures (such as Tony the Tiger and Chester Cheetah), product jingles, and product-defined situations. Marketing experts are keenly aware of the possibilities here, as a Saatchi & Saatchi advertising executive puts it:

> Marketers have here an unparalleled opportunity to get kids actively involved with brands—Brand characters, brand logos, brand jingles, brand videos—by cutting, pasting, and coloring these elements. Advertisers can then give kids public places to post these characters and also provide activities for kids to do together. And all, of course, within the brand environment by using brand spokescharacters or other brand icons (Erica Gruen, cited in Center for Media Education 1996b).

To see what CME is talking about, visit Kellogg's Web site (www.kelloggs.com), shown in Figure 8.1. It's an intriguing and visually stimulating environment that's fun to explore. At every turn, there's a branded environment to experience. You'll have fun online, but you're going to do it with Snap, Crackle, and Pop as your guides and confidants (Montgomery 1996).

Goal 3: Draw Kids into Flow Experiences Involving Product Themes.   University of Chicago anthropologist Mikael Czikszentmilhalyi—it's pronounced cheek-zent-mill-hall-yee—has a word for it: flow.

According to Czikszentmilhalyi, one characteristic of deeply rewarding play is that it fully engages us—we don't notice the passage of time. We feel empowered, at the apex of our mastery. It's one of life's optimal experiences, one in which what matters is not so much the goal that is attained, but rather the experience itself. In Czikszentmilhalyi's words, flow is a state in which "people are so involved in an activity that nothing else seems to matter; the experience is so enjoyable that people will do it even at great cost, for the sheer sake of doing it" (Czikszentmilhalyi 1990: 4).

Flow is not easily achieved, but there is ample evidence that computers can provide optimal conditions for it. Computers facilitate the construction of microworlds (Rieber 1992), which are sharply delimited play zones full

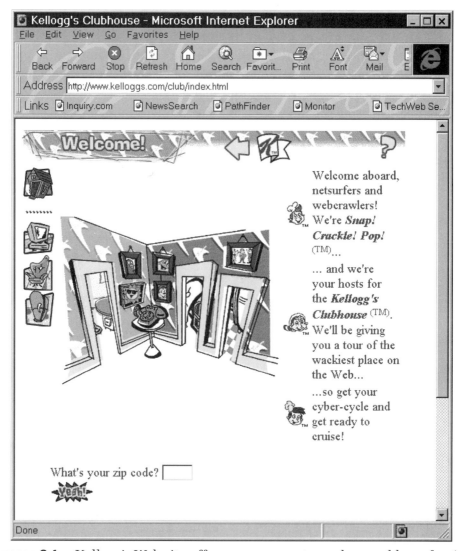

FIGURE 8.1   Kellogg's Web site offers many ways to explore and have fun in a consistently branded environment.

of highly manipulatable tools—a children's sandbox is a perfect example. In microworlds, flow experiences bring about learning on a scale that is virtually impossible to achieve in other states.

Advertisers know Czikszentmilhalyi's work very well—and they're creating Web-based microworlds that try to engage kids in flow experiences. But the purpose isn't merely to give kids a good time. It's to get them involved in flow experiences in which the advertiser's characters, logos, slogans, and products are indistinguishable from the game that's being played.

That's why games are so prominent at Web sites aimed at children. For example, Kellogg's Web site features Java games, such as the maze shown in Figure 8.2, that invite children to play in a thoroughly branded environment.

FIGURE 8.2   Children's Web sites use state-of-the-art technology to offer fun, engaging games with brand-related themes.

The reward of this game is a cybersnack—a bowl of cereal that magically disappears before your eyes.

As a further incentive to get kids involved in playing games, corporate sites aimed at kids typically offer prizes that children find nearly irresistable, such as compact disc players and other electronic goodies.

Goal 4: Develop a Lasting Relationship.   A major drawback of television, radio, and magazine advertising is that it's one-way. Apart from mail-in offers, there's no way to get children involved in an enduring, *high-touch* relationship with an advertiser. But the Internet offers many opportunities to lure children into lasting relationships with advertisers, including e-mail, mailing lists, bulletin boards, and downloadable games that push advertising slogans into their faces at every turn. Erica Gruen, Director of Saatchi & Saatchi Interactive, says that "There is nothing else that exists like [the Web] for advertisers to build relationships with kids" (cited in Center for Media Education 1996a).

If your kids register for a site, you can expect that they'll receive unsolicited e-mail—perhaps from a cartoon character spokesfigure, who will invite the child to return to the site and play games for valuable prizes, such as portable compact disc players.

The Mountain Dew Extreme Network

Now that you know what corporations are up to on the Web, let's have a look at a site that does an impressive job on all four goals. It's called the Mountain Dew Extreme Network (www.dewbeep.com), which is aimed at boys from roughly 14 to 18 years of age. I think you'll be impressed at the way they've used technology to get your kids engaged with their product themes.

Joining the Mountain Dew Extreme Network will cost you $29 and ten proof-of-purchase labels from PepsiCo products. And when you send them in, you can become a member of the Mountain Dew Extreme Network. What do you get for your money? Access to a password-protected Web site (Figure 8.3) and—get this—a beeper. Yes, a fully functional beeper.

You've Got a Call!   The beeper's yours, and you can use it to keep in touch with your buds—but they've got your number. Once per week, you get a message on your beeper that tells you to call a toll-free number, where

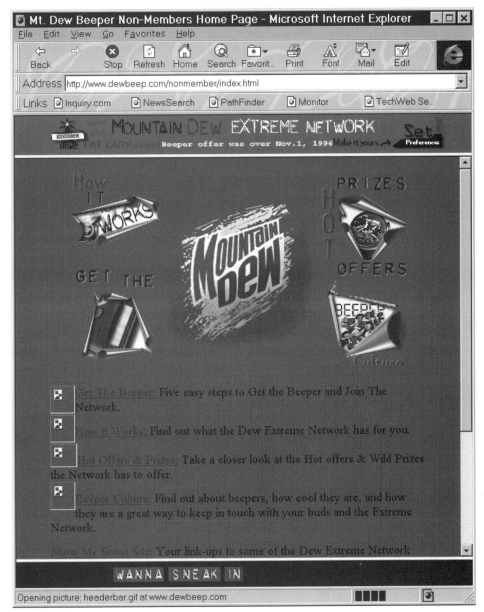

FIGURE 8.3   Mountain Dew's Extreme Network site (www.dewbeep.com) has two versions, one for members with beepers and one for browsers without beepers.

you learn about a prize or some other offering. The company promises not to call kids during school hours. If you're under 18, you need a parent's signature to apply—but according to the Center for Media Education, the application form doesn't say anything about the weekly marketing calls.

Nonstop Shopping.   This is a perfect example of the basic strategy that corporations are using to attack our children: Use technology to get kids hooked into a permanent, unavoidable relationship with commercial sponsors, one that consumes the child's time and intrudes on otherwise noncommercial settings. According to the Center for Media Education, a media watchdog group that has taken the leadership in protecting children's privacy online:

> The Mountain Dew Extreme Network is not a commercial on a TV channel that can be changed, nor an ad on a page that can be turned; this is unavoidable, commercial manipulation. Mountain Dew wants to set the agenda to nonstop shopping for our nation's teens. It won't matter if they are in summer school, hiking in a park, taking violin lessons, or visiting a museum (Center for Media Education 1996a).

Just What Kind of Status Symbol Is This, Anyway?   The Extreme Network site explains why you'd want a beeper: "The cell [cellular phone] is more a Mom and Dad thing. . . . The beeper's easier not to forget and carry. Plus, it's the baddest." What's the allusion here? Plainly, to the culture of drugs and gangs that has taken over so many of America's schools. Perversely, carrying a beeper—one of several technologies used by drug dealers to stay one step ahead of the police—has become a status symbol, and PepsiCo is more than willing to cash in on the trend.

Don't bother writing or calling PepsiCo to complain. At this writing, a message had appeared on the Extreme Network's home page announcing that the beeper offer expired November 1, 1996. What's next, PepsiCo?

Fighting Back

Leading the fight against online exploitation of children is the Center for Media Education, a nonprofit, public-interest organization founded in 1991. CME seeks to improve the quality of electronic media for children, families, nonprofit organizations, and the general public.

A Foretaste of the Future Information Superhighway?

It isn't fun to think about, but Fortune 500 companies are coming to see that the Internet is the perfect medium for microtargeted advertising. And even though the Internet's tradition defines users as people to be connected, we're going to be treated, increasingly, as consumers to be targeted.

That's the message of Jeff Johnson, former Chair of the Computer Professionals for Social Responsibility (CPSR), a Palo Alto, CA-based organization that examines the impact of computer technology on society. In a worst-case scenario prediction of what might happen if corporations effectively take over the Net, Johnson (1995) paints a picture that's disturbingly close to what we're seeing in this chapter.

"Ideally," says Johnson, "the Internet would provide a free market in which buyers could compare products, get the information they need, and make wise purchasing decisions. But that's not what corporations want," Johnson says. "They want captive markets—consumers who buy based on habit and on a lack of information about competitors."

The Mountain Dew Extreme Network perfectly exemplifies what Johnson is talking about. The corporate sites of the future, Johnson warns, will lure you with "bait-and-list fronts," sites that appear to promise you something cool, and then measure the heck out of everything you do so that your data can be packaged and sold to direct-marketing firms. And the icing on the cake? To get you to sign up for something, such as a mailing list, so that they can get their product into your face at every conceivable opportunity.

As part of the organization's Action for Children in Cyberspace project (www.tap.epn.org/cme/acc.html), CME studied children's Web sites for six months. The result? Several complaints to the U.S. Federal Trade Commission (FTC) regarding the manipulation of children online and the invasion of their privacy, as well as an important report, titled *Web of Deception: Threats to Children from Online Marketing* (Center for Media Education, 1996a).

The CME has called on the FTC to conduct a full-scale investigation of online marketing directed toward children, and has identfied a list of objectionable practices. In addition, the CME has made a number of specific recommendations for reform.

Joining the CME in this effort are The American Academy of Child and Adolescent Psychiatry, The American Psychological Association (APA), the Consumer Federation of America (CFA), and the National PTA.

The CME's List of Objectionable Practices.   In its study, CME identified the following objectionable practices:

▶ Using surveys and the lure of prizes and games to elicit personal information from children
▶ Monitoring children's online activities and compiling detailed personal profiles that are then sold to market research firms
▶ Using this information to design personalized ads aimed at individual children
▶ Designing advertising environments to capture children's attention for extended periods of time
▶ Integrating advertising and content
▶ Creating spokescharacters to develop special interactive relationships with kids

What Are the CME's Recommendations?   The Center for Media Education urges the Federal Trade Commission to adopt the following rules:

▶ Personal information should not be collected from children, nor should personal profiles of children be sold to third parties.
▶ Advertising and promotions should be clearly labelled and separated from content.
▶ Children's content areas should not be directly linked to advertising.
▶ There should be no direct interaction between children and product spokescharacters.
▶ There should be no online microtargeting of children and no direct-response marketing.

The Marketing Industry Reacts.   Industry reaction, predictably, was to downplay the threat and play up the industry's ability to regulate itself. John Kamp, Senior VP of the American Association of Advertising Agencies, stated that the proposed rules could have a "chilling effect" on Internet advertising, since it's impossible to determine if a World Wide Web surfer is 16 or 60 (quoted in Thyfault 1996). Meanwhile, in a preemptive strike, the AAAA and the Association of National Advertisers recommended that consumers be able to prevent online marketers from selling their names. Other industry organizations made similar recommendations.

KidsCom, the subject of a CME complaint to the FTC in May 1996, has made many changes to its site in response to public criticism. For example, advertisements are clearly distinguished from content by means of a special icon, and the site promises not to sell kids' names to any third party.

Apparently, the site still collects a great deal of information about visiting kids, and uses it to develop and display targeted advertisements. Parents will need to consider carefully whether these measures allay their concerns.

Children's Privacy Protection and Parental Empowerment Act of 1996.

On May 22, 1996, Representative Bob Franks (R-NJ) introduced a bill titled The Children's Privacy Protection and Parental Empowerment Act of 1996, which is designed to prevent the collection and dissemination of information about children without parental consent. The bill is intended to:

► Prohibit the sale or purchase of personal information about children without parental consent
► Require list brokers and solicitors to disclose to parents, upon request, the sources and content of personal information in files about their children
► Require list brokers to disclose to parents, upon request, the names of persons or entities to whom they have distributed personal information on that parent's child
► Prohibit prisoners and convicted sex criminals from processing the personal information of children
► Prohibit any exchange of children's personal information that one has a reason to believe will be used to harm or abuse a child

In a letter to Representative Franks, the Center for Democracy and Technology noted that the well-intentioned legislation might backfire in that it would actually increase the amount of data collection online. In order to determine whether a site was collecting data on children, it would have to require registration of all participants—the alternative could well be making a criminal out of someone who did not realize that his Web server was creating a list of everyone who logged on to the site, adults and children alike.

What Should You Do?

Now that you've read this chapter, I sincerely hope that you won't let your children roam the Internet without supervision. You can take some action right now to help improve this situation, and you can spend some time with your kids at some Web sites that are really worth visiting. In addition, you can get technology on your side.

Take Action Now.   My recommendations are those of CME (1996d):

▶ Teach your kids that they should never give your personal information in cyberspace, in the same way that they shouldn't speak to strangers.
▶ Make other parents aware of the dangers of online marketing targeted to kids.
▶ Educate your local school board, PTA, and children's advocacy groups regarding the dangers of online marketing aimed at children.
▶ Write complaint letters to the Federal Trade Commission.
▶ Supervise your children's time online, and make sure that schools aren't allowing kids access to commercial kids' sites.
▶ Get involved with Web sites that employ objectionable practices; try to get them to see that what they're doing is wrong.

Find Noncommercial Sites to Visit.   There are plenty of places for kids online that don't try to transform them into consumption machines:

▶ Boston University's Center for Scientific Visualization offers a number of great kids' games (http://www.bu.edu/Games/games.html).
▶ NASA's Jason Project (http://seawifs.gsfc.nasa.gov/JASON/HTML/JASON.html). The Jason Project is designed to bring the thrill of exploration and discovery to students around the world. At this wonderful site, you'll find a number of expeditions, including a visit to a recent volcanic eruption in Iceland. You'll find plenty of interactive features here, including a bulletin board for students and teachers.
▶ Just for Kids! (http://www.nsf.gov/od/lpa/nstw/kids/start.htm). Developed by the National Science Foundation, this site offers engaging explorations of scientific subjects.
▶ PBS Electronic Field Trips (http://www.pbs.org/insidepbs/learningservices/eft.html). These electronic field trips are designed to harness the

Internet's power to take kids to new places. A current exhibit: Wild Wings Heading South, a visit to the Bosue del Apache National Wildlife Refuge in New Mexico.

References

Center for Media Education. 1996. *Web of Deception: Threats to Children from Online Marketing*. Washington: Center for Media Education. Online document (http://epn.org/cme/cmwdecov.html).

Center for Media Education. 1996b. "And Now a Web from Our Sponsor: How Online Advertisers Are Cashing In on Children." *infoActive* 2:2, pp. 1–10. Online document (http://epn.org/cme/infoactive/22/22nweb.html).

Center for Media Education. 1996c. "Children's Advocacy Group Asks Federal Trade Commission to Rule against Deceptive Internet Site Targeting Children." Online document (http://tap.epn.org/cme/cmcftcpr.html).

Center for Media Education. 1996d. "The Deceiving Web of Online Advertising." Pamphlet.

Czikszentmilhalyi, Mikael. 1990. *Flow: The Psychology of Optimal Experience*. Chicago: University of Chicago Press.

Johnson, Jeff. 1995 "Info 'Hypeway': A Worst-Case Scenario." *Electrical Engineering Times* (August 28, 1995).

Montgomery, Kathryn C. 1996. "Children in the Digital Age." *The American Prospect* (July/August 1996), pp. 69–74.

Nielsen Media Research. 1996. "What Did Kids Do before the Internet, Grandpa?" Marketing Tools (March/April 1996).

Paulson, Mary. 1996. "Advertisers Target Cybertots." *PC Magazine Online* (April 26, 1996). Online document (http://www.pcmag.com/news/trends/t960426b.htm).

Perkins, M. 1996. "Mining the Internet." *The Red Herring* (March 1996).

Rieber, L.P. "Computer-Based Microworlds: A Bridge between Constructivism and Direct Instruction." *Educational Technology Research & Development* 40:1, pp. 93–106.

Thyfault, Mary E. 1996. "Internet Data Gathering Rules Sought—Chilling Effect Feared by Industry Groups." *Information Week* (June 10, 1996).

PART II

Get Technology on Your Side

CHAPTER 9

Create and Organize Industrial-Strength Passwords

An important key to protecting your privacy online: Creating and using good passwords. In Chapter 1, you learned why this is so important, and you also learned good techniques for creating your own passwords.

Although these techniques are good, bear in mind that many service providers recommend changing your password at least once per month. Since it's tedious to come up with a new password that often, you may wish to consider using a program capable of generating truly random passwords.

Such a program not only frees you from the task of creating a password, but it also gives you an additional measure of protection. A truly random password cannot be guessed by a password-cracking program—at least, not without putting the equivalent of all of the CIA's and KGB's fastest computers to work for several months.

The one drawback of random passwords (such as zra~4%_n9u) is that they're hard to remember. For this reason, you may wish to store your password in a password reminder application, such as Password Book or Password Master. These programs run on your computer. They're password-protected, too, to make sure that no one but you can access your Internet passwords. You'll still have to remember one password, but you don't have to change it once you've created it (unless you have reason to believe that somebody saw you type it).

This chapter introduces two of the Internet privacy programs that you'll find on this book's CD-ROM, Random Password Generator and Password Book. Both are shareware applications. If you're not familiar with shareware, please read the sidebar, "Understanding Shareware." I would like to ask all readers to please register your programs if you decide to use them beyond the free evaluation period.

Introducing Random Password Generator

Created by Timothy Hirtle, a San Diego, CA-based programmer, Random Password Generator gives you a secure way to create new passwords for any purpose, including Internet access. The program won the coveted *Windows* magazine Superior Shareware award in August 1995.

Random Password Generator creates passwords using up to 96 available characters, including uppercase and lowercase letters, and special characters such as punctuation marks. Because the program selects these characters using true randomization, there is virtually no chance that somebody could guess your password by running a password-cracking program.

Program Requirements.   Random Password Generator requires Windows 3.1 or Windows 95. In addition, it requires that you've installed a file called VBRUN300.DLL in your Windows System directory. Chances are that you already have this file. If you don't have this file, the program will inform you the first time you try to run it. You can download the file from the Internet (try www.shareware.com).

TIP   **To obtain VBRUN300.DLL, use your Web browser to access www.shareware.com, and search for** vbrun300.zip. **Download this program, decompress it using a decompression program such as WinZip, and install the file.**

Registration.   You may use Random Password Generator for 30 days without obligation. During the free evaluation period, you may create up to 25 passwords at a time. (After registration, the program can generate up to

Understanding Shareware

To market commercial software, you need lots of help: Attorneys, marketing consultants, advertisers, banks, distributers, packagers, technical writers, venture capitalists, clerical help—the list goes on. That adds considerably to the price of software. Perhaps it's worth it. But in all honesty, do you always get your money's worth? How many commercial programs have you purchased that didn't live up to expectations, leaving you with a worthless software package taking up space on your bookshelf?

Thanks to shareware authors, there's another way. Shareware authors distribute evaluation versions of their programs freely, using the Internet, CD-ROM, and computer bulletin boards (BBSs) for this purpose. Typically, the evaluation version of the program is a full-featured version of the software. You're free to evaluate the program for a stated period, generally 30 days. At the end of this period, you should either remove the program from your computer or pay the registration fee—which is generally very reasonable, since the author doesn't have to pay all the overhead that goes along with a commercial software business.

Note that shareware programs aren't in the public domain. (The authors of *public domain* programs specifically renounce all rights to these programs; you can do anything you want with them.)

There's always the chance, of course, that people will keep on using shareware programs even though they haven't paid the registration fees. For this reason, most shareware authors program reminders of various sorts into their creations—Random Password Generator, for example, displays a message every few minutes reminding you that the program isn't registered. Some programs are time-locked, meaning that they just stop working after the 30-day period is up.

For readers of this book, I hope that reminders won't be necessary, and that you'll register the programs that you wind up using. Is it worth the money? You bet. I think you'll agree after trying these programs that they're as good as, or better than, many of the commercial programs you've used. Please support the shareware programs by registering the software that you find useful.

1,000,000 passwords in a single pass.) At the end of 30 days, you must register the program to continue using it. To register, send $15 (plus $3.50 for U.S. shipping or $5.00 for international shipping) to:

Timothy L. Hirtle
P.O. Box 710911
San Diego, CA 92171-0911

TIP For more information on Random Password Generator, check out Tim's Web site (http://ourworld.compuserve.com/homepages/hirtle/htm). From this site, you can download the latest version of the program

Installing Random Password Generator

To install Random Password Generator on your system, do the following:

1. Insert this book's CD-ROM in the disc drive.
2. Open the PassGen folder.
3. Locate the file Install.exe.
4. Double-click this file. Windows will start the Install program.
5. Follow the on-screen instructions. When asked, let Install create Program Manager icons for you.

Creating Industrial-Strength Passwords with Random Password Generator

Internet service providers (ISPs) need to provide their clients with randomly generated passwords—and they need to come up with lots of them. That's why Random Password Generator can create up to 1,000,000 randomly generated passwords. As an Internet user, you don't need so many. Still, if you're planning to change your password every month, as many ISPs suggest, it's nice to have a program such as this to create truly random passwords when you need them. As you'll see, Random Password Generator is simple to use.

Running Random Password Generator.   To start Random Password Generator, do one of the following:

▶ In Windows 3.1, use the Program Manager to locate the the Random Password Generator program group, and double-click the Random Password Generator icon.

▶ In Windows 95, click Start Programs and choose Random Password Generator.

You'll see the Random Password Generator registration box, shown in Figure 9.1.

If you would like to register the program now, just click Order Form. You'll see an order form that you can fill out, print, and mail.

To continue with the program without registering, click Continue. You'll see the main Random Password Generator window, shown in Figure 9.2.

Selecting the Characters to Use.   To create an industrial-strength password for Internet access, you need to know which characters you can use. Most Internet service providers enable you to construct passwords using uppercase letters, lowercase letters, numbers, punctuation marks, and some special symbols. If you're not sure which characters you can use, call your Internet service provider's technical support hotline.

FIGURE 9.1   Use this dialog box to register your copy of Random Password Generator.

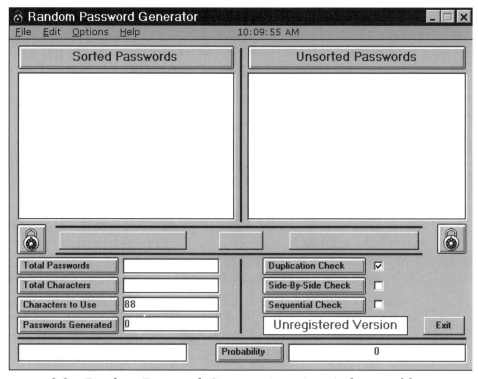

FIGURE 9.2   Random Password Generator's main window enables you to create as many as 25 passwords at a time during the free evaluation period.

To choose which characters to use:

1. Choose Options Characters, or press Ctrl + A. You'll see the Characters dialog box, shown in Figure 9.3. Note the buttons below the check boxes. These buttons enable you to quickly deselect all the numbers, lowercase letters, uppercase letters, or special symbols.
2. Choose the characters that you want to use.
3. Click Accept.

Choosing Options.   You can choose several options to increase the security of your passwords.

▶ **Duplication Check**—If you're creating a large number of passwords, select this option to make sure that the list does not contain any duplicates.

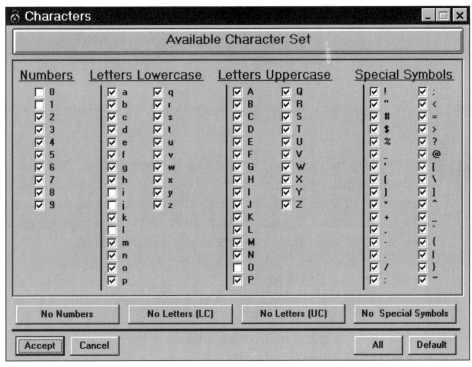

FIGURE 9.3   Before constructing your passwords, choose the characters that your service provider tells you that you can use in an Internet password.

▶ **Side-by-Side Check**—This option checks to see whether any password contains repeated characters that are adjacent to each other (such as "bb"). If so, it changes the repeated character to something else.

▶ **Sequential Check**—This option checks to see whether any characters appear in sequence (for example, "123"). If so, it changes the sequence to something else.

For Internet passwords, the default setting—Duplication Check only—is fine.

Determining the Number of Passwords to Create.

You can create up to 1,000,000 passwords with Random Password Generator, but chances are you won't need so many. If you're changing your password every month, try creating 12. To choose the number of passwords to create, type a number in the Total Passwords box.

Determining the Total Number of Characters to Use.   You must now decide how long your passwords should be. Your passwords should be at least 8 characters in length, and preferably 10 or 12. The longer the password, the less the chance that someone could guess it or happen upon it by accident.

To choose the length of your password, type a number in the Total Characters box.

TIP **After typing this number, look at the Probability box. This tells you the probability that somebody could guess your password. If you chose a password 10 characters in length, the probability is pretty small! Try changing the Total Characters to 1, 2, and 4 to see what happens. As you can see, the longer the password, the more secure it is.**

Creating the Passwords.   To create your passwords, just click Execute. You'll see the passwords in the Sorted Passwords and Unsorted Passwords panels (see Figure 9.4). These panels contain exactly the same passwords—it's just that they're alphabetized in one panel, while in the other panel they're shown in the order they were created.

TIP **Please don't use any of the passwords that you see in Figure 9.4. Bear in mind that lots of people have a copy of this book!**

Saving Your Passwords to a File.   You can save your sorted or unsorted passwords to a file. To do so, click the Save Sorted to File or Save Unsorted to File. You'll see the Save Unsorted File dialog box, shown in Figure 9.5. Type a name for the file, and click OK.

CAUTION   Bear in mind that you've saved your passwords to a text file, which any knowledgeable user can open and read. If you think there's any reason to think that somebody might snoop through your system looking for your passwords, be sure to store them in a secure password storage program such as Password Book, the next program to be discussed in this chapter.

Exiting Random Password Generator.   To exit Random Password Generator, click the Exit button.

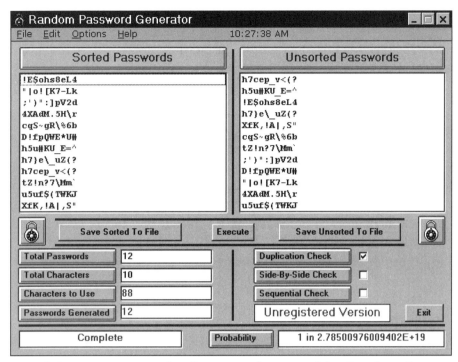

FIGURE 9.4   A year's worth of passwords created by Random Password Generator (please don't use any of these).

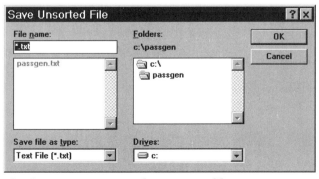

FIGURE 9.5   Saving your passwords to a text file.

Introducing Password Book

The creation of PrimaSoft PC, Inc., a small British Columbia-based software company, Password Book is a useful application that can do much more than store your Internet passwords. It's a great place to store any sensitive number that you don't want prying eyes to see, such as credit-card and PIN numbers. You can password-protect your copy of Password Book so that only you can open the program.

TIP **You can also use Password Book to store the user names and passwords that you create to enter registered Web sites. After you stop using cookies, you'll find, these sites no longer permit you to log on automatically, so you'll need to remember your user name and password to gain access to these sites. Password Book provides a great way to store and retrieve them.**

What You Need to Run Password Book.
Password Book is a 16-bit application that runs on Windows 3.1 and Windows 95. The program doesn't run on Windows NT.

Registering Password Book.
Password Book is a shareware application that you may evaluate for a period of 30 days, from the date of first installation. After 30 days, you can't enter any new data, but you can still see the data you've entered.

Registration is currently $17. You can register in any of the following ways:

▶ Mail a check or money order to PrimaSoft PC, Inc., P.O. Box 456, Surrey, BC V3T 5B7 Canada.
▶ Call 1-604-951-1085 to purchase the program with a Visa credit card.
▶ By means of a First Virtual account (see http://www.fv.com) and on-site registration (http://www.infohaus.com/access/by-seller/PrimaSoft_Inc).
▶ By clicking the Register button on the registration screen that appears when you start or quit Password Book. You'll see an on-screen registration form that you can print and mail. Alternatively, you can encrypt your order form so that you can e-mail it to PrimaSoft, PC, without fear that someone could read your credit-card number while the form is on its way to its destination.

TIP Password Book is just one of many organizer programs that PrimaSoft PC distributes as shareware. From the company's Web site (www.primasoft. com), you can download and evaluate organizers for your car, wine cellar, books, movies, stamps, coins, and more. You may wish to access Prima-Soft PC's Web site to make sure you have the most recent version of this application.

Installing Password Book

To install Password Book on your computer, do the following:

1. Insert this book's CD-ROM in the disc drive.
2. Open the Passbook folder.
3. Locate the file Install.exe.
4. Double-click this file. Windows will start the Install program.
5. Follow the on-screen instructions.

Storing Your Internet Passwords in Password Book

Now that you've installed Password Book, you can use the program to store your Internet passwords. This program also enables you to store other sensitive information, such as PIN numbers.

Running Password Book

To start Password Book, do one of the following:

▶ In Windows 3.1, find the Password Book program group and double-click the Password Book icon.

▶ In Windows 95, click Start Programs and choose Password Book.

After you start Password Book, you'll see the Password Book registration window, shown in Figure 9.6.

To register the program, click Order Form. To continue without registering yet, click OK. You'll see the Password Book Table of Contents, shown in Figure 9.7.

FIGURE 9.6   You can register Password Book by using this window.

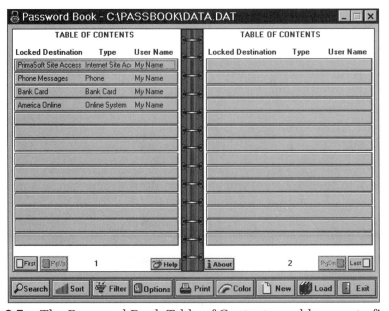

FIGURE 9.7   The Password Book Table of Contents enables you to find your passwords quickly.

Understanding the Password Book Table of Contents. The Table of Contents enables you to quickly choose any of the passwords you have created. To show you how this works, Password Book comes with four sample records. To access the America Online record, just click its button. After clicking one of these buttons, the Password Book opens, as if you were opening a loose-leaf binder (see Figure 9.8). This is called the Detail window.

Deleting the Sample Records. After looking at the sample records in the Detail window, delete them. To do so, follow these instructions:

1. In the Detail window, click First to access the first page.
2. Click Delete until you have deleted all the sample records.

To return to the Table of Contents, just click the Table of Contents button.

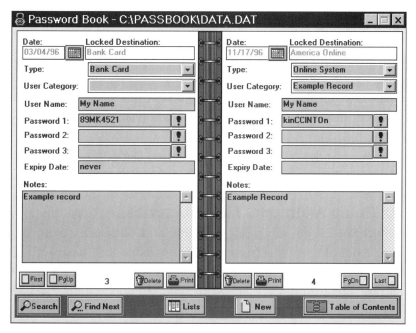

FIGURE **9.8** After you click one of the entries, Password Book's Detail Window opens like a loose-leaf binder.

Creating Your First Password Entry.   Now that you've deleted the sample records, you can create your first Password Book entry. In the Table of Contents view, click the First button. If you're looking at the Detail view already, just click First. You'll see two blank records. (If they're not blank, delete them according to the instructions in the previous section.)

To create your first record, do the following:

1.   Next to the Date box, click the Calendar icon to display the Calendar (see Figure 9.9).
2.   Just click Send to enter today's date in the Date box.
3.   In the Locked Destination box, type the name of your Internet service provider.
4.   In the Type box, choose Internet Access from the list box.
5.   Leave the User Category box blank. (This box enables you to accommodate multiple users, but that's beyond the scope of our interests here.)
6.   In the User Name box, type the user name you use to log on to the Internet.
7.   In the Password 1 box, type the password you use to log in to your Internet account.
8.   In the Expiry date, type the date on which you should change your password.
9.   If you created a secure password with Random Password Generator, open your saved password file with the Notebook utility. Then use the Windows clipboard to copy your passwords into the Notes box. When your current password expires, you can change it to one of the additional ones.
10.   Double-check your typing. A completed Detail view record is shown in Figure 9.9.

Defining Additional List Categories.   To get the most out of Password Book, you may wish to define additional Password Type categories. For example, my electronic-mail user name and password differ from the ones I use to log in to my Internet service provider. You may wish to define a new Electronic-Mail password type. To create a new password type, follow these instructions.

To define additional Password Type categories:

1.   In the Detail view, click List. You'll see the Lists dialog box, shown in Figure 9.10.

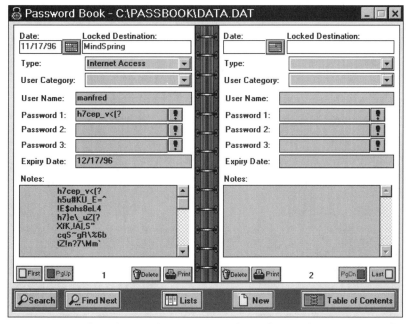

FIGURE 9.9   Completed Detail view record, with Random Password Generator passwords pasted into the Notes area via the Windows clipboard. The Calendar enables you to enter today's date easily.

2. Make sure the Password Type option is selected.
3. In the New Item box, type the name of the list type you want to define. This will appear as an option in the Type list box when you create new records.
4. To add your new item to the list, click Add.

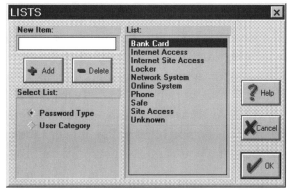

FIGURE 9.10   You can define additional Password Types in this dialog box.

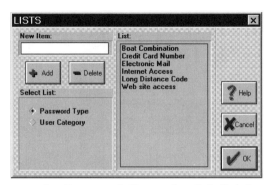

FIGURE 9.11   Here are the Password Types that I defined.

5. Repeat Steps 3 and 4 to define as many password types as you wish. Figure 9.11 shows the password types I defined (including the combination for my sailboat's lock).

6. If you would like to delete any of the existing items, select an item and click Delete.

Generating Passwords.   Random Password Generator, discussed earlier in this chapter, is the best choice for creating truly random passwords. If you've decided not to register Random Password Generator, you can use Password Book to generate passwords. The password generation method is not as good as the one used by Random Password Generator, but the passwords produced by Password Book are still far superior to those you can create manually. To generate a password, do the following:

1. Next to one of the Password boxes (Password 1, Password 2, or Password 3), click the exclamation point. You'll see the Generate Password dialog box, shown in Figure 9.12.

2. In the How Many to Generate area, click 1, 5, or 10 passwords. You'll select only one of them, but clicking 5 or 10 gives you many to choose from.

3. In the Password Length area, choose a length for your password. The default number, 10, is a good choice. The longer the password, the smaller the chance that somebody could guess it by running a password-guessing program.

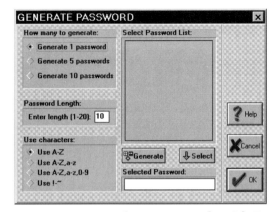

FIGURE **9.12**   You can generate random passwords with Password Book, but they aren't quite as good as those created by Random Password Generator.

4. In the Use Characters area, click the option corresponding to the permissible characters you can use. If there are no restrictions, use A-Z, a-z, 0-9.
5. Select your favorite password out of the ones you've generated, and click Select.
6. Click OK to confirm your password and place it in the Password text box.

Navigating within Password Book.   After you have created many password and other entries in Password Book, you may wish to take advantage of Password Book's navigation tools to find your way around. In the Detail view, you can click the following buttons:

▶ **First**—Go to the first page.
▶ **PgUp**—Display the previous page.
▶ **PgDn**—Display the next page.
▶ **Last**—Go to the last page.

Searching for Passwords.   If you can't find the password you're looking for, you can search for it. To do so, click the Search button. You'll see the Search dialog box, shown in Figure 9.13. In the Text to Find box, type the text you're looking for. In the Scope area, just leave the setting to All Fields. Click OK to begin the search. Password Book will show you the first record, if any, that matches what you've typed. To repeat the search, click Find Next.

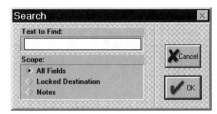

FIGURE 9.13   You can search for your password using this dialog box.

Password–Protecting the Password Book Application.   After you have entered many passwords and other secret numbers in Password Book, you should protect your database from prying eyes. You can do this by assigning a password to Password Book. In order to gain access to Password Book, you must type this password. There's no way to read the database files without Password Book, because this disk file is encrypted.

CAUTION   This is one password you can't afford to forget! If you forget your Password Book password, there's no way you can gain access to the records you've created. To make sure you don't forget, I recommend that you create your password by using the first-letter-of-each-word-in-a-sentence technique, introduced in Chapter 2. For example, the password "ydg2cwtt" comes from the following sentence: "You don't get two chances with this thing."

To define your password, do the following:

1. In the Table of Contents, click Options. You'll see the Options dialog box, shown in Figure 9.14. This dialog box enables you to choose what's displayed in the Detail view records, including the date format. For now, though, set your password.
2. In the Set Password area, click Password, and click the Set Password button. You'll see the Enter/Change Password dialog box, shown in Figure 9.15.
3. In the Enter new password box, type your password.
4. In the Confirm new password box, type your password again. Password Book will not accept your password unless you type it the same way twice.
5. Click OK.

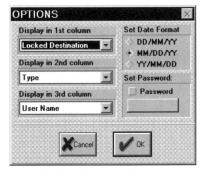

FIGURE 9.14 The Options dialog box enables you to select a password to gain entry to Password Book.

After you define a password, you'll have to type it again to gain access to Password Book. Figure 9.16 shows the dialog box that appears when you start Password Book. To gain entry into the program, type your password and click OK. Better not forget your password!

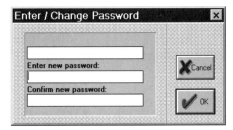

FIGURE 9.15 Don't forget *this* password!

FIGURE 9.16 You must supply your password to enter Password Book.

TIP If you tried to define your password but Password Book doesn't demand it when you start the program, you must have pressed Cancel at some point while you were using the Options dialog box. Pressing Cancel at any time cancels the whole operation. Repeat the password-definition procedure, and be careful not to press Cancel.

From Here

You've taken the first step toward ensuring your privacy while using the Internet. In the next chapter, you'll learn how to secure your entire system against intrusion.

10

Secure Your System

Your own computer system is probably the greatest threat to your privacy. If others have access to your system, or if you leave your computer unattended sometimes, a knowledgeable user could access and read your e-mail, see which Internet sites you've been visiting, or even send electronic mail messages or Usenet posts that appear to come from you. You'll be very wise to secure your system so that unauthorized people can't gain access to it.

TIP **Do your children use your computer? Win-Secure-It is an excellent tool for restricting access to programs or data that you don't want your kids to mess around with, whether it's work that you've taken home or Internet applications you don't want them to run (such as a Usenet newsreader). With Win-Secure-It, you don't have to worry about your kids damaging important files.**

This chapter fully covers an excellent security program for Windows 95 systems, called Win-Secure-It. The accolades are numerous, but they're worth quoting here. According to an *InfoWorld* review (June 10, 1996), Win-Secure-It is a "high-quality file-protection tool—it prevents accidents and casual snooping." According to The Shareware Tip of the Day (May 15,

1996), Win-Secure-It "supplies protection against unwanted intruders accessing items you choose to protect . . . a MUST HAVE tool for anyone who tries to protect files and work data."

Win-Secure-It is a complete security solution for your desktop computer. It enables you to do the following:

▶ Establish differing levels of access to your system. You're the administrator, and you have full access. To gain access as administrator, you have to type the correct password.

▶ Guests and other users enter via their own password. They can access only those system resources that you want them to see. If you wish, you can hide entire directories so that they don't appear at all—your guests won't even know they're there.

▶ An activity log provides a complete audit trail. If anyone has tried to access your system or do something you forbade them to do, you'll know it.

▶ If you suspect that someone such as a coworker has been snooping in your machine, you can set up a "stealth mode" that will log this person's actions and provide you with incontrovertible evidence.

This chapter is designed to show you how to secure the system you use for Internet access. You'll learn how to make sure that no one but yourself can gain access to your electronic mail, Usenet postings, and the sites you've visited on the World Wide Web.

CAUTION   Please note that Win-Secure-It is designed to protect your system against casual intruders, not professionals. Computer experts and investigative agencies possess the means to bypass this program's safeguards. There are programs you can use to encrypt selected files and directories with a deeper level of security, as discussed in the following chapter.

Introducing Win-Secure-It

The maker of Win-Secure-It, Shetef Solutions, Inc., is a Haifa, Israel-based software company that was founded in 1996. Win-Secure-It is a shareware application, which you'll find on the CD-ROM included with this book.

How Win-Secure-It Controls Access to Your System.   Win-Secure-It comes with two default access types, Administrator (that's you) and Guest. You can define additional users by name. For example, suppose your 12-year-old plays games on your computer. You can set up a user name for your son. In the next section, you'll learn how you can define differing levels of protection for each user you've defined.

Win-Secure-It's Four Levels of Protection.   For each user, you can define four types of protection:

▶ **Completely hiding files and folders**—As far as your coworker or kids know, the hidden files and folders don't exist.
▶ **Blocking any access to selected files**—Others accessing your system can see the files but they can't access them.
▶ **Allowing read-only access to selected files**—This setting enables guests to access the data in files, but they can't be changed.
▶ **Just monitoring file and data usage**—This is an excellent setting when you're trying to find out whether someone's been snooping in your computer. You can print out the evidence and confront the person!

TIP **To prevent a coworker from reading your e-mail or looking at where you've been surfing, you can completely hide your e-mail folder, browser folder, and the various places where your browser leaves traces of your surfing activity. (You'll learn more about this later in this chapter.)**

What You Need to Run Win-Secure-It.   Win-Secure-It is a 32-bit application that is designed to run on Windows 95 systems. It's not compatible with Windows NT, for reasons you'll appreciate after running the program—it goes *mano a mano* with the Windows registry and other system-level aspects of the Windows 95 operating system. This prevents all but the most technically informed intruders from circumventing your defenses.

In addition, Win-Secure-It requires an 80386 or later microprocessor.

Registering Win-Secure-It

You can use Win-Secure-It for a 30-day period in order to evaluate the program. After this time, you should erase it or register. In the unregistered version of Win-Secure-It, all the features work, but there are limitations concerning how many files and folders you can hide. To get full functionality from the program, you need the registered version.

CAUTION   If you decide to erase Win-Secure-It after installing it, do not simply erase the Win-Secure-It folders and files. Open the Win-Secure-It folder and run the Uninstall program you'll find there.

To register Win-Secure-It, do one of the following:

▶ Open the file ORDER.TXT in your Win-Secure-It folder after installing the program, print and fill out this form. Send the form with $29 in cash, money order, or a personal check to the following address:
    Yonat Dascalu
    10 Azmaut Street
    Ness-Ziona 74010
    Israel
▶ Access PsL Online (http://206.109.101.6/cgi-win/psl_ord.exe/ITEM1465) and order using your MasterCard, American Express, or Discover credit card. You can also call PsL at 1-800-242-4775 during business hours (Central Standard Time).

In return, you'll receive a user's manual, free technical support, and notice of program updates.

Planning Your Security Configuration

Before you get started, spend a few minutes to plan your security configuration. By default, Win-Secure-It defines two user names:

▶ **Administrator**—This is you, the system's owner. The administrator always has full access to the system.
▶ **Guest**—This is the default guest's user name. You can limit your guest's access to the system. This should give the lowest level of access.
▶ **Additional users**—You can define additional user names for others who use your system. For example, if you have children, you can define user names for them and specifically limit what they can do and what they can see.

Give some thought now to how you can protect your Internet data from prying eyes. With your program manuals and Windows Explorer to guide you, locate the following:

▶ The name of the folder where your browser stores its cache and history list. (These folders contain data that could enable a snooper to find out where you've been surfing.)
▶ The full path name (file name and location) of your e-mail program. You should hide this program so that nobody can send e-mail in your name.
▶ The name of the folder where your e-mail files are stored. You should hide these files so that nobody can copy your stored e-mail to a floppy disk.
▶ The full path name of any other programs that you don't want a guest to run. For example, if you don't want your kids to access Usenet, or if you'd prefer that nobody snoops to see which newsgroups you've been accessing, you can hide your Usenet folder.

After you hide files and folders, they don't exist, so far as your guest is concerned. They're also invisible to the operating system, including MS-DOS. Since a hidden file can't be found, no program can run it.

Installing Win-Secure-It

To install Win-Secure-It on your computer, do the following:

1. Insert this book's CD-ROM in the disc drive.
2. Open the SecureIt folder.
3. Locate the file setup.exe.
4. Double-click this file. Windows will start the Install program.
5. Follow the on-screen instructions. When asked, let Install create Program Manager icons for you.

After installing Win-Secure-It, you'll need to restart your system.

Configuring Win-Secure-It

When you start your system after running Win-Secure-It, you'll see a dialog box prompting you to create an Administrator's password. At this point, you should define your Administrator's password and choose system configuration options.

Defining the Administrator's Password.   To define the Administrator's password, simply click OK and type the password you want to use to gain full access to your computer. You'll be asked to type it twice in order to verify it.

TIP   Be aware that you can't gain full access to your system if you lose or forget your password. However, you shouldn't use a password that's obvious, either. The best bet, as recommended in Chapter 1, is to use the first letters of a sentence you aren't likely to forget, such as "my 27-foot boat sails the Chesapeake Bay" (m27fbstCB). I recommend that you write the password down and hide it someplace.

Using the Check-In Screen.   After you've defined your password, Win-Secure-It shows you the Password Verification screen, shown in Figure 10.1. This is what you'll normally see when you start Windows.

At this point, you also have an opportunity to choose configuration options. To do so, click the check box, type your password, and click OK. You'll see the Select User's Configuration dialog box, shown in Figure 10.2.

FIGURE **10.1**   The Password Verification screen enables you to type your Administrator's password.

FIGURE **10.2**   This dialog box enables you to define new users and choose which files and folders they can see.

Defining Guest Access.   One of the options on the Password Verification screen is the Guest login. You should begin by defining a low level of access for any guest on your system. Once you've done this, you can define other user names if you wish.

To define the Guest entry in the Select User's Configuration dialog box:

1.   Highlight Guest, and click Select. You'll see the Configuration For dialog box, shown in Figure 10.3. This dialog box has a number of tabs you can click. By default, you see the Alerts page. Skip this for now.

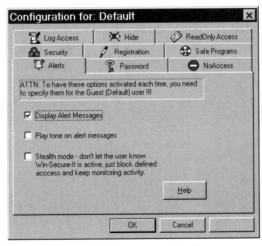

FIGURE **10.3**   Configuration for dialog default alert screen.

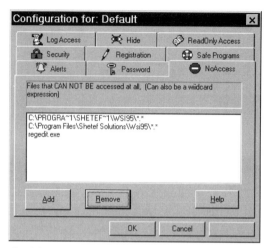

FIGURE 10.4   Use the No Access page to completely hide files and folders.

2. Click No Access. You'll see the No Access page, shown in Figure 10.4.
    Note that Win-Secure-It and the Windows registry are already on this list.
    Hiding these files prevents your guest from disabling Win-Secure-It.
3. To add a file or folder to the No Access list for this guest, click Add. You'll
    see the New Path Expression dialog box, shown in Figure 10.5.

    Here, you can type DOS expressions if you wish. But the easiest way is
    to use the Pick a File or Pick a Folder button, which enables you to browse
    for the files or folders you want to hide.

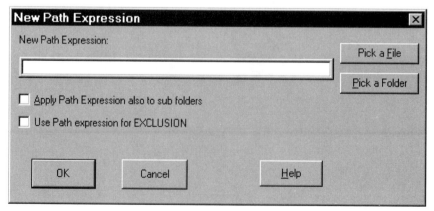

FIGURE 10.5   Use this dialog box to identify the files or folders you want to
hide.

To hide a file, click Pick a File and use the dialog box to locate and select the file you want to hide. Click OK.

To hide a folder, click Pick a Folder and use the dialog box to locate and select the folder you want to hide. Click OK. If you would like to hide all the subfolders (subdirectories) within this folder, click Apply Path Expression also to subfolders.

4. To define read-only files or folders, click the Read Only tab and use the methods you learned in Step 3.

5. To define a password for your guest user, click Password. Type the password twice to verify, and click OK.

6. Click Finish to complete this user's configuration.

TIP   When you're choosing files to hide or mark for read-only access, you can use DOS wildcards. For example, use the expression *.TXT to hide or mark as read-only all the text files on your computer.

Defining Additional Users

Once you've defined the guest user with the minimum level of access to your system's files and folders, you can define additional, named users with just the level of access you desire. To do so, follow these instructions:

1. Log in as Administrator, and click the Configuration check box. In the Select User's Configuration dialog box, select Guest, and then click Duplicate. This duplicates the Guest settings.

2. In the New User Name dialog box, type the user name and click OK. Now you'll see the user name in the Configuration dialog box.

3. Select the new user name, click Select, and modify the file restrictions as you wish.

What Happens When a Security Violation Occurs

Now that you've defined the Guest access, you can test Win-Secure-It. In Windows 95, choose Start Programs Win-Secure-It Check In, and choose Guest from the check-in list box. Type the guest's password. Try accessing something that's forbidden! You'll see the dialog box shown in Figure 10.6.

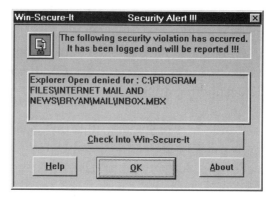

FIGURE 10.6   This is a no-no!

The next time you log on as Administrator, you'll see the Access Log Information (Figure 10.7), which shows you all the attempts that have been made to access forbidden files or directories on your system. The log also shows incorrect password entries, so you'll know immediately if somebody has been trying to gain access to your system by trying to guess your password.

Using Stealth Detection

Do you suspect that someone has been snooping in your computer? Like to know for sure? You can use Win-Secure-It's stealth mode to find out.

FIGURE 10.7   The Access Log shows all the attempts to access restricted resources.

You'll set up the stealth mode by completely hiding the fact that Win-Secure-It is running. No password dialog box will appear when the person starts the computer. There won't be any warning, audible or visible, when the person tries to access hidden files or folders. Later, you can log on as Administrator. You'll see the Access Log dialog box, which reveals whether the suspected person has accessed any of the files or folders you've identified as sensitive.

To set up the stealth mode, do the following:

1. In Windows 95, choose Start Programs Win-Secure-It Check In Win-Secure-It, and log in as Administrator. Be sure to check the Configuration Modifications check box.
2. In the Select User Configuration dialog box, choose Guest, and click Select. You'll see the Configuration dialog box.
3. Click Log Access, and choose the files and folders that you want to log. Users won't be prevented from accessing these files, but their accesses will be logged.
4. Click Alerts. Click Stealth mode, and make sure that the alerts are deactivated.
5. Click Security, and deselect the Ask for Password on Startup option.
6. Click OK.
7. Click Finish.

Try it out. Restart your computer. It will restart in the default Guest mode. Then try to access some of the files you've marked for logging. Then log in as Administrator. You'll see a log that shows all the accesses to the files you've marked for logging.

If you would like to confront the person who did this, select the information in the Access Log, copy it to the clipboard, and paste it into your word processing program. You can then print the information.

From Here

You've secured your system against casual snoopers, such as coworkers or kids. Nevertheless, you should realize that a professional snooper could penetrate Win-Secure-It's defenses, and gain access to hidden files. To gain a greater measure of protection, you should encrypt sensitive files and directories. On to Step 3!

Encrypt Sensitive Files and Directories

Programs such as Win-Secure-It can secure your system against casual snoopers, such as curious bosses, coworkers, and kids. But they don't offer enough protection to safeguard your system against professional intruders.

To protect your computer system against expert snoopers, you may wish to add file-encryption capabilities to your system.

A variety of programs are available that add file-encryption capabilities to your comptuer. Some of them work at the operating system level, adding encrypt and decrypt commands to file-management programs (such as File Manager or My Computer). Others work within applications, such as Microsoft Word, adding secure encryption and decryption capabilities.

In this chapter, you learn how to use Cryptext, a powerful file-encryption program that blends seamlessly with the Windows 95 operating system. After installing Cryptext, you can right-click any file and choose Encrypt or Decrypt from a pop-up menu. Also covered in this chapter is TSS PGPWord 7.0, a shareware utility that adds very secure encryption/decryption capabilities to Microsoft Word 7.0. This program is included on this book's CD-ROM.

I'm Encrypting My Data.
Does This Mean I'm a Criminal?

Some people seem intent on demonizing computer users who encrypt their files. The philosophy is that people would not want to use this technology unless they have something to hide, such as pornographic pictures. According to the misguided advice of one management consultant, an employee found to possess encrypted files should be terminated immediately!

One does not need to be a drug dealer or pornography collector to have valid reasons for encrypting files. My office computer, for example, contains student grade records dating back several years. I wouldn't want anyone accessing those files, for any reason—it's confidential information. The same goes for reference letters, performance evaluations, drafts of potentially patentable ideas, and many other sensitive documents.

If you're in business, you need to consider how common business espionage is. Would you like your business correspondence, letters, memos, reports, and proposals to fall into your competitors' hands? Chances are you already shred printed documents so that they cannot be obtained by "dumpster diving." Then why leave unprotected files on your computer, where they could be easily accessed and read by a reasonably knowledgeable intruder?

Consider, too, what might happen if your computer is stolen. Notebook computer theft is very common! Would you want some stranger—a criminal, at that—reading love letters to your spouse, detailed itineraries for upcoming trips (including hotel reservations and credit-card numbers), and your daily journal?

There are many valid reasons for wishing to protect your files from prying eyes. To be sure, this same technology can also be used by people engaging in illegal activity. But demonizing people who encrypt their files is like criticizing a family that purchases deadbolts to keep their house locked in a crime-filled neighborhood. To be sure, criminal activities sometimes go on in locked houses.

But taking the locks away would victimize the broad majority of innocent people, who simply want to protect themselves from unwanted intrusions.

How Encryption Works

Encryption has been known since the time of Caesar, and it has long been a mainstay of military intelligence. An encrypted document can't be read by anyone who does not possess the *key*, or the formula that's used to translate the original text into *ciphertext* (the encrypted text). A simple encryption method, called rot13, was once popular on Usenet. rot13 works by rotating or moving each character 13 places to the right in the alphabet. That's the

You Can't Export That!

The United States government defines encryption technology as munitions. That's right—armaments. In order to export programs that employ anything other than relatively weak levels of encryption (a key of fewer than 40 bits), you have to get a permit from the State Department—and if you don't, fines and imprisonment await you.

It's understandable that paranoia abounds in government circles concerning encryption—after all, it's widely believed that the Allied victory in the European war was directly linked to cracking the Nazi's encryption code. (Allied commanders knew just when and where Hitler was going to move his troops—so accurately, in fact, that the Allies had to pretend not to know.)

But the ban on exporting encrypted software is ridiculous. That cat's already out of the bag—strong encryption technology has diffused worldwide, and anybody who wants to obtain it can do so without difficulty. Meanwhile, U.S. companies that would like to include strong encryption in their programs are losing an estimated $6.9 billion annually as non-U.S. companies fill the gap.

Don't expect reform soon. The U.S. government, faced with mounting losses in its war against drugs, and an increasing threat of terrorism at home, wants to require the publishers of encrypted software to give a copy of the key to an "independent" government agency, which will enable the U.S. government to break coded communications after a valid warrant has been obtained. But what is to guarantee that the government will follow its own rules there?

key. To decrypt the text, you apply the key in reverse, by moving the characters back 13 places in the alphabet. rot13 was once used to shield youthful eyes from articles that might contain adult language. The idea was that knowledgeable Usenet users would know the key, but kids wouldn't.

Effective encryption requires a longer key and, of course, you have to keep it secret. In general, the longer the key, the harder it is to break the encryption. A 40-bit key can be broken fairly easily by a powerful computer that just runs through all the possibilities. A 160-bit key would require millions of computers to do the job.

Introducing Cryptext

Cryptext is a freeware utility for Windows 95 and Windows NT that provides a very high degree of protection for your files. The program employs a 160-bit key, meaning that it is virtually impossible to access the data that you've encrypted with this program (see the following sidebar).

Cryptext was created by N.J. Payne, an Australian programmer. The program is freeware and is freely available to anyone who wishes to use it.

How Hard Is It to Break into a File That's Encrypted with Cryptext?

Cryptext uses 160-bit encryption, meaning that there are 2^{160} possible combinations. Assuming that there are one billion computers on Earth, that every single one of them is devoted solely to breaking your key, and that each computer can test one billion combinations per second, it would take 100,000,000,000,000 years to break your key. That's about 1,000 times greater than the estimated age of the universe.

There are other ways to break into somebody's encrypted files, though. You can try to guess the password they use to access the file—that's easy, if they've used a nonrandom password of some kind. Spies use electromagnetic detection devices to reveal keystroke patterns. And authorities use contempt-of-court citations to keep you in the cooler until you cough up the password!

Obtaining Cryptext.   I'm sorry to say that this book's CD-ROM does not include a copy of Cryptext due to U.S. export restrictions—which is actually quite hilarious, since the program comes from Australia. In other words, U.S. export restrictions have prevented me from placing a foreign program on our CD-ROM out of the fear that it would fall into foreign hands.

You can obtain Cryptext from many online sources, such as Shareware.com (www.shareware.com), Tucows (www.tucows.com), or the program's home page (www.pcug.org.au/~njpayne/). Download the file to a temporary directory, and decompress it using WinZip.

Installing Cryptext.   After you have unzipped the files in the temporary directory, installing Cryptext is easy. Just use My Computer to locate and display the icon of cryptext.inf. Right-click the file, and choose Install from the pop-up menu.

TIP   In order to install Cryptext to Windows NT, you must have administrator's privilege. Cryptext is a shell extension and only administrators have the right to modify the shell.

Running Cryptext

After you install Cryptext, you'll find Encrypt and Decrypt options appear on pop-up menus within My Computer and Windows Explorer (see Figure 11.1). These options enable you to encrypt or decrypt a file as if these functions were extensions of Windows 95 or Windows NT.

Creating Your Password.   The first time you use Cryptext to encrypt a file, you will see the Change Encryption Password dialog box, shown in Figure 11.2. Type your password twice (to verify it). This establishes your password for accessing all encryption and decryption operations. Be sure to write it down somewhere!

Encrypting a File.   To encrypt a file, do the following:

1.   Right-click the file in a My Computer or Windows Explorer window. You'll see the Enter Encryption Password dialog box, shown in Figure 11.3.

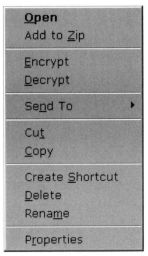

FIGURE 11.1   Cryptext modifies Windows 95 so that new commands appear on the Windows Explorer pop-up menu.

2. If you're encrypting an executable file, click Encrypt executable files.
3. In the Password box, type your password.
4. Click OK.

After you encrypt the file, the file's icon changes to one showing a lock (Figure 11.4). In order to read or use this file, you must decrypt it.

FIGURE 11.2   Use this dialog box to define your password for all encryption and decryption operations.

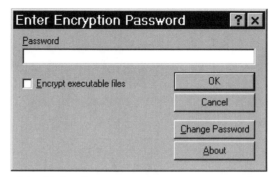

FIGURE 11.3   Use this dialog box to enter your password.

Decrypting a File.   To decrypt a file, do the following:

1. Right-click the file in a My Computer or Windows Explorer window.
    You'll see the Enter Encryption Password dialog box, shown in Figure 11.3.
2. In the Password box, type your password.
3. Click OK.

    After you decrypt the file, you will see the file's normal icon again.

Introducing TSS PGPWord 7.0

Programs such as Cryptext provide encryption and decryption capabilities at the file management level. If you frequently use Microsoft Word version 7.0 for Windows 95, you may find it convenient to use TSS PGPWord 7.0. This

FIGURE 11.4   This icon tells you that the file is encrypted.

program automatically encrypts and decrypts documents as you open and close them in Microsoft Word. The following section introduces TSS PGP-Word 7.0, a program created by TSS Software (Total System Solutions, Inc.).

Isn't Word's Password Protection Sufficient?

If you're an experienced Word user, perhaps you know that you can save your documents with a password. Theoretically, no one can open your documents unless they type the password. What you may not know is that Word's built-in password protection is very easily circumvented. Widely circulated on the Internet is a freeware program called Word for Windows Password Cracker. (This program is included with TSS PGPWord, just in case you'd like to see for yourself how easy it is to crack Word's standard password protection.) A commercial program called WDPASS for MS Word is also available for professional snoops and law enforcement agencies. Either of these programs can be used to crack password-protected Word documents in a matter of minutes.

Program Requirements.   TSS PGPWord 7.0 enhances Microsoft Word 7 for Windows 95 so that it includes additional File Menu commands for encryption and decryption. In order to run TSS PGPWord, you need the following:

▶ Microsoft Windows 95 or Windows NT
▶ Microsoft Word 7 (or later) for Windows 95
▶ Pretty Good Privacy 2.3a or higher installed on your system. If you don't have PGP (a freeware utility), PGPWord will help you obtain it.

TIP PGP has a rather unsavory reputation among some computer users because it is too difficult to use. But you don't need to use PGP directly in order to make full use of TSS PGPWord, which configures PGP automatically.

Installing TSS PGPWord

TIP Before installing the version of TSS PGPWord on this book's CD-ROM (version 7.0), access the TSS PGPWord Website (ourworld.compuserve.com/homepages/TSS). Check to see whether a new version is available.

To install TSS PGPWord on your computer, do the following:

1. Insert this book's CD-ROM in the disk drive.
2. Open the PGPWORD7 folder.
3. Locate and double-click SETUP.EXE.
4. Follow the on-screen instructions.

NOTE If TSS PGPWord didn't find a copy of PGP on your system, you'll see instructions on how to obtain this program by downloading it from the Internet. You can also choose Start Programs TSS PGPWord, and choose Web Links for Free Download of PGP.

NOTE The software included with this book (and extensively discussed in Part II) is designed to work with Windows 95 systems. However, some of the programs will work with Windows 3.1. If you're using some other type of computer, you can still make use of all the strategies discussed in Part I of this book. These strategies make use of the Internet software that you're already using.

Purchasing TSS PGPWord.   The evaluation copy of TSS PGPWord is fully functional, except that you cannot encrypt documents longer than one page. (You can decrypt documents of any size.) Purchasing is easy; you'll receive an authorization code that unlocks the program's full capabilities. You'll also receive free upgrades for the life of the product.

To purchase your copy of TSS PGPWord, do the following:

▶ Start Word. You need to have the program running so that you can enter the authorization code that the phone operator will give you.
▶ Call 800-814-2300 (or 718-375-2997) and pay the fee (currently $19.95) with Visa, MasterCard, American Express, Discover, or Diners Club. You can call Sunday through Thursday 9 A.M. to 9 P.M., or on Friday between 9 A.M. and 5 P.M. (EST).

You can also purchase by fax (718-375-6261)—but you'll still have to call to get the authorization number.

Encrypting and Decrypting Documents with TSS PGPWord 7.0

After you install TSS PGPWord, the program seamlessly integrates and configures PGP and Word alike. You can ignore PGP and just use Word as you always did. However, you'll find a new option—TSS PGPWord— on the File menu. When you choose this option, you see the dialog box shown in Figure 11.5. However, you can pretty much ignore this option— PGPWord operates automatically when you close and open documents.

TIP If you would like to encrypt all the files you create with Microsoft Office applications (not just your Word files), be sure to visit the TSS home page, mentioned earlier. One company is planning a utility that will provide on-the-fly encryption and decryption for all Office applications.

Creating a Password.   Before you begin working with TSS PGP-Word, you need a password that you can use to encrypt and decrypt your documents. No one will be able to open this document unless they have the password.

You can use Random Password Generator, discussed in Chapter 10, to create a password for this purpose. Just be sure to write the password down somewhere that's secure from intruders. If you forget your password, there is absolutely no way that anyone, including the makers of TSS PGPWord, can open your document again!

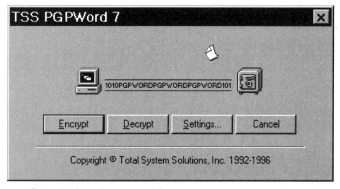

FIGURE 11.5   This dialog box enables you to save and retrieve encrypted documents with Microsoft Word for Windows.

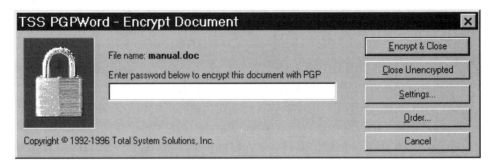

FIGURE 11.6   Use this dialog box to encrypt a Word document.

Encrypting a Document.   To encrypt the current document, do the following:

1.   Save the document using the File Save command, or click Save.
2.   Close the document by choosing File Close or clicking the Close button. You'll see the TSS PGPWord—Encrypt Document dialog box, shown in Figure 11.6.
3.   Type your password, and click Encrypt and Close.

Opening an Encrypted Document.   To open an encrypted document, do the following:

1.   Choose File Open, or click Open on the toolbar. (Don't choose the document's name from the File menu—this won't work.)
2.   You'll see the TSS PGPWord—Decrypt Document dialog box, shown in Figure 11.7.

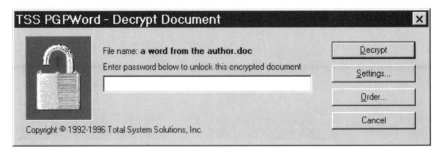

FIGURE 11.7   Use this dialog box to decrypt a Word document.

> ## File Encryption/Decryption Utilities for Windows 3.1 and Macintosh Users
>
> If you're using Windows 3.1 or a Macintosh, check out the following utilities, which can be downloaded from Shareware.com (www.shareware.com):
>
> ▶ PGP Assistant (Windows 3.1)—Here's a Windows 3.1 interface for the PGP software discussed in this chapter. It provides easy-to-use tools for encrypting and decrypting files with this powerful encryption technology.
> ▶ MacPGP Kit (Macintosh)—This is a set of programs designed to work with MacPGP. It supports many PGP functions, including encrypting and decrypting files.

3. Type your password.
4. Click Decrypt. TSS PGPWord decrypts the document and displays it on-screen.

From Here

Now that you've secured your system against casual and professional snoopers, you've taken important steps against somebody snooping into what you've been doing online. But there's still a security hole in your system: Anyone who wishes to do so, and has the requisite technical knowledge, can recover the files you've deleted. In the next chapter, you'll learn how to erase files so that they're not recoverable under any conditions.

CHAPTER 12

Ensure Total Deletion of Unwanted Files

Computer disk drives are an open invitation to snoopers who would like to violate your privacy. That's because they retain data that you thought you had deleted. A knowledgeable snooper can recover this data quite easily.

In order to secure your system against professional as well as amateur snoops, you need to learn new data-deletion techniques. Instead of using the Windows deletion utilities, such as the Recycle Bin, you'll learn how to use file-wiping software that fully and permanently erases a file.

However, you'll also learn in this chapter that merely deleting files is not enough.

This chapter introduces a variety of file-wiping utilities that you'll find on this book's CD-ROM. When used regularly, they can give you a measure of protection against snooping that is not provided by Windows.

Why a Normal File Delete Erases Very Little

Let's say you've written a confidential performance evaluation. It's something you just don't want somebody to see unless they've a right to do so. You've printed a copy and sent it up the line. Now you want to make sure it's erased. So you drag it to the Recycle Bin, and then empty it. Is it deleted?

Not necessarily. When you delete a file using Windows, the operating system does not actually erase the data. Typically, all that is erased is the first character of the file name. In addition, the operating system makes the space occupied by the file available for other data. In time, this space will be overwritten, and the data won't be fully recoverable. But this is a process that could take days, or weeks. In the interim, a knowledgeable snooper could easily restore all or part of sensitive files that you thought you had deleted.

Wiping Files Is the First Step.   To eradicate most traces of a file, you should erase files using a *wipe program.* This is a utility that doesn't just delete the first character of the file's name. It overwrites the entire area occupied by the file with new, meaningless data. The best wipe programs are rather slow because they do this several times.

Why is it necessary to overwrite the space several times? A single pass by a wipe program may not be sufficient to completely eradicate the traces of a sensitive file. Once a magnetic medium has been exposed to a magnetic field, the resulting structure is remarkably persistent. Several passes by the wiping software may be needed to destroy all traces of the prior structure.

Why Wiping Isn't Enough.   You will be wise to use a wipe program to erase sensitive data when you're finished with it. But you'll also be wise to recognize that wiping alone does not fully secure your system against knowledgeable snoopers. Wipe utilities do nothing to safeguard you against four potential sources of persistent data:

▶ **Swap Files**—Graphical user interfaces such as Windows 95 are inherently insecure because they write large *swap* files to disk. These files are written to bring about an apparent increase in the system's memory size. Because they remain on disk after the user quits Windows, they could retain sensitive information that the user imagined had been completely deleted.

▶ **Temporary Files**—Word-processing and other application programs typically create temporary files (with the extension *.tmp) while you're working. They may leave these files intact when you quit—particularly if your system crashes before you're able to shut down the program properly.

▶ **Slack Space**—When an operating system assigns space to a file, it allocates a fixed number of disk sectors or clusters to this file. The space actually alloted is larger than the file itself. When you wipe the file, the wipe utility erases only the portion of the cluster that was occupied by the file. The *slack space*, or the portion of the cluster from the end of the file to the end of the cluster, is not affected by the wipe operation. This space may contain remnants of previous data, and this could be recovered by a knowledgeable expert.

▶ **Empty Space**—The "empty" space on your drive might prove to be full of files that were not completely deleted previously.

If you've been working with very sensitive data, you need to do the following to fully secure your system:

1. Wipe the data with a good wipe utility.
2. Wipe temporary files.
3. Erase all the tips on your hard drive.
4. Erase the free space on your hard drive.
5. Shut down Windows and erase the swap file.

The CD-ROM included with this book contains two utilities that can help you secure your system against snoopers: ZAPFILE, a package of DOS file-wiping utilities; and Mutilate, a Windows 95 front-end program (interface) that is designed to run ZAPFILE from within Windows.

Introducing ZAPFILE

ZAPFILE is a suite of freeware DOS utilities created by Mark Andreas. No registration is required, but Andreas retains the programs' copyrights and asks that they be redistributed for noncommercial purposes only.

What's in ZAPFILE?   ZAPFILE consists of the following DOS programs:

▶ **ZAPFILE.COM**—This program hinders undeletion efforts by thoroughly overwriting the file, changing its file size to 0 bytes, changing the file's date/time stamp to 1/1/1980, renaming the file to a 1-character file name, and deleting the file. All that's left is the sector number where the file began, but the rest is wiped.

▶ **BIGFILE2.COM**—This program enables you to see what's stored, without your knowledge, in the free space on your drive. It transforms this free space into one gigantic file, which you can open with a text editor. Chances are you will see some data that you thought you had deleted.

▶ **ZAPEMPTY.COM**—This program wipes the free space on your drive.

▶ **ZAPSWAP.COM**—This program overwrites the Windows swap file (386spart.par), but without altering the file's size, disk position, or date/time. This is needed because Windows expects to find these values intact the next time it starts. *Do not run this program from within Windows!*

▶ **ZAPTIPS.COM**—This program deletes all the space from the end of existing files to the end of disk clusters (slack space).

To install ZAPFILE, do the following:

▶ On your hard drive, create a folder to store the ZAPFILE programs.
▶ Place this book's CD-ROM in the disc drive.
▶ Open the ZAPFILE folder.
▶ Copy all the files in the ZAPFILE folder to the folder you created.

NOTE Of the five ZAPFILE utilities, the one you'll use most often is ZAPFILE, the file deletion utility. You can run this program from DOS, but the best way to run it is to use Mutilate, a Windows program that makes use of ZAPFILE. Mutilate is described in the next section. For information on using the other utilities, see "Running the ZAPFILE utilities," later in this chapter.

Introducing Mutilate

Mutilate is a Windows 95 front end (interface) for DOS file-wiping programs, including ZAPFILE.

Registering Mutilate. Mutilate is a shareware program. You may evaluate the program free of charge for a period of 30 days. Subsequently, you are required to register if you find the program useful. To register, please send $15 to:

Craig Christensen
P.O.Box 30593
Spokane, WA 99223-3009

Program Requirements. Mutilate is a 32-bit application that requires Windows 95. Since it's designed to work with DOS file-wipe applications, there's no point to installing the program on a Windows NT system. In addition, you need a DOS file-wipe program. Mutilate has been
tested with the following: ZAPFILE.COM, Mark Andreas's DOS file-wiping
program, included on this book's CD-ROM.

Pretty Good Privacy is the respected file encryption/decryption program
that can't be included on this book's CD-ROM due to export restrictions. To
obtain a copy of PGP, access http://web.mit.edu/network/pgp.html.

To install Mutilate, follow these instructions:

1. Place this book's CD-ROM in the disc drive.
2. Open the Mutilate folder.
3. Double-click Setup.exe.
4. Follow the on-screen instructions.

Wiping Files with Mutilate

In this section, you learn how to wipe files with Mutilate and ZAPFILE.
This combination gives you a good level of protection from snoopers who
may try to recover deleted data from your drive.

Running Mutilate for the First Time. To run Mutilate, choose
Start Programs Mutilate. When you run Mutilate for the first time, you'll
see the Select Wiper dialog box (see Figure 12.1) prompting you to enter the
name and path of your DOS file-wiping program. If you've stored ZAPFILE
in a directory called C:\zapfile, type the following: c:\zapfile\zapfile.com.

Note that you can also include *switches.* A switch turns on an optional
feature of the program.

Of interest here is ZAPFILE's ability to wipe files more than once. For
maximum protection, you should wipe files at least twice. In the British secret service, files are wiped six times! This is overkill for most purposes,

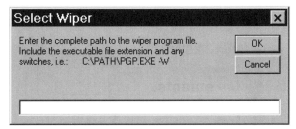

FIGURE 12.1   Mutilate's Select Wiper dialog box enables you to identify the location of your DOS file-wipe program.

however. Note that wiping is much slower than deleting, and wiping more than once takes proportionately longer.

To control the number of times ZAPFILE wipes a file, type a forward slash followed by a number from 1 to 255. The following switch instructs ZAPFILE to wipe files twice: c:\zapfile\zapfile.com /2.

If you would like to run Mutilate with Pretty Good Privacy's file-wipe utility, be sure to include the wipe switch. If you've stored Pretty Good Privacy in a directory called c:\pgp, type the following: c:\pgp\pgp.exe -w.

When you've finished showing Mutilate where your DOS file-wipe utility is located, click OK.

Deleting Files Completely.   To delete files with Mutilate, open the program by choosing Start Programs Mutilate. You'll see the Mutilate window, shown in Figure 12.2. You should use Mutilate for all your file deletion operations.

To wipe a file with Mutilate, do the following:

1. To choose the drive, select a drive from the drive selection box (at the bottom of the left panel).
2. In the Folder window, find and select the folder that contains the file or files you want to wipe.
3. In the File Type box (below the folder window), select the file type (you can choose from all files [*.*], text files [*.txt], Pretty Good Privacy files [*.pgp], JPEG graphic files [*.jpg], or GIF files [*.GIF]. If you don't see the file type you want, you can type directly in this box. For example, to show temporary files, type *.TMP.

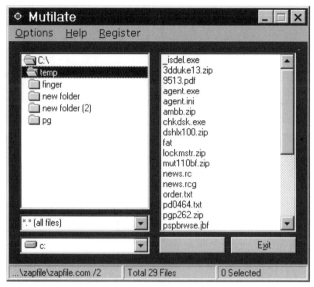

FIGURE 12.2   Mutilate's window gives you a mini-Windows Explorer that enables you to locate and wipe unwanted files.

4. In the file list, select the files you want to wipe. To select more than one file, hold down the Ctrl key to select the files you want, or hold down the Shift key and click to select a series of files. Press Ctrl + A to select all the files.

5. To start wiping, click Mutilate. (This button is dimmed until files are selected.) You'll see the warning shown in Figure 12.3.

6. If you're sure you want to wipe this file completely, beyond recovery, click OK.

Wiping Temporary (*.TMP) Files.   If you've been working with sensitive data, you should know that many programs create temporary files

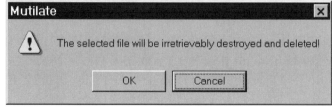

FIGURE 12.3   Are you sure?

that may persist after you've exited an application. To see just how many temporary files there are on your hard drive, do the following:

1. Click Start Shut Down, and choose Restart the computer in MS-DOS mode.
2. In MS-DOS, type cd\ to display your hard drive's root (top-level) directory.
3. Type dir *.tmp /s /b and press Enter.

You'll see a list of all the temporary files on your hard drive.

Now that you know where the files are located, you can delete them. However, be sure to do this from DOS. Some of the temporary files are created by Windows applications. If you delete these files while Windows is running, you may crash the applications or Windows.

For more information on running ZAPFILE from DOS, see the next section.

Running the ZAPFILE Utilities

To run the ZAPFILE utilities from DOS, be sure to quit Windows and restart your computer in MS-DOS mode. Do not run the ZAPFILE utilities from a DOS window inside Windows. If you do, you could cause your applications or Windows to crash.

CAUTION   **Don't switch off your computer while one of these utilities is running. Be aware that some of them take a very long time to finish. However, if you get tired of waiting and switch off your computer, you could scramble some of the data on your hard drive. Don't run these utilities unless you have lots of time available and you feel that you have a genuine need to do so.**

Running ZAPFILE from DOS.   To wipe a file using ZAPFILE, do the following:

1. Switch to ZAPFILE's directory. If ZAPFILE is in the directory c:\zapfile, type cd c:\zapfile and press Enter.
2. Type zapfile followed by a slash and the number of wipes you want, as well as the file name and path (for example, zapfile /2 c:\windows\temp\ eval.tmp).

Note that you can't use DOS wildcards with ZAPFILE. That's why it's better to run ZAPFILE with Mutilate—unless you're trying to delete temporary files. Always wipe temporary files from DOS.

Zapping Your Disk's Slack Space.   To wipe the slack space on your drive between the ends of files and the ends of disk clusters, switch to the ZAPFILE directory, type zaptips at the DOS prompt and press Enter.

CAUTION   Note that ZAPTIPS takes a very long time to run. Don't interrupt it while it's running, or you could scramble some of the data on your drive.

Zapping Your Disk's Empty Space.   To wipe the empty space on your drive, switch to the ZAPFILE directory, type zapempty at the DOS prompt and press Enter.

CAUTION   ZAPEMPTY takes a long time to run. Don't interrupt it while it's running, or you could scramble some of the data on your drive.

Setting Your Virtual Memory.   To prepare Windows for secure swap-file deletion, you need to set the swap file to a fixed size. This prevents Windows from deleting the file insecurely and preventing the wipe program from fully eradicating the data.

To set a fixed size for your Windows swap file:

1. Click Start Settings Control Panel. You'll see the Control Panel dialog box.
2. Double-click System. You'll see the System Properties dialog box.
3. Click the Performance tab.
4. Click Virtual Memory. You'll see the Virtual Memory dialog box.
5. Click Let me specify my own virtual memory settings.
6. In the Minimum and Maximum boxes, type the same number (in megabytes). Try a figure that matches or exceeds the amount of RAM in your computer, such as 32.
7. You'll see a warning box that your choices may degrade system performance. Click Yes to continue. As long as you set aside enough disk space for the swap file, you shouldn't see any noticeable change in Windows performance.
8. Click Yes to restart your system with your new virtual memory settings.

Zapping Your Windows Swap File.   To wipe your Windows swap file after a session working with sensitive data, do the following:

1. Click Start Shut Down, and click Restart the computer in MS-DOS mode.
2. In MS-DOS, switch to the directory in which you stored the ZAPFILE utilities.
3. Type zapswap, and press Enter.

CAUTION   Do not run ZAPSWAP from within Windows. The result would be analogous to tearing the wings off an aircraft while it is in flight! Always restart your computer in MS-DOS mode to work with ZAPSWAP.

File-Wiping Utilities for Windows 3.1 and Macintosh

If you're not using Windows 95, I recommend the following utilities (all available from www.shareware.com):

▶ Flamefile (Macintosh)—This drag-and-drop file-wiping utility conforms to U.S. Department of Defense wipe specifications. If you like, you can play a sound while a file is being flamed.
▶ WipeForWin (Windows 3.1)—This program adds a file-wiping extension to the Windows 3.1 File Manager. It doesn't work with Windows 95.

From Here

By following this chapter's suggestions, you can safeguard your system against snoops. But you're not done yet. Without your knowledge, your Internet browser has been documenting just where you've been on the Internet—the sites you've seen, the files you've downloaded, and even the search terms you've typed into search engines. In Chapter 13, you learn how to clean up your browser's trails.

Clean Up Your Browser's Trails

This is really depressing. While I'm typing these words on my Macintosh, I'm watching the screen of my Windows 95 system, just to my left. It's scrolling, displaying an absolutely unbelievable amount of data—megabytes' worth. What's in this data?

▶ Every URL that I have accessed using Internet Explorer since I installed the program

▶ Every query I've done with Alta Vista and other search engines, including the search terms

▶ Everything I've ever typed and uploaded in forms documents, including my Visa and American Express card numbers

▶ Everything I typed when I participated in Web-based chat rooms

Let's just put it this way. By examining the files Internet Explorer has secretly stored on my disk, a knowledgeable intruder could put together a shockingly accurate picture of what I've been doing with my computer over the past couple of years—what subjects I've been researching, what type of information I've been searching for, which sites I've visited.

Don't believe it? Take a look at Figure 13.1. Here's the record of my Internet Explorer usage when I was researching the chapter on children's pri-

```
IEClean30 demonstration
File  View  Click here first!
e Query "children's ad...on=caribbean&rtype=index&rinfo=Hotels&return_url=/bin/concierge.cgi?de
stNum=33&hotelNum=156&searchTerms={month}%20attribList}%20dec}%20{region}%20regionList}%20Caribbean
}%20%20{activities}%20attribList}%20sail}%20{}%20%20{}%20{}%20%20{weather}%20weatherList}%20{7%}%20t
o%2085}}&sail&type=cost&priorityNum=2&priorityList=region%20weather%20activities%20cost%20
ambiance&destination=Destination%20Finder&title=Bitter End Yacht Club&locator_file=&locator=&pa
th=destinations/caribbean/Virgin_Gorda¶K◊◆\B◊$Jþ`ÿⅰ⌐æ2|þñ⌐ⁿ ◊Ⅰ║ ◊■⌐ NE_?dn◊Visited: http:
//altavista.digital.com/cgi-bin/query?pg=q&stq=40&q=%22children%27s+advocates%22+Internet+pedop
hiles¶¶AltaVista Search: Simple Query "children's ad...s&Region="caribbean&rtype=index&rinfo=Hot
els&return_url=%2Fbin%2Fconcierge.cgi%3FdestNum%3D33%26hotelNum%3D156%26searchTerms%3D{month%25
20attribList%2520dec}%2520{region%2520regionList%2520Caribbean}%2520%2520{activities%2520attrib
List%2520sail}%2520{}%2520%2520{}%2520{}%2520%2520{weather%2520weatherList%2520{7%%2520to%2520
5}}%26sail%3Dsail%26type%3Dcost%26priorityNum%3D2%26priorityList%3Dregion%2520weather%2520activ
ities%2520cost%2520ambiance%26destination%2520Destination%2520Finder&title=Bitter%20End%20Yacht%2
0Club&locator_file=&locator=&path=destinations%2Fcaribbean%2FVirgin_Gorda¶¶destinations/caribbe
an/Virgin_Gorda      ...9◊ñⁿⅰ♣♦↓þ |ⁿⅼÿⅰ⌐ ◄◊^ùⁿⅰ⌐ⁿ ⌐◊ ⌐%0¶¶◊Visited: http://www.netm
ind.com/cgi-bin/uncgi/url-mind?resppage=http://www.webaid.com/a-rspnse.html&required-email=bp◊v
irginia.edu&url=http://www.webaid.com/reference/r-introd.html¶◊◊►⌐ þ⌐ ◊' jùⁿⅰ⌐ⁿ' jùⁿⅰ⌐◊┤||NR⌐⌐◊ ?
◊;¶¶⌐lg◊Visited: http://www.netmind.com/cgi-bin/uncgi/url-mind?resppage=http%3A%2F%2Fwww.webaid.
com%2Fa-rspnse.html&required-email=http%3A%2F%2Fwww.webaid.com%2Freference%2
Fr-introd.html¶¶URL-minder E-Mail Address Double-Check◊◊◊pⁿd⌐hùⁿⅰ⌐⌐hùⁿⅰ⌐⌐◊┤|NR⌐⌐◊ N◊¶N┤◊ kg◊
Visited: http://www.netmind.com/cgi-bin/uncgi/url-mind-confirmed?verified-email=bp◊virginia.edu
&required-email=bp◊virginia.edu&url=http://www.webaid.com/reference/r-introd.html&resppage=http
://www.webaid.com/a-rspnse.html¶◊◊┤◊pC◊ⁿuÿⁿⅰ⌐◊C◊ⁿⅰuÿⁿⅰ⌐?%⌐◊R⌐⌐◊ ◊¶■◊Visited: http://altav
ista.digital.com/cgi-bin/query?pg=q&what=web&fmt=.&q=graphics+visual++web++page+design+exciteme
nⁿⅰ⌐░█◊└ⁿⅰ⌐l¶U◊⌐◊◊ SEN◊║⌐Q◊ⅼⅰⁿⅰNⅰchst◊┤/Altavⅰⁿⅰtasⅰdigⅰ┤ⅰ⌐♪pA/cgi-bin/query?pg=q&what=web
&fmt=.&q=graphics+visual+%2Bweb+%2Bpage+design+excitement+interest¶¶AltaVista: Simple Query web gra
phics visual +web ... st...6◊◊|╪◄ⁿⅰ-pⁿ⌐◊ⁿⅰⁿⅰ⌐◊ⁿⅰAⁿⅰ⌐ⅼ;%⌐◊R⌐⌐◊ ◊N¶■◊h◊Visited: http://altavista.di
gital.com/cgi-bin/query?pg=q&what=web&stq=10&fmt=.&q=graphics+visual++web+design+exciteme
nt+interest¶¶AltaVista: Simple Query Microsoft Internet st...◊◊◊ ┃þ`ⅰⅼ⌐ⁿⅰⁿⅰ⌐◊ⁿⅼⅰ⌐ⁿⅰ⌐◊┤|R◊ⁿⅰ⌐ⁿⅰ VEⁿ
!⌐h◊Visited: http://altavista.digital.com/cgi-bin/query?pg=q&what=web&stq=10&fmt=.&q=graphics vi
sual+%2bweb+%2bpage+design+excitement+interest¶¶AltaVista: Simple Query graphics visual +web .
..6◊◊┤◊░┤þ°ⅼⁿⅰ⌐◊~ëÿⁿⅰ⌐◊ⁿⅼ%⌐◊R⌐⌐◊ ◊N¶■◊h◊Visited: http://altavista.digital.com/cgi-bin/query?p
g=q&what=web&stq=20&fmt=.&q=graphics+visual++web++page+design+excitement+interest N◊◊►ⁿⅰ ▄ⁿⅰyⁿⅰ⌐ⁿⅰE
ëÿⁿⅰ⌐◊ⁿⅰ⌐◊ VEⁿ¶h◊Visited: http://altavista.digital.com/cgi-bin/query?pg=q&what=web&stq=10&fmt=.&q
fmt=.&q=graphics+visual+%2bweb+%2bpage+design+excitement+interest¶¶AltaVista: Simple Query grap
hics visual +web ...◊◊┤◄◊◄♣pⁿ⌐900ÿⁿⅰ⌐◊áⁿⅰaX0ÿⁿⅰ⌐◊┤|R◊R⌐⌐◊ ┃;¶h◊Visited: http://altavista.digital
.com/cgi-bin/query?pg=q&what=web&fmt=.&q=graphic+design¶¶AltaVista: Simple Query graphic design
lle windows◊◊prᵣ◊ⁿⅰ⌐◊ rᵣ◊ⁿⅰ⌐◊⌐ⅼⁿⅰ⌐%R◊R⌐⌐◊ =?¶U◊Visited: http://altavista.digital.com/cgi-bin/query?
pg=q&what=web&fmt=.&q=graphic+design+web¶¶AltaVista: Simple Query graphic design webdows!!◊◊┤ⁿⅰ⌐◊
┤ⁿ◊ⁿⅰ⌐◊◄l┤ⁿⅰ⌐◊┤|R◊R◊R⌐◊ ┃?¶.¶,i◊Visited: http://altavista.digital.com/cgi-bin/query?pg=q&what=web
&stq=10&fmt=.&q=graphic+design+web¶¶AltaVista: Simple Query graphic design web¶¶◊◊┤ⁿⅰ⌐◊
¬┤ⁿⅰ┤◊╵♣¬◊UR⌐◊ |9¶|un◊Visited: http://guide-p.infoseek.com/Titles?col=WW&sv=IS&lk=noframes&gt=
web+graphics+design¶¶Infoseek Guide : web graphics design ver.NASHVILLE◊◊►◊♦◊²⌐þ◊╵◊░◊◊┤⌐◊
◊⌐%⌐UR⌐◊ ⌐9¶|sn◊Visited: http://guide-p.infoseek.com/Titles?st=web+graphics+design&col=WW&st=1
0&sv=IS&lk=noframes¶¶Infoseek Guide : web graphics design◊◊►E!¶◊R►┤ ┃R⌐⌐◊◊ⁿ9¶|qn◊Visited: http:/
/guide-p.infoseek.com/Titles?qt=web+graphics+design&col=WW&st=20&sv=IS&lk=nofra
mes¶¶Infoseek Guide : web graphics design◊◊*E!⌐p¦Rₑ ┃R⌐ⁿⁿⅰ⌐◊◊ ⁿ9¶|qn◊Visited: http:/
/guide-p.infoseek.com/Titles?qt=web+graphics+design&col=WW&st=30&sv=IS&lk=noframes¶¶Infoseek Gu
ide : web graphics design, 6/30/96"◊◊$◊◊◊þ ▓
                              íⁿⁿ◊   ▓▓
                          ◊ⁿ⌐◊┃ᵣRZXR⌐⌐◊ ▓E¶◊ Oq◊Visited: http://www.l
ycos.com/cgi-bin/pursuit?query=web+design+graphics+advice+rules+principles+fundamentals¶¶Lycos
search: web design graphics advice rule...6◊◊┤◊◆,◊pqⁿⅰ√¿íⁿⅰ◊¥¼íⁿⅰ⌐◊||>"XR⌐⌐◊◊ <¶◊◊Oq◊Visited: htt
p://www.lycos.com/cgi-bin/pursuit?first=11&maxhits=10&minterms=1&minscore=0.01&terse=standard&q
uery=design+proportion+balance¶¶Lycos search: design proportion balance6◊◊┤◊◆┤þⁿ╵◊◄¼◊ⁿⅰ⌐◊◄◊¼◊ⁿⅰ
◊◄RᵣJYR⌐⌐◊ <¶◊!ⁿⅰ⌐◊r◊Visited: http://www.lycos.com/cgi-bin/pursuit?first=21&maxhits=10&minterms=1&
minscore=0.01&terse=standard&query=design+proportion+balance¶¶Lycos search: design proportion b
alance6◊◊ñ◊◄<þⁿⁿⅰQⁿⅰ◊áⁿⅰ⌐◊◊áⁿⅰ⌐◊nùÿYR⌐⌐◊ <¶◊ár◊Visited: http://www.lycos.com/cgi-bin/pursuit?firs
t=31&maxhits=10&minterms=1&minscore=0.01&terse=standard&query=design+proportion+balance¶¶Lycos
search: design proportion balance6◊◊¼◊Dⁿþ ñⅼⁿⅰⁿⁿⅰ◊⌐þⁿⅰⁿⁿⅰⁿⅰ◊ⁿⅰ⌐◊ <¶◊!ⁿⅰr◊Visited: http://www.
lycos.com/cgi-bin/pursuit?first=41&maxhits=10&minterms=1&minscore=0.01&terse=standard&query=des
ign+proportion+balance¶¶Lycos search: design proportion balance6◊◊¼◊↑pα=¦6Añ⌐◊◊¦6Añ⌐◊◊M3¥R⌐⌐◊
◊◊ <¶◊◊r◊Visited: http://www.lycos.com/cgi-bin/pursuit?first=51&maxhits=10&minterms=1&minscore
=0.01&terse=standard&query=design+proportion+balance¶¶Lycos search: design proportion balance6◊
◊d◊◊I◊þ ¦ñⁿⅰⁿⅰ◊ ¦ñⁿⅰⁿⅰ◊L◊⌐YR⌐⌐◊ <¶◊ ir◊Visited: http://www.lycos.com/cgi-bin/pursuit?first=61&
maxhits=10&minterms=1&minscore=0.01&terse=standard&query=design+proportion+balance¶¶Lycos searc
h: design proportion balance6◊◊l◊◊♣p δ¼◊áⁿⅰ⌐◊◄¼ÿ◊áⁿⅰ◊¼-YR⌐⌐◊ <¶◊¼◊Visited: http://www.lycos.
com/cgi-bin/pursuit?first=71&maxhits=10&minterms=1&minscore=0.01&terse=standard&query=design+pr
oportion+balance¶¶Lycos search: design proportion balance6◊◊t◊◊◊þ◊ ¦ñⁿⅰⁿⅰ◊ ¦ñⁿⅰⁿⅰ◊-99YR⌐⌐◊ <¶
!◊r◊Visited: http://www.lycos.com/cgi-bin/pursuit?first=81&maxhits=10&minterms=1&minscore=0.01&
terse=standard&query=design+proportion+balance¶¶Lycos search: design proportion balance6◊◊◊◊◊♣
p úBeúⁿⅰ⌐◊ úBeúⁿⅰ⌐◊┤|>¼◊ZR⌐◊◊ <¶◊%s◊Visited: http://www.lycos.com/cgi-bin/pursuit?first=91&maxhit
s=10&minterms=1&minscore=0.01&terse=standard&query=design+proportion+balance¶¶Lycos search: des
ign proportion balance◊◊◊◊♣t◊pⁿDm¼◊áⁿⅰ◊ otⁿ◊áⁿⅰ◊◊GYR⌐⌐◊ ⌐Eⁿ'┃r◊Visited: http://the-tech.mit.edu
/cgi-bin/HyperNews/get/KPT/general/67.html¶¶What proportion do you begin with when design...MP
Article7◊■◊◊♣◊pá¦│ dúⁿⁿⅰ◊á¦⌐ dúⁿⁿⅰ◊┃¼◊ZR⌐◊◊ √<¶◊$s◊Visited: http://www.lycos.com/cgi-bin/pursuit?
first=101&maxhits=10&minterms=1&minscore=0.01&terse=standard&query=design+proportion+balance¶¶L
ycos search: design proportion balance7◊◊£◊◊♣þ ¦▓◄úñⁿⅰ◊ ¦▓◄úñⁿⅰ◊┃│◊ZR⌐◊◊ √<¶◊$s◊Visited: http:/
/www.lycos.com/cgi-bin/pursuit?first=111&maxhits=10&minterms=1&minscore=0.01&terse=standard&que
ry=design+proportion+balance¶¶Lycos search: design proportion balance
```

FIGURE 13.1 Internet Explorer keeps a detailed record of every last byte that you upload to the Internet via this program.

vacy on the Net. There are lots of search terms connected with this subject. Did I keep my nose to the grindstone? Nope. I spent some time browsing Caribbean resort hotel sites, and got off on a long tangent concerning excellence in Web page design. Obviously, I'm a problem employee!

And that's not all. Netscape and Internet Explorer both keep copies of virtually everything you download from Usenet newsgroups and Web sites, including graphics. A knowledgeable intruder—or an amateur who knows a few tricks—could put together a portrait of your Internet browsing habits in just a few minutes.

This chapter shows you how to use NSClean or IEClean. These shareware programs clean up the myriad files left behind by Netscape (NSClean) or Internet Explorer (IEClean). Included on this book's CD-ROM are demo versions of these programs. They enable you to view the contents of Netscape's or Internet Explorer's files, but you can't delete them. You need the registered version to delete the files.

CAUTION   Please note that neither NSClean nor IEClean can eradicate the traces of your Internet surfing that are left behind on your service provider's or employer's computer. What these programs can do is eradicate the trails on *your* computer, meaning that they're inaccessible to anyone trying to snoop on you by accessing your PC. These programs provide some protection against snooping kids or coworkers, but they can't protect you if an investigator accesses your service provider's records. In addition, NSClean or IEClean can't protect you if someone is performing a live tap on your Internet connection.

Introducing NS Clean and IE Clean

If you use Internet Explorer or Netscape, and you're concerned about the trails these browsers leave behind, you'll want to take a look at one of the following programs (located on this book's CD-ROM):

▶ **NSClean (demo version)**—Works with the 32-bit version of Netscape Navigator 3.0 (for Microsoft Windows 95 and Windows NT).

▶ **IEClean (demo version)**—Works with the 32-bit version of Internet Explorer 3.0 (for Microsoft Windows 95 and Windows NT).

Both of these programs hunt down the files that your browser leaves here and there on your hard drive, and enable you to view their contents. You can view the following:

Which Files Can You View?   The demo versions of NSClean and IEClean are designed to show you how much data both browsers store concerning your Internet activity. You'll be very surprised to find out what someone could learn about you from this data.

With the full, registered versions of these programs, you'll be able to view the following files:

▶ **Newsgroup information**—Both Netscape and Internet Explorer keep detailed records of which newsgroups you've accessed, which headers you've downloaded, which GIFS or JPEGs you've seen. The purpose of this tracking is to prevent you from seeing a read article's header the next time you access the newsgroup. That's convenient, but these records would enable an intruder to tell exactly what you've read when you've accessed Usenet. Netscape's newsgroups database (see Figure 13.2) shows which newsgroups you've accessed and which news items you've seen. Internet Explorer's news database is much more insidious: It not only contains records about which newsgroups you've accessed and which articles you've read, but it also contains the full text of these articles, including graphics files—even if you thought you had deleted these files. Were you to download some illegal pornography quite by accident, you could still be incriminated by this database, which keeps a bit-by-bit copy of everything you've accessed.

```
You have viewed the following in these newsgroups:

news.announce.newusers: 1-2615,2618-2638,2649,2655-2656
news.newusers.questions: 1-380099,420702,420864,421014,421049,421181,421205
news.answers: 1-82925
rec.boats.cruising! 27329
```

```
  Note that not only the newsgroups you visited have been listed. The actual
message numbers you've read are stored also. This feature of Netscape is
used so you don't read old messages again, and that's useful. But the
message numbers could be used by a snooper to see what you're "into" as
well. NSClean lets you decide if you want to keep or wipe this information.
```

FIGURE **13.2**   Your browser keeps detailed records of which Usenet newsgroups you've visited—and even which articles you've read.

▶ **URL window**—Both programs keep records of recently visited sites in a drop-down list box attached to the Location box (Netscape) or the Address box (Internet Explorer). To cover your tracks fully, you should clear these—and you can't do it from within the program. Figure 13.3 shows NSClean's view of my URL window.

▶ **History database**—Both programs keep records of the URLs you have accessed in this and previous sessions. Internet Explorer's history database is unusually large and detailed. Figure 13.1 shows the appalling detail of Internet Explorer's history database.

▶ **User ID**—In both Netscape and Internet Explorer, you're asked to state your name and e-mail address for identification purposes. Under certain circumstances, Internet sites can extract this information without your knowledge.

▶ **Cookies**—As you learned earlier in this book, many Web sites store information about your browsing habits on your own hard drive. Figure 13.4 shows my most recent crop of Internet Explorer cookies.

▶ **Cache directory**—Both programs store recently accessed HTML files, as well as GIF and JPEG graphics, on your hard drive. The purpose of the cache is to speed the retrieval of these sites if you access them again; the browser can retrieve the text and graphics from your hard drive rather than the Internet. However, the cache could also be used to reconstruct your browsing activity.

```
Netscape has records of the following sites in your URL window:

URL01: http://my.yahoo.com/
URL02: http://www.digicrime.com/
URL03: http://www.bulletproof.com/
URL04: http://altavista.digital.com/
URL05: http://www.hotbot.com/
URL06: http://www.yahoo.com/
URL07: http://www.bigbook.com/
URL08: http://www.jasmin.com/cgi-bin/kids.cgi
URL09: http://www.ici.net/customers/twu/Java/cookies.html
URL10: http://www.stpt.com/

-----------------------------------------------------------------
The sites listed above can be viewed by anyone who has access to your
computer, such as your family, your employer or snoopers. If you should
end up at a site you might consider embarassing or just don't want others
to know about, only NSClean can wipe out the listing so no one else can
see what sites you visit if you want NSClean to do so. NSClean can kill
all listings yet leave your default home page settings undisturbed.
```

FIGURE 13.3   The drop-down list under the Location or Address box contains recently accessed sites.

```
Your user information as known by Netscape:

Sig File:
User Org: Galactor Syndicate
Address : nobody@nothing.net
Username: None of your business
Reply to: nobody@nothing.net
_____
   NSClean allows you to change your email ID to an alias which will help to
prevent web sites and newsgroups from knowing your true identity. The above
information is gathered by combinations of cookies, javascripts, perl scripts
and so-called "pull-tags." NSClean lets you be someone else or yourself when
you want to be by simply checking or unchecking the "Use alias User ID while
online" option of NSClean. This goes a long way to enhancing your privacy.
```

FIGURE 13.4   A few days' worth of Internet Explorer cookies.

What You Can Do with the Full Registered Version.   With the full version of NSClean or IEClean, you can do any of the following:

▶ **Use an alias user ID while online**—Changes your user name and e-mail address to something bogus so that Internet sites cannot determine your identity without your knowledge.

▶ **Kill records of news site visits**—Completely obliterates your tracks through Usenet.

▶ **Kill records in history database**—Removes all traces of your previous browsing.

▶ **Kill records in URL window list**—Blanks the drop-down list box attached to the Location or Address box.

▶ **Kill records in cookie list file**—Deletes all the cookies from your hard drive (see Figure 13.5).

▶ **Kill cache containing old activity**—Deletes copies of HTML, graphic, and other files that you have recently accessed.

▶ **Kill all your Favorites or Bookmarks settings**—Favorites (Internet Explorer) and Bookmarks (Netscape) are saved URLs that appear in your Favorites or Bookmarks menu. Although storing these items in these menus enables you to return to these sites, you may wish to delete them if you want to fully cover your tracks.

Can't I Just Delete These Files Manually?   You could, but it's a very tedious job—they're scattered all over your hard drive. Worse, Internet Explorer's cache files are stored in hidden directories that are very difficult

```
Here is your Cookie data file. Note that you can't edit it. The sites
below have put this information into your machine with or without your
knowledge and left it there planning to retrieve information from your
machine at a future time ... IEClean can remove them if you wish.

Client UrlCache MMF Uer 3.2 ◆◆←•▶▐◙α≪◆♣ρôQ◙◥◡◥6↑┬◖❘KüE✱◥◙◙▶p!↑▐8p!↑▌cookie:anyuser@www.globa
ltrak.net/anyuser@www_globaltrak.txt◠◆♣pôL óc◥6↑┬◖◡.dᚴ↑┬◙◙▶p!$▐❘p!$▌cookie:anyuser@ad.doubl
eclick.net/anyuser@ad_doubleclick.txtó◆◖◆◆p➄α┌◥6↑┬◖◡`8£8S◥◙◙▶q!8❘◀q!8▌cookie:anyuser@focal
ink.com/anyuser@focalink.txtó◆➄kkt◥6↑┬◖�📂r·᛫᛫◖◡◥◙◙▶r!b◖◀r!b◖cookie:anyuser@software.net/anyus
er@software.txtleclick.txtó◆
               p➄jkt◥6↑┬◖❘∰M└≪≌◡◙◙▶r!≡◀◀r!≡◀cookie:anyuser@infoseek.com/anyuser
@infoseek.txtcrawler.txtíp➄r·kt◥6↑┬◖◐£up↑◙◙▶v!Of◖v!Ofcookie:anyuser@amazon.com/anyuser@amaz
on(1).txt➄pie ᵟ£➄6↑┬◖◡ ♠᛫q◡◙◙▶v!`v◖v!'vcookie:anyuser@hotbot.com/anyuser@hotbot.txtt.txtÜ◆⅞℮
Gαᛁ┬X┌◡┐◖C┌r ᛁ$δS┐◙◙▶m!♣oδ᛫n!♣ocookie:anyuser@nytimes.com/auth/auth.txtúiCαᛁ┬X┌◡┐◖C┌r ᛁ$δS┐◙◙▶m!
♣oδ᛫n!♣ocookie:anyuser@nytimes.com/anyuser@nytimes(1).txt➄ieá└┬X┌◡┐◖◡ ♠᛫q◡◙◙▶n!:δcookie:
anyuser@hotbot.com/anyuser@hotbot.txt%◆◀£Q└a└☐X┌◡┐◖᛭,δ◆↑◙◙▶o!᛫δo!᛫δcookie:anyuser@www.digi
crime.com/anyuser@www_digicrime.txt➄i^C̈_X┌◡┐◖C┌r ᛁ$δS┐◙◙▶p! ᛙr◖p!᛭rcookie:anyuser@disney.com/
anyuser@disney.txt£è^C̈_X┌◡┐◖C┌r ᛁ$δS┐◙◙▶p!Kw◖p!Kwcookie:anyuser@adobe.com/anyuser@adobe.txtᵢ
æ‖á²‖◖v ᛁ◥◖❘KüE✱◥◙◙▶p!�
æ▾p!⌠æcookie:anyuser@www.kelloggs.com/anyuser@www_kelloggs(1).txtClie
nt UrlCache MMF Uer 3.2 ◆▶
_____
 IEClean can remove these cookies so you can't be tracked. Best of all,
set MSIE to just accept cookies rather than getting frustrated clicking
them a
```

FIGURE 13.5   IEClean shows what's actually in Internet Explorer's secret files.

to access unless you have special software or advanced technical knowledge. By running NSClean or IEClean periodically, you delete all the sensitive files with just one simple click of the mouse. *Voilà!*

Registering NSClean or IEClean.   To register your copy of NSClean or IEClean and receive a fully functional version of the program, do one of the following:

▶ Visit www.axxis.com/cgi-bin/order-clean. You can order using your credit card through this secure site.

▶ Call 801-523-8221. In Europe or Asia, call 44 115 956-8823.

Currently, NSClean and IEClean are priced at $40.

TIP For the latest info on IEClean and NSClean, see their home pages (www. wizvax.net/kevinmca/).

Installing NSClean or IEClean

To install the demo version of NSClean or IEClean, do the following:

▶ Place this book's CD-ROM in the disc drive.

▶ Open the folder containing the version of the program you want to install (NSClean or IEClean).

▶ Double-click SETUP.EXE.

▶ Follow the on-screen instructions.

Running NSClean or IEClean

To run NSClean or IEClean, just click Program Start and choose NSClean or IEClean from the menu. Then do the following:

▶ From the View menu, choose Examine your Netscape files (NSClean) or Examine your Internet Explorer files (IEClean). You'll see a submenu that enables you to choose which files you want to view.

▶ Choose one of the files. You'll see the file's contents on-screen.

CAUTION   Internet Explorer's History database file is very large, and there's no way to stop IEClean from scrolling through the file until the program reaches the end of this file. Don't choose this option unless you've some time to kill!

When to Use NSClean or IEClean

These programs can eradicate the trails left behind on your PC by Netscape and Internet Explorer. You may wish to consider running the appropriate version of the program in the following situations:

▶ You are sharing your computer with someone and do not wish this person to know anything about your browsing habits.

▶ You're about to let a child use your computer, and you don't want to leave any trails to adult-oriented sites.

▶ You are responsible for an Internet-connected PC that's made available in a public setting, such as a library. A user who violates usage policies by accessing adult sites, or a prankster who's hoping to embarrass you, may leave behind bookmarks or other trails that would be discernible to subsequent users.

▶ You are taking your computer into a shop for maintenance and do not want the technicians to have a little fun by probing into your online browsing habits.

Although NSClean and IEClean can do much to clear up your browser's trails, there's another privacy-compromising trace you're leaving behind: cookies. In the next chapter, you'll find out what cookies are, what threats they pose to your privacy, and how you can eliminate them.

CHAPTER 14

Kill Your Cookies

Cookies, introduced in Chapter 6, are text files that Web servers can use for a variety of purposes—including establishing your identity. Chapter 6 discussed the benefits and perils of cookies. In this chapter, you learn how to put technology to work to eliminate cookies.

To deal with cookies through technical means, you have four choices;

1. **Turn off automatic downloading of cookies in Netscape Navigator and Microsoft Internet Explorer**—The disadvantage here is that both programs ask you for confirmation before rejecting a cookie. Some sites hit you with repeated requests. Soon, you'll get tired of confirming the deletions, and switch off this feature. (Almost certainly, this is what was intended.) Also, in both browsers, turning off automatic cookie downloading does not prevent the programs from uploading cookies that have already been stored on your hard drive.

2. **Delete cookie files at the beginning of each session**—This prevents Web sites from storing long-term information about your identity and preferences. However, it enables Web sites to store temporary information that persists only during the current operating session.

3. **Use a cookieless browser**—If you would like to dispense with cookies altogether, use a browser that does not know how to send or receive them.

Ariadna, the Russian browser discussed in the next chapter, is a cookie-less browser with many of the advanced features of Netscape Navigator 2.0, including tables and Java.

4. **Use PGPcookie.cutter**—This shareware application from PGP, Inc., enables Netscape users to selectively block or allow cookies, just as you wish.

TIP Deleting your cookies does have some costs. If you follow the instructions in this chapter, be aware that neither Netscape Navigator nor Microsoft Internet Explorer will be able to log you in to registered sites automatically. You'll have to type your user name and password manually.

How Netscape Navigator Stores Cookies

Netscape Navigator (through version 3.0) stores cookies in a file called cookies.txt (see Figure 14.1).

TIP Cookies.txt is something of a security risk, as you can see from Figure 14.1. I've registered for several sites. Were the screen shot wide enough, you'd be able to see the user name and password I use to log on to those sites. If a knowledgeable hacker got into my system while I was away from my desk, this information could be obtained very easily simply by printing or copying the file.

You can delete this file at any time. Doing so effectively prohibits Web servers from collecting previously stored information. However, doing so does not prevent Web servers from creating a new cookies.txt file and storing new information in it.

How Internet Explorer Stores Cookies

Internet Explorer (version 3.0) stores cookies in a special directory that is automatically created within your Windows directory (see Figure 14.2). It's called Cookies, naturally. Each cookie is written individually to a text file.

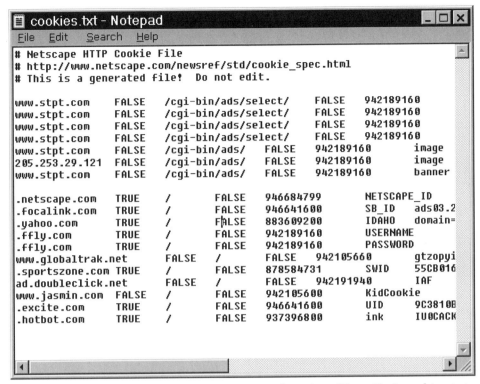

FIGURE **14.1**   Netscape Navigator stores cookies in a file called cookies.txt.

The Internet Explorer Cookie Killer

On the CD-ROM packaged with this book, you'll find a file called IE-KILL. BAT designed to work with Windows 95. The file contains the following:

```
@echo off
if not exist c:\windows\cookies\*.txt go to noexist
erase c:\windows\cookies\*.txt
echo Internet Explorer cookies deleted!
goto end
:noexist
echo You have no Internet Explorer cookies.
:end
@echo on
```

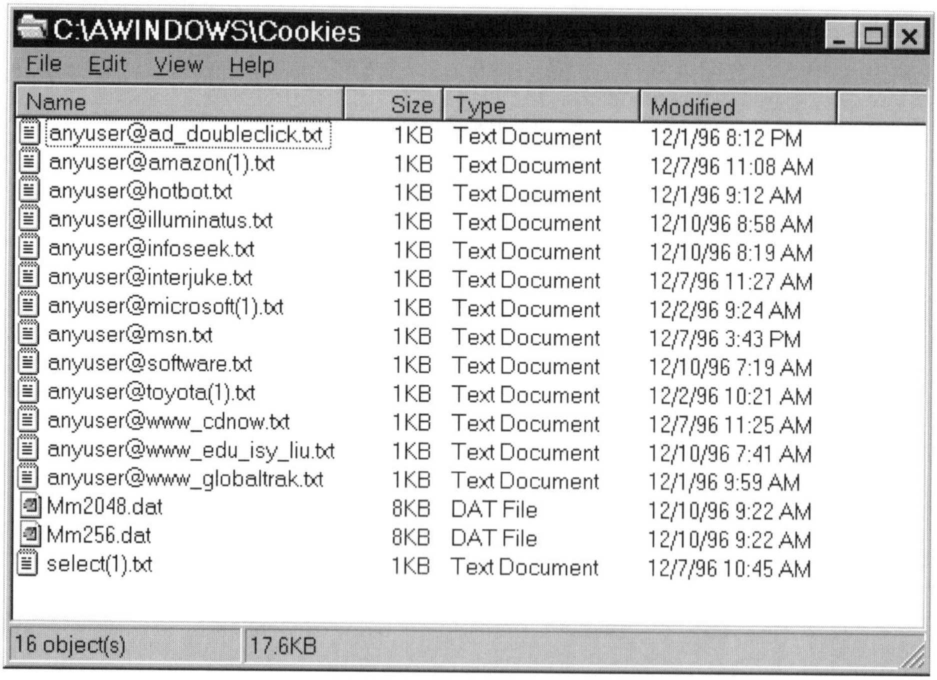

FIGURE 14.2   Internet Explorer stores cookies in the \windows\cookies directory.

In English, this little batch file says, in effect, "If there are no text files in the Cookies directory, display 'You have no Internet Explorer cookies.' If one or more text files exist, wipe them out and display 'Internet Explorer cookies deleted.'"

There's a lot to be said for this approach. It prevents Web servers from storing long-term information about you. At the same time, it enables Web servers to store temporary cookies, which are very useful for a number of applications that directly benefit Web users. One example: The shopping carts used in many commercial Web sites. To shop at these sites, you place items in a virtual shopping cart, and you don't pay until you've finished selecting items. Cookies make shopping carts possible.

TIP   This little batch program will not work correctly if you installed Windows to a directory other than c:\windows. To make the file work, you must edit the file and type in the correct path to the \cookies. directory. For exam-

ple, if you installed windows in c:\windoze, you must replace the two references to c:\windows\cookies*txt with c:\windoze\cookies*.txt.

To make sure this batch file will work correctly, open an MS-DOS window, type the following, and press Enter:

dir c:\windows\cookies*.txt.

If you see the message "Path not found," then you probably installed Windows in a directory other than c:\windows, or you're not using the current (3.0) version of Internet Explorer. If you see a file name or "File Not Found," then everything's hunky-dory.

If the test works, try running this batch file. Using My Computer or Windows Explorer, simply locate and double-click this file. You'll see an MS-DOS window. If the file deleted one or more cookies, you'll see the message, "Internet Explorer cookies deleted!" If there were no cookies, you'll see the message "You have no Internet Explorer cookies." Just click the Close box to close the MS-DOS window. To make sure the batch file worked correctly, open the c:\windows\cookies directory, and make sure there are no text files present.

To include this program in your AUTOEXEC.BAT file, see the section titled "Including the Cookie Killers in your AUTOEXEC.BAT file," later in this chapter.

The Netscape Cookie Killer

Like the Internet Explorer cookie killer, the Netscape cookie killer is located in the Kill Cookies folder of this book's CD-ROM. It's called NS-KILL.BAT, and it contains the following:

```
@echo off
if not exist c:\progra~1\netscape\cookies.txt go to noexist
erase c:\progra~1\netscape\cookies.txt
echo Netscape cookies deleted!
goto end
:noexist
```

echo You have no Netscape cookies.
:end
@echo on

In English, this little batch file says, in effect, "If the Netscape cookie file doesn't exist, display 'You have no Netscape cookies.' If it *does* exist, wipe it out and display 'Netscape cookies deleted.'"

TIP **Like IE-KILL.BAT, this file assumes that cookies.txt is located in the default installation directory (c:\program files\netscape\cookies.txt). To make sure this batch file will work on your computer, open an MS-DOS window, type the following, and press Enter:**

dir c:\progra~.1\netscape\cookies.txt

If you see the message "Path not found," then you probably installed Windows in a directory other than c:\windows, or you're not using the current (3.0) version of Netscape. If you see a file name or "File Not Found," then everything's hunky-dory.

If the test works, try running this batch file. Using My Computer or Windows Explorer, simply locate and double-click this file. You'll see an MS-DOS window. If the file deleted one or more cookies, you'll see the message, "Netscape cookies deleted." If there were no cookies, you'll see the message "You have no Netscape cookies." Just click the Close box to close the MS-DOS window. To make sure everything worked correctly, open the c:\Program Files\Netscape directory and make sure there's no cookies.txt.

To include this program in your AUTOEXEC.BAT file, see the next section titled, "Including the Cookie Killers in your AUTOEXEC.BAT file."

Including the Cookie Killers in Your AUTOEXEC.BAT File

If you've tested the cookie killers and found that they're working on your system, add them to your AUTOEXEC.BAT file.

To add the cookie killers to your AUTOEXEC.BAT file:

1. Use Windows Explorer or My Computer to copy IE-KILL.BAT and NS-KILL.BAT to the root directory of your hard drive (C:\).
2. Choose Start Run, and type sysedit in the Open box. You'll see the System Configuration Editor, shown in Figure 14.3.
3. If necessary, bring the AUTOEXEC.BAT window to the foreground.

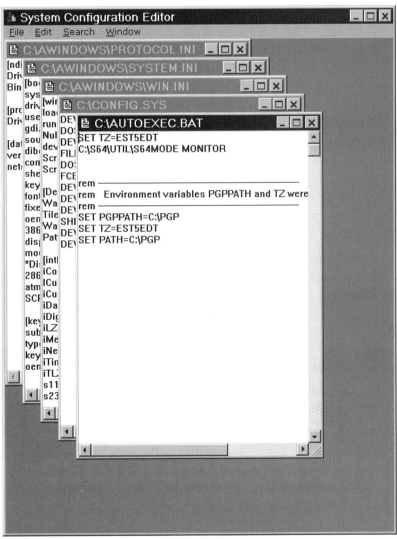

FIGURE 14.3   The Windows 95 System Configuration Editor enables you to edit system files.

If no AUTOEXEC.BAT file is visible, exit the program and go to the section called "Creating AUTOEXEC.BAT."

1. Press the down arrow until you reach the end of the file, and then press Enter.
2. Type CALL IE-KILL, and press Enter.
3. Type CALL NS-KILL, and press Enter.
4. Choose File Save.
5. Choose File Exit.
6. Restart your system.

Your cookies are deleted if you had any.

Creating AUTOEXEC.BAT.   This section is for readers whose systems lack AUTOEXEC.BAT. To create the file, do the following:

1. Open the Windows Notepad accessory.
2. Type CALL IE-KILL, and press Enter.
3. Type CALL NS-KILL, and press Enter.
4. Choose File Save.
5. Name the file AUTOEXEC.BAT.
6. Save the file in your hard disk's root directory. If the file already exists, choose Cancel, and quit Notepad without saving. Return to the previous

PGPcookie.cutter Lets You Control Cookies

To gain more control over cookies, consider PGPcookie.cutter, a program marketed by PGP, Inc. PGPcookie.cutter is a plug-in that works with Netscape Navigator and Internet Explorer. It provides a control panel that enables users to block or allow specific cookies. Unlike the cookie-prevention features built into current browsers, PGPcookie.cutter enables you to allow full cookie functionality for trusted sites, while preventing unwanted cookies from sites you haven't approved. Not yet available at this writing, the program can be downloaded from PGP's Web site (www.pgp.com). The registration fee is slated to be $19.95.

section ("Adding the Cookie Killers to AUTOEXEC.BAT") and follow the instructions there.

From Here

If you would rather browse without leaving any cookie trails whatsoever, consider installing and running Ariadna, the cookieless browser described in the next chapter.

CHAPTER 15

Use a Cookieless Browser

I n Chapter 14, you learned a number of ways you can kill the cookies that your browser leaves on your hard disk. But there's another way—avoid them altogether.

The key here is to use a *cookieless browser*—a browser that doesn't respond to server requests concerning cookies and doesn't write them to your hard drive.

Where do you get a cookieless browser? Right on this book's CD-ROM, which contains a copy of AMSD Ariadna. This browser isn't technologically retrograde—it can handle tables, Java, and typefaces, enabling you to see Web-page designs in all their glory (or stupidity, as the case may be). It just doesn't handle cookies, a feature that Ariadna's designers haven't had time to implement. For privacy-conscious Internet users, the *lack* of this feature is actually a plus!

This chapter introduces Ariadna, shows you how to install the program on your hard drive, and runs down the basics of using the program. I'm assuming that you've already learned the basics of using a cookieful browser such as Netscape Navigator or Microsoft Internet Explorer, so I'll just highlight the procedures that differ somewhat from what you're used to.

Introducing Ariadna

Ariadna is a full-featured Web browser created by Advanced Multimedia Systems Design (AMSD), a Russian software development firm. The program is available for Windows 95 and Windows NT. Developed from scratch and written in C++, AMSD does not depend on legacy code from NCSA Mosaic, like most other browsers. The program is fully optimized to take advantage of the advanced characteristics of the 32-bit Windows operating environment. The project leader is Artem A. Bovin, and the lead programmers are Maxim Y. Kaikin and Oleg G. Zakharov.

Admittedly, Ariadna has a few rough edges—but they're forgivable. In the dialog boxes, the English isn't so hot, a fact that I personally find endearing rather than offensive. It takes some *chutzpah* for a tiny Russian company to take on the likes of corporate giants Netscape and Microsoft! Not so endearing is the fact that Ariadna doesn't cope well with some rarified video systems, such as my Portrait display monitor. But I wouldn't go so far as an ill-tempered Belgian commentator, who rather uncharitably branded the program an *amateuristische kopie* (amateurish copy) of Netscape. Maybe it's amateurish to leave out cookies—or maybe it's a plus, depending on one's point of view!

Remember, too, that the version of Ariadna on this book's CD-ROM is beta software. You should think twice about running Ariadna if you've got some valuable work going in other applications. Although I haven't experienced any crashes with Ariadna (yet), a small software firm such as AMSD simply doesn't have the resources to check the program out on every conceivable computer system.

TIP **To get the latest copy of Ariadna, use your existing browser to log onto AMSD's home page (www.amsd.ru). The version of Ariadna on this book's CD-ROM is the latest available at this writing (version 1.2 beta b1). Be aware, though, that AMSD didn't leave out cookies because of privacy concerns—they left them out because they haven't had time to implement them. A future version of Ariadna may not ignore cookies the way the current version does.**

As you might expect, Ariadna really shines when it comes to displaying Russian. The program automatically reads from any of five Russian keyboard layouts in any font, and can recognize the character set automatically if the correct HTML tags are used.

Ariadna's Features.   Feature for feature, Ariadna is a worthy competitor to Netscape Navigator and Microsoft Internet Explorer. The program supports:

▶ All the main Internet protocols (the Web, FTP, Gopher, Telnet, and local files)
▶ Simultaneous downloading of text and graphics
▶ Attractive formatting of HTML heading tags to increase document legibility
▶ Java (requires installation of the freeware Java Developer's Kit)
▶ PNG graphics (a graphics format that is expected to replace the inferior and copyrighted GIF format)
▶ Built-in Mailto e-mail replies
▶ Tables (with up to 100 levels of internal nesting)
▶ Font faces, sizes, and colors
▶ Built-in Internet telephony (AMSD EasyTalk)
▶ Well-conceived bookmark capabilities (better than Netscape)
▶ Sophisticated Russian language display capabilities

What Ariadna doesn't do, arguably, you don't need. Not included are the following:

▶ **Frames**—No huge loss here, since many Web users find frames aesthetically displeasing and difficult to use. Sites that employ frames generally make a nonframes version available, and Ariadna will display this version by default.
▶ **Security**—Ariadna can't establish a secure connection with a commercial Web service. This isn't the browser to use if you like to surf with your Visa card in hand.
▶ **GIF animations**—Personally, I think this is reason enough to use Ariadna. I just hate all those cute little winkies that say, "Here! Me! Buy this!"
▶ **Plug-ins**—Ariadna can work with external helper programs, but it can't run Netscape plug-ins. This probably isn't the best browser to use if you're addicted to multimedia—but considering how long it takes to

download multimedia files on slow modem lines, this isn't a big loss for many users.

▶ **JavaScript**—Ariadna can work with Java—but not its insecure little sister, JavaScript. As explained in Chapter 7, this is actually an advantage. In the beta version, though, Java isn't particularly stable, and I don't recommend that you install it.

▶ **Cookies**—Ariadna does something completely wonderful with server cookie downloads and requests: It ignores them. As a result, processing occurs much more rapidly, since there's a lot less overhead as you're downloading a page. What's not to like about this? Very little. You won't be able to take advantage of page customization features, and you'll have to supply your login name and password when you log on to subscription services.

Ariadna's Requirements.   Ariadna requires a 486DX33 PC or better, with at least 8 MB of RAM. The program also requires Windows 95 or Windows NT. It does not run on Windows 3.1 systems.

Installing Ariadna

Ariadna comes with an automatic installation utility that installs the program quickly. In order to set up Java, though, you may have to download some additional software

Running SETUP.   To install Ariadna on your Windows 95 or Windows NT system, do the following:

1. Insert this book's CD-ROM in the drive.
2. Open the Ariadna folder.
3. Double-click SETUP.EXE.
4. Follow the on-screen instructions.

Installing the Java Developer's Kit (JDK).   To use Java with Ariadna, you must install the freeware Java Developer's Kit (JDK). However, I've found that the beta version of Ariadna isn't particularly stable after installing Java, so you may want to think twice about installing it.

To install the Java Developer's Kit, do the following:

1. Important: From the Ariadna folder on this book's CD-ROM, copy JDK-1_0_2-win32-x86.exe to your computer's root directory (c:\). You must run this file from your root directory so that Java will install it to c:\java. If you install the Java software elsewhere, Ariadna won't be able to find it.
2. Locate and double-click this file. This will unpack the files to c:\java.
3. Delete the JDK-1_0_2-win32-x86.exe file from your root directory.
4. Note: If Ariadna doesn't run Java applets, the problem probably lies in your having installed an earlier version of Java. To remedy the problem, do the following:
5. From the Start menu, click Run. You'll see the Run dialog box.
6. Type sysedit, and click OK. You'll see Sysedit, a Windows application that enables you to edit your system files.
7. Click the AUTOEXEC.BAT window.
8. Determine whether there's a SET CLASSPATH line. If so, delete it.
9. Type SET CLASSPATH c:\java\lib\classes.zip.
10. Type SET PATH c:\java\bin.
11. Choose File Save.
12. Restart your computer.

Running Ariadna

Once you've installed Ariadna, you run it as you would any other browser. First connect to the Internet, and then start the program.

To start Ariadna, click Start Programs AMSD Ariadna. You'll see Ariadna on-screen, as shown in Figure 15.1. By default, the program displays AMSD's home page, in Moscow, as its default start page. Click English—unless, that is, you know Russian and would like to browse the Russian version!

TIP **You may wish to check out the Ariadna home page (www.amsd.com/Ariadna/ariadna.htm, shown in Figure 15.2) to see whether there's a more recent version of Ariadna available. Just make sure it's still cookieless!**

Learning Ariadna's Interface

I'm assuming that you've already used another Web browser—probably Netscape Navigator or Microsoft Internet Explorer—and that you're familiar

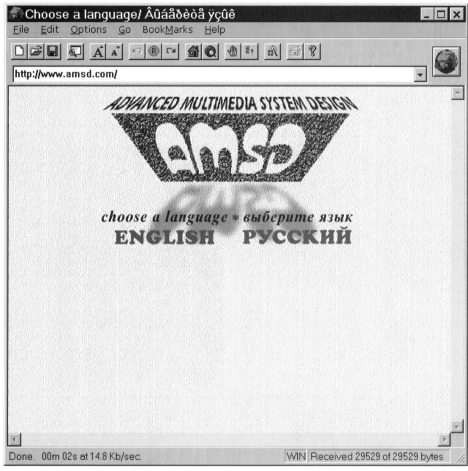

FIGURE 15.1   Ariadna's default start page is AMSD's home page in Moscow.

with the basics. My purpose here isn't to fully document this program, but rather to point out the features you're most likely to use. You can explore the rest of the program on your own—and as you do, you won't be leaving behind a trail of cookies!

Using the Toolbar.   Ariadna's toolbar gives you quick access to the commands you're most likely to use. From left to right, here's what they do:

▶ **New Browser**—Open a new document window.
▶ **Open File**—Open a local file (a file located on your system).

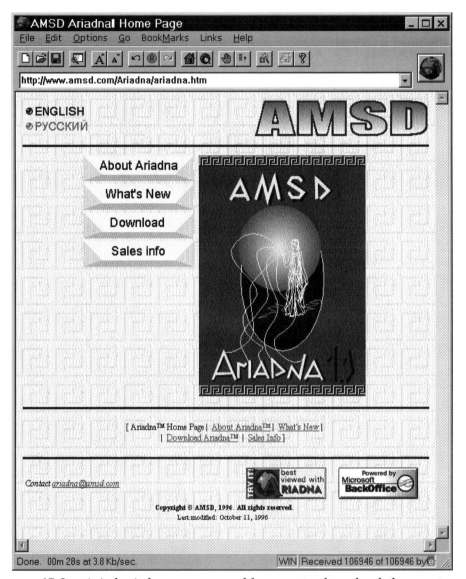

FIGURE 15.2   Ariadna's home page enables you to download the most recent version.

- ▶ **Save As**—Save a document to disk, in HTML or plain text formats.
- ▶ **View Source**—View the source HTML code of the current document.
- ▶ **Enlarge Fonts**—Increase the current display font size.
- ▶ **Decrease Fonts**—Reduce the current display font size.
- ▶ **Back**—Go back to the previous page.

Who's Ariadna?

In Greek mythology, Ariadna is the daughter of King Minos, whose curse it was that his wife should give birth to a monster, half man and half bull. To house this monster, the Minotaur, Minos had Daedalus construct a labyrinth—a house with "innumerable paths of deception," according to Ovid. Daedalus himself was barely able to return to its entrance.

The labyrinth was indeed a maze from which few returned, since the Minotaur had a very nasty habit of consuming all those who entered. Desiring to rid Athens of this cursed creature, the hero Theseus arrived to enter the labyrinth, where by force of arms he planned to dispatch the beast. Falling in love with this brash young fool, Ariadna gave him a ball of yarn—which enabled the victorious Theseus to find his way out of the maze. In the same way, Ariadna helps you find your way through the Web.

▶ **Reload**—Retrieve a fresh copy of the document from the network.
▶ **Forward**—Redisplay a page you had previously displayed but went back from.
▶ **Home**—Return to the current default start page.
▶ **Search Page**—Search the Internet.
▶ **Insert Bookmark**—Bookmark this page.
▶ **View Bookmarks**—Open the Bookmarks window.
▶ **URL Wizard**—Decode the current page's URL so that you can see the various parts of the URL differentiated (protocol, host, and path).
▶ **Print**—Print the current document.
▶ **Help**—Display Ariadna's help pages.

TIP If you forget what a button does, just move the mouse pointer to the button. You'll see a tool tip that names the button.

Using the Keyboard. I've got one heck of a repetitive strain injury—but not from my keyboard. It's from using the mouse! That's why I really appreciate the neat way that Ariadna implements keyboard commands. Table 15.1 contains a list of keys you can press to access Ariadna's features.

Using the Pop-Up Menu. When you click the right mouse button within Ariadna's window, you see a pop-up menu (see Figure 15.3). Just

---

Table 15.1   **Ariadna's Keyboard Shortcuts**

Open a new browser window	Ctrl + N

File Commands

Open a local file	Ctrl + F
Save document as an HTML file	Ctrl + A
Save document as a text file	Ctrl + T
Print the document	Ctrl + P

Editing Commands

Cut selection to the Clipboard	Ctrl + X
Copy selection to the Clipboard	Ctrl + C
Paste selection	Ctrl + V
View source	Ctrl + E
View document information	Ctrl _ L
Enlarge fonts	Ctrl + Gray plus
Decrease fonts	Ctrl + Gray minus
Restore default font size	Ctrl + Gray asterisk

Navigation Commands

Access current hyperlink	Enter
Go back	Ctrl + Left arrow
Reload current document	Ctrl + R
Go forward	Ctrl + Right arrow
Return to default start page (home page)	Alt + H
Go to default search engine page	Alt + S
Stop loading document	Esc
View recent browsing history	Ctrl + H

Bookmark Commands

Add current document to Bookmark menu	Ctrl + D
View Bookmark window	Ctrl + B

---

what's on this menu varies, depending on the context. Here's what you'll find on the various versions of the menu:

▶ **Go back**—Same as clicking the Back button.
▶ **Go Forward**—Same as clicking the Forward button.
▶ **View History List**—Displays a list of recently accessed sites.

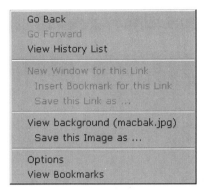

FIGURE 15.3 Ariadna's pop-up menu.

▶ **New Window for this Link**—Opens this link in a new window.

▶ **Insert Bookmark for this Link**—Adds a bookmark to your Bookmarks menu.

▶ **Save this Link as**—Same as clicking the Save As button.

▶ **View this Image Display**—The current in-line image in a new Ariadna window.

▶ **Save this Image as**—Saves the current image to your disk.

▶ **View background**—Displays the background graphic.

▶ **Options**—Displays the Options dialog box.

▶ **View Bookmarks**—Displays the Bookmarks dialog box.

Cookieless Browsing with Ariadna

As previously mentioned, I'm assuming that you've used Netscape Navigator or Microsoft Internet Explorer previously, so you need only a quick rundown of Ariadna's features.

Changing the Default Start and Search Pages. Chances are that you'll want to see something besides AMSD's home page every time you start Ariadna. You may also wish to change the default search page. To change the default start and search pages:

1. Choose Options Preferences. You'll see the Options dialog box. Click the General tab to see the General page, shown in Figure 15.4.

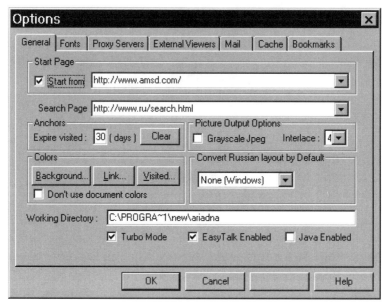

FIGURE 15.4   You can change Ariadna's default start and search pages.

2. In the Start Page area, type the new start page's URL in the text box next to Start From. I changed mine to www.stpt.com (Starting Point), which is a really cookie-intensive site. You won't believe how much faster it loads with Ariadna!

3. In the Search Page area, type the new search page's URL in the text box next to Search Page. I like www.hotbot.com.

4. Click OK.

Ariadna Browsing Tips.   If you're making the transition from Netscape Navigator or Microsoft Internet Explorer to the cookieless Ariadna, here are a few tips concerning Ariadna features that aren't obvious on the display window:

▶ To reload a page, just click the Reload button—or click the Ariadna program icon.

▶ To access a URL by typing it, you don't have to type the protocol (http://). Ariadna supplies this automatically.

▶ If you access a page with forms, remember that you can't upload the text in a form box by pressing Enter. Ariadna uses Enter to activate hyperlinks. Click the Submit or Send button instead.

▶ To revisit a site you previously visited, click the down arrow to the right of the URL location box, and choose the site from the list. Alternatively, choose View History, or just click Ctrl + H. You'll see the History window, shown in Figure 15.5. Choose a site from the list, and click Go To.

Ensuring Your Privacy with Ariadna

Like Netscape Navigator and Microsoft Internet Explorer, Ariadna keeps a record of the sites you've visited. This could be a privacy concern, especially if you share your computer with somebody, have a snoopy boss, or let your kids use your computer. But here Ariadna has another feature that you will like: You can disable the cache. In addition, you can clear the history list, effectively covering your tracks.

Disabling the Cache.   Browsers use a cache—a section of your hard disk that is set aside for storing copies of recently accessed Web pages—in order to speed a browser's apparent operation. When you revisit a previously visited site, the browser checks with the site to determine whether

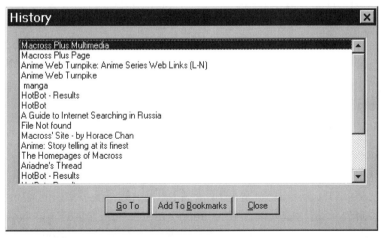

FIGURE 15.5   Ariadna's History window enables you to return to previously accessed sites.

the page has been altered since you last accessed it. If not, the program loads the document from your hard drive rather than retrieving it from the network. Since your hard drive is a lot faster than the network, it seems as if your browser is running much faster. The only problem is that all those documents provide snoops with a verifiable trail that documents your browsing habits.

Unlike Netscape Navigator and Microsoft Internet Explorer, Ariadna enables you to turn off caching entirely. The result is that the program seems to run much more sluggishly when you're returning to previously accessed sites. If you're concerned that a coworker or someone else might be trying to document your browsing habits, though, it's worth it. (Just bear in mind that your Internet service provider's server may also have a record of your browsing habits, so this measure is effective only against people snooping around in your own computer system.) To disable the cache:

1. Choose Options Preferences. You'll see the Options dialog box. Click the General tab to see the General page, shown in Figure 15.4.
2. Click the Cache button. You'll see the Cache options, shown in Figure 15.6.
3. Select Disabled.
4. Click OK.

Clearing the History List.   To finish covering your Ariadna tracks, be sure to erase the history list. You can do so from within Ariadna (choose Options Preferences, click General, and click Clear in the Anchors area), but a snooper could recover this file. It's best to use Mutilate, introduced in Chapter 12, to delete this file so that it cannot be recovered. To do so, quit Ariadna, open Ariadna's folder with Mutilate, and wipe the file HISTORY.DAT. (If you see CACHE.DAT, wipe this too.)

Organizing Bookmarks with Ariadna

Ariadna's Bookmarks dialog box enables you to organize your bookmark items. This section briefly covers this feature, which differs from similar features in Microsoft Internet Explorer and Netscape Navigator. Specifically, the folders you create in the Bookmarks dialog box don't appear as menu items on the Bookmarks menu. Still, you can use the Bookmarks dialog box to organize and store lots of bookmarks.

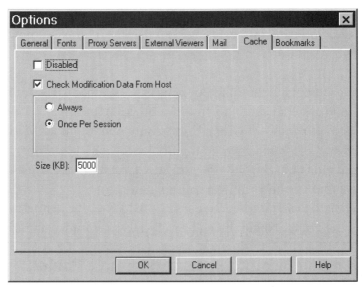

FIGURE 15.6 With Ariadna, you can completely disable caching, eliminating one of the trails most browsers leave behind that could be used to document your browsing habits.

Chances are you're thinking of organizing your bookmarks because your Ariadna bookmark menu is full of unorganized links, like the one shown in Figure 15.7.

Here, you see two types of links: Most pertain to Japanese animation (anime), but there's a link to a search engine, too. Your first step is to organize your existing bookmarks into folders. You may then wish to create new folders.

FIGURE 15.7 A disorganized bookmark menu.

Creating New Folders.   Your first step is to create new folders, in which you can store existing bookmarks. To create a new folder at the top level:

1. Choose Bookmarks View Bookmarks, or choose Ctrl + V. You'll see the Bookmarks Manager shown in Figure 15.8. In the left panel, you see the existing folders—of which there's only one, the BookMarks Library. In effect, this is the top level of the Bookmarks menu. In the right panel, you see the bookmarks that are currently stored in this folder—yes, they're the ones that currently appear on the menu.
2. To create a new folder, choose Edit Add New, or just press Ctrl + N. You'll see the Folder Name dialog box. Type a new folder name, and click OK.

Dragging Existing Bookmarks into a Folder.   Once you've created a folder, it's easy to place existing bookmarks into it. Just select the bookmarks in the bookmarks list (the right panel of the Bookmarks window), and drag the selection to the folder.

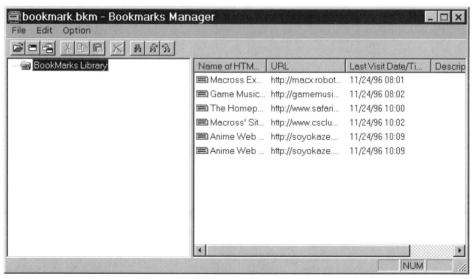

FIGURE 15.8   The Bookmarks window enables you to organize your bookmarks.

Choosing Which Folder to Display.   After you organize your book-marks, you can choose which folder to display. To choose the folder to display:

1. In the Bookmarks window, choose Option. You'll see the Options dialog box.
2. In the From Folder box, type the name of the folder you want to display on the Bookmarks menu.
3. If this folder contains subfolders, and if you would like the Bookmarks menu to contain the sites stored in these folders, click Recursive. In the Quantity box, choose the maximum number of sites you want to display.
4. Click OK.

Saving Your Changes.   When you're finished making changes to the Bookmarks dialog box, choose File Save to save your changes.

Accessing a Bookmarked Site.   Once you've stored a site in a folder within your Bookmarks dialog box, you must open the Bookmarks dialog box to visit the site again.

To go back to a bookmarked site:

1. Choose Bookmarks View Bookmarks, or press Ctrl + B. You'll see the Bookmarks dialog box.
2. Click the folder that contains the bookmark item.
3. Double-click the bookmark item. This closes the Bookmark window and tells Ariadna to retrieve the item from the network.

Configuring Ariadna to Work with Helper Applications

Ariadna doesn't work with plug-ins, so you need to configure the program to work with helper applications. These are widely available for downloading on the Web.

Understanding MIME Types.   To configure Ariadna to work with helper applications, you must first understand how MIME types work. MIME types are names that identify the type of data a browser is downloading. For example, a WAV audio file has the MIME type audio/x-wav. To get Ariadna to start a helper application automatically when the program encounters a file of this type, you must associate this MIME type with a program that can play a WAV file.

Chances are you already have most of the programs you need to configure Ariadna to work with the most commonly encountered MIME types. The following lists the MIME types you need to configure in order to cope with most of the Web's multimedia:

MIME Type	Recommended Application
audio/x-wav	Windows Sound Recorder
video/x-wav	Windows Movie Player
video/x-msvideo	Windows Movie Player
zipfile/zipfile	WinZip

Associating Applications with MIME Types.   To associate an application with a specific MIME type, do the following:

1. Choose Options Preferences, and click the External Viewers tab. You'll see the External Viewers page, shown in Figure 15.9.

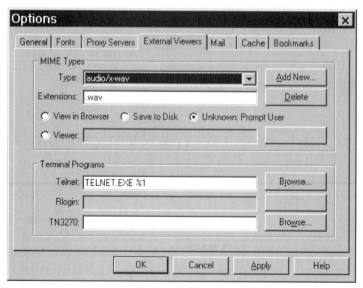

FIGURE 15.9   Use this dialog box to associate applications with MIME types.

2. In the Type box, choose the MIME type you want to configure.

3. Click Viewer.

4. Click the Browse button. You'll see an Open dialog box.

5. Use the Open dialog box to locate and select the application for this MIME type. For sounds, look in the Windows directory and choose PLAYER.EXE. For movies, look in the Windows directory and choose MPLAYER.EXE.

6. Click Open to choose the selected application.

7. Repeat steps 2 through 6 for additional MIME types.

8. Click OK when you're done.

Sending E-Mail with Adriana

Although Ariadna doesn't include full send-and-receive mail capabilities, you can use the program to respond to Mailto links. You may encounter these links in Web documents. They display a Mail dialog box, enabling you to send e-mail to the page's author. In addition, you can originate mail to anyone. You'll need an e-mail program to receive mail, however.

Configuring Ariadna to Send E-Mail.   Before you can send e-mail with Ariadna, you must first configure the program for sending mail. To configure Ariadna to send mail:

1. Choose Options Preferences, and click the Mail tab. You'll see the Mail page, shown in Figure 15.10.

2. In the Your Name area, type your name.

3. In the Your Email area, type your e-mail address.

4. In the SMTP Server area, type the Internet address of the computer your service provider uses to send your mail. (Note: This may be different from the POP3 server that's used to receive your mail.)

5. Click OK.

Responding to a Mailto Link.   If you see a link on a Web page that enables you to send e-mail to the page's author, click the link. You'll see the Send Mail window, shown in Figure 15.11. Type a subject line, as well as a message, and click the Send button.

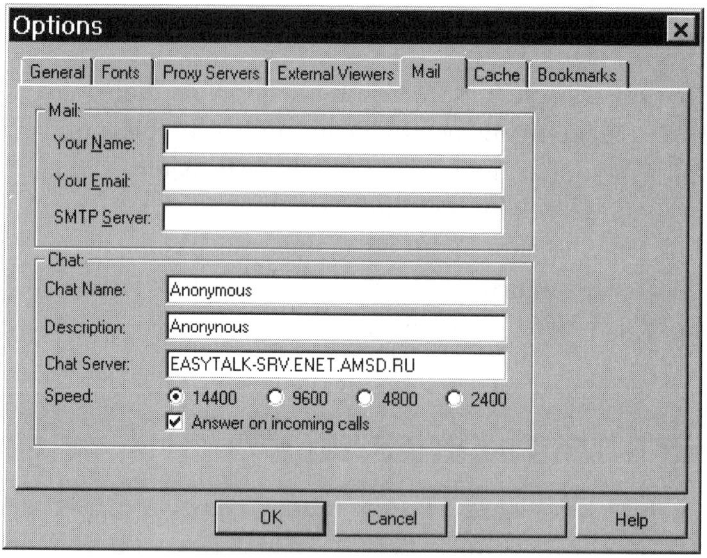

FIGURE 15.10 Use this dialog box to configure Ariadna's e-mail capabilities.

FIGURE 15.11 You can send mail using this Ariadna window.

Sending E-Mail to Anyone.   Did you just come across a link that you'd like to tell somebody about? You don't need to switch to your e-mail program to do so. First, select the URL and press Ctrl + C to copy it to the Clipboard. Then choose File Send E-Mail. You'll see the Send Mail window. Type the recipient's e-mail address and subject. In the Mail Content area, type a message. Press Ctrl + V to paste the URL into the message if you wish. Click Send when you're done.

From Here

Congratulations! You've learned how to use technology to cover your tracks on the Web. In this next chapter, you learn how to reduce your online visibility while using Usenet newsgroups.

CHAPTER 16

Post Anonymously

Many people do not realize that when they post messages to Usenet, they are publishing. That's right, *publishing*.

Posting a message to Usenet is akin to printing out your message—complete with your name and e-mail address—and taping it to the inside of a New York City subway car. Even if you leave off your e-mail address and put a bogus name in your message, it's a trivial matter to trace a message's origin. Every step of the way, computers that forward Usenet messages add lines to the *header* (the "envelope" in which your Usenet message is enclosed). Every message you send can be traced back to you.

Not only are you making your message public, but you're also making it retrievable from massive Usenet databases. Services such as Alta Vista (altavista.digital.com) and Deja News (www.dejanews.com) enable anyone with Internet access to quickly assemble all of your Usenet posts. From this information, an intruder could quickly learn your place of employment, your hobbies and interests, your political leanings, and other highly personal information—some of which could be highly damaging. Suppose a would-be employer found out that you had posted messages to alt.support.depression—and decided against hiring you!

As millions of Internet users have recently discovered, posting to Usenet carries another peril: junk e-mail. Programs exist that enable scum-level marketers to gather hundreds of thousands of e-mail addresses from Usenet, which they then transform into mailing lists that they sell for as little as $50 per pop. Every small-time crook in the country has seemingly discovered that there's money to be made in junk e-mail. I can't believe that anyone in their right mind would respond to junk e-mail, but the theory is, Hey, the list cost me only $50, so if I get three suckers to pay me $25 each for my herbal lust inducer, I've made a profit.

Faced with these facts, most Internet users sadly conclude that it just isn't worth posting to Usenet. That's the conclusion I've reached—reluctantly. I've been an enthusiastic proponent of Usenet since 1989, and wrote what I think is one of my best books on Usenet (*The Usenet Book,* published by Addison-Wesley in 1994). But I don't post to Usenet anymore. And I'm not alone. People who know what Usenet was like back in its glory days—a communication system founded on the principle that people could pool information and help each other—feel that Usenet has fallen so far that there's little worth salvaging.

If you disagree, perhaps you'd like to learn how to safeguard your anonymity when you post to Usenet. Truth to tell, this is a highly controversial subject, thanks to the obnoxious and often illegal behavior of users who hide behind anonymity to threaten, harass, defame, curse, and litter newsgroups with hate-ridden messages. Still, there are valid reasons to post anonymously: You don't have to be a cyberterrorist to possess defensible reasons for covering your tracks.

This chapter explains the various ways you can hide your identity when you post to Usenet. As in other Part II chapters, I'm assuming that you've already tried Usenet, and that you've learned the basics of using a newsreader (such as Free Agent or the newsreader that's built into Netscape Navigator or Microsoft Internet Explorer).

CAUTION **Although this chapter shows you how to post to Usenet with varying levels of anonymity, your news-reading and file downloading actions leave a trail on your ISP's server. This trail could be accessed by someone with a valid court order and the information could be used against you.**

The Anonymity Controversy

Anonymous posting isn't universally admired. For many Internet users, including influential *Wall Street Journal* columnist Walter Mossberg, anonymous posting is little more than an attempt—at best—to evade accountability. At its worst, it's a cover for a spectrum of illegal activities (see the sidebar, "Crime under the Guise of Anonymity"). In many Usenet newsgroups, those who post opinions anonymously may be accused of cowardice, or worse, by users who believe that you should back up your opinions with your name. According to the enemies of anonymity, it facilitates wrongdoing by enabling people to evade responsibility for their speech. For those opposed to anonymity on the Internet, the possibility

Crime under the Guise of Anonymity

Anonymous speech is socially desirable; it provides an important counterforce to political, social, and religious oppression. When coupled with Internet technology, however, the price of anonymity rises steeply—so steeply, in fact, that many voices call for criminalizing anonymous speech on the Internet.

- ▶ **Cyberblackmail**—According to a recent report in the *London Times*, computer hackers have been using anonymous remailers to threaten banks, brokerage houses, and other financial institutions. In their messages, they detail precisely how they are going to shut down the firm's trading network. According to the report, the blackmailing hackers have been paid up to $20 million per incident to desist.
- ▶ **Hate speech**—Under the guise of anonymity, thousands of individuals seem unable to resist the temptation to indulge themselves in the most atrocious hate speech, which riddles Usenet newsgroups.
- ▶ **Industrial espionage**—According to official estimates, thieves steal more than $10 billion of sensitive data annually, including trade secrets, new product plans, company financial data, litigation records, stolen credit-card information, and pirated software. Using anony-

(continued)

that wrongdoing will occur provides sufficient grounds to deny anonymity to everyone.

But this logic strains credibility: One could just as well argue that privacy should not be permitted in hotel rooms simply because so many of them have been used for adulterous liaisons. The question is, Do the advantages of anonymity provide a counterbalance to the undeniable excesses?

Reasons abound for arguing that preserving anonymity—despite the very real potential for abuse—is essential to the preservation of free speech. U.S. Supreme Court Justice J.P. Stevens put this point eloquently in a recent decision upholding anonymous pamphleteering in an Ohio election. According to Stevens, the most important function of anonymity is that it provides a "shield from the tyranny of the majority." Without anonymity,

mous remailers, this information can be sent to information brokers without leaving a trace.

▶ **Intellectual property infringement**—A software publisher that licenses a patented encryption algorithm was stunned to find code containing the algorithm posted to Usenet and bulletin boards worldwide. The code had been sent from an anonymous remailer and was untraceable. Intellectual property holders cannot protect themselves against infringement when they cannot identify the infringers.

▶ **Sexual harassment**—Women who make their presence known on the Internet may be the victims of concerted harassment under the cloak of anonymous remailers, receiving threats, obscene pictures, and abusive language (in response to a mildly profeminist post, for example, one woman received a message describing her as a "hairy-legged feminazi").

▶ **Spamming**—Anonymity is appealing to Usenet spammers, who post unwanted material to hundreds or even thousands of Usenet newsgroups.

▶ **Stock market manipulation**—When the Solomon-Page Group, Ltd., was in the midst of an initial public offering (IPO) of stock, a forged message appeared on Usenet falsely accusing the firm's president of criminal activity and fraud. The firm's shares plunged in price nearly 45 percent in the ensuing month. The culprit? Unknown, but probably somebody who planned to sell the stock short (in short selling, you can make money if a stock price goes down).

Stevens argues, the personal costs of dissent rise unacceptably. In addition, a person may have valid grounds for separating an argument from his or her personal identity: It provides a way for a writer who may be personally unpopular, Stevens writes, "to ensure that readers will not prejudge her message simply because they do not like its proponent."

The following uses of online anonymity would seem to be justified in the name of human freedom:

▶ You are living abroad under an oppressive regime. You and your friends are trying to expose the regime's behavior to the world by means of anonymous posts. You want to be sure that the secret police cannot trace your posts to your computer.

▶ A woman in a conservative state in the U.S. south is bisexual, and she is interested in wicca. She posts anonymously because she could lose her job and even suffer grave personal danger were her interests known to her neighbors or employer.

▶ You are recovering from drug abuse or alcoholism. You want to use the Internet to discuss your recovery, and receive support from others in recovery, but you do not want your employer or coworkers to find out.

▶ You are working for a major corporation and you have discovered solid evidence of crass design negligence, which has already resulted in several injuries. You want to make this information known but you do not want to suffer the penalties that whistle-blowers typically endure, including lawsuits and the total loss of your career.

Debate will no doubt continue on the ethics and morality of anonymous posting. For now, you need to consider whether you want to expose yourself to the risks of revealing your identity on Usenet. In the next section, you'll learn that there are varying levels of anonymity on Usenet. You'll learn how to choose the one that's right for your purposes.

The Six Levels of Anonymity on Usenet

On Usenet, you will find six distinct levels of anonymity, ranging from disguising your identity within a message (but still leaving trails that could be followed) all the way to military-strength anonymity, which enables you to post in such a way that it is quite impossible to determine where your message came from.

▶ **Level 1: Omitting Your Identity from a Message**—You can gain a small measure of anonymity by configuring your newsreader to attach a pseudonym and bogus e-mail address to your messages. However, an investigator could easily determine your identity from the header information in your message (see Figure 16.1). This message, posted to misc.test, contains a phony name and e-mail address, but the message's true origin is contained in other header lines: You can tell precisely when it was sent (November 30, 1996 at 20:14 GMT), and from where (one of Mindspring's dialup nodes).

How anonymous is this post? Not at all. To be sure, a court order would be required to determine who was using this Mindspring dialup node at this time. If you posted using your employer's computer, however, your

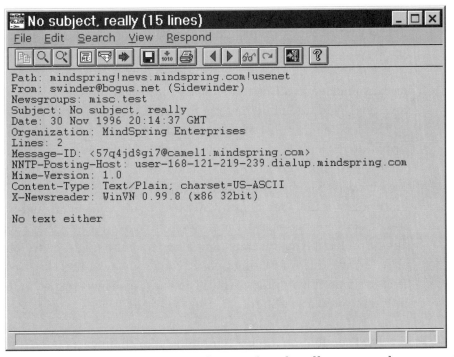

FIGURE 16.1   Even if you post with an online handle, or pseudonym, and use a phony e-mail address, the message's origin is clearly displayed in the header.

employer might not feel the need to obtain a court order to determine who posted this particular message. And if you made the post from a computer at work, chances are this computer is connected to a local area network (LAN)—and it would require very little work to determine which computer was used to originate the message. In sum, using a phony name and e-mail address gives you no protection from anyone armed with a subpoena, or an employer bent on snooping around in your computer files.

This level of anonymity may be sufficient, however, for a person who wants to contribute something perfectly innocent—such as a recipe—without the risk of winding up on some idiot's junk e-mail list. When coupled with Level-2 anonymity, this approach gives some measure of protection against casual snooping.

▶ **Level 2: Keeping Your Posts Out of the Databases**—A major concern for anyone posting to Usenet is that anyone can research your past Usenet posts, and compile a dossier of everything you've contributed. Search services such as Deja News have been roundly criticized for compiling these archives. Still, they provide a useful resource for people innocently looking for information.

If you would like to keep your posts out of at least some of these databases, you can add a line to the header information that is sent along with your post. Add the following line of text: X-no-archive: yes

The problem is, most newsreaders don't enable you to edit header information directly. An exception is WinVN, the newsreader that's included with this book's CD-ROM. The use of WinVN for anonymous Usenet posting is discussed later in this chapter.

Coupled with Level-1 anonymity (removing your name and e-mail address from your messages), the X-no-archive header provides some measure of protection against amateur snoopers, who might be trying to profile you based on your Usenet posts. Note, however, that the use of this header is purely voluntary; Alta Vista and Deja News respect it, but there's nothing to stop a search service from ignoring it.

▶ **Level 3: Pseudoanonymous Remailers**—For three years (1993 to 1996), anonymous posting was virtually synonymous with a site called anon.penet.fi, which recently closed down. The site's Internet address is virtually synonymous with the term *anonymous remailer*, a free computer service that enables you to send electronic mail to a Usenet newsgroup or to an e-mail recipient without creating a trail back to your true identity.

The work of Johan Helsingius, anon.penet.fi provided some 700,000 Internet users with a means of sending anonymous e-mail messages and Usenet posts. The system also provided a means by which you could receive a reply—but this compromised its privacy, as you'll see.

Here's how anon.penet.fi worked. You established an account, using your real name and e-mail address. When you sent your message or post to anon.penet.fi, the service stripped it of its header information. Instead, it substituted your account name (such as 31-0987@anon.penet.fi). Any Internet user could reply to your message; the reply went back to Finland, where it was matched again to your real e-mail address, and forwarded on to you.

The problem here lies in the fact that the service keeps records linking every user's name and e-mail address with a specific anon.penet.fi account. This means that the site's administrator could be pressured to reveal the connection. For this reason, systems of this type are called *pseuodoanonymous remailers*. They give the appearance of anonymity—but in fact, the system administrator could be forced to reveal a user's identity. And that is precisely what happened to anon.penet.fi.

In early 1995, the Church of Scientology was trying to determine who posted a number of sensitive Church documents to the Internet. The posts had been made via anon.penet.fi. A complaint was made to the Finnish authorities, who demanded that Helsingius reveal the name and e-mail address of the person responsible for the posts. Believing that he had no other choice, Helsingius complied. After additional threats were made to force Helsingius to reveal his users' identities, he shut down the system.

Other pseudoanonymous remailers have appeared since anon.penet.fi's demise, such as Mailmasher (to be discussed later in this chapter). Everyone who makes use of a pseudoanonymous remailer must bear in mind that the system administrator can be forced to reveal your identity. It would not be wise to use an anonymous remailer when your career is at stake. Note, however, that some pseudoanonymous remailers claim to give a higher degree of anonymity by using encryption and other techniques that make a user's true identity unavailable to the system administrator.

▶ **Level 4: Web-Based Anonymous Remailers**—Unlike pseudoanonymous services such as anon.penet.fi, true anonymous remailers strip off the original message headers and save absolutely no information about the sender. Especially when combined with *chaining*, a technique in which a message is routed through several anonymous remailers, there is a very high degree of likelihood that the message cannot be traced to its origin. The down side of this is that no one can reply to your message.

The lowest level of anonymous remailer anonymity is provided by Web-based services such as Replay (www.replay.com/remailer/anon.html), shown in Figure 16.2, or Jim Wise's Anonymous Mail (www.arch.columbia. edu/~jim/anon/). To send your message, you type the newsgroup or e-mail address, the subject, and the message body. You then choose two

---

Guidelines for Anonymous Posting

Anyone posting anonymously to Usenet should observe the following guidelines:

▶ **Use anonymity only when it is appropriate to do so**—Valid reasons include posting personal information, whistle-blowing information, or opinions that could get you into trouble with your employer or a conservative community bent on violent reprisals.

▶ **Do not use anonymity as a cover for illegal or immoral actions**—The use of anonymous remailers for harassment, provocation, libel, defamation, software piracy, or other abusive actions will convince would-be site managers that it's not a good idea to make anonymous remailing services available. In addition, do not use anonymity to evade Usenet customs (such as avoiding excessive cross-posting, or posting binaries to nonbinary newsgroups).

▶ **Do not use anonymity as a cover for bigoted opinion or hate speech**—This is one of the worst forms of cowardice to be seen on the Internet, and you will be justifiably flamed.

▶ **Don't include a signature**—Obviously, there's no point in posting anonymously if you include identifying information of any kind.

(continued)

remailers, and click the submit button. Where's the privacy hole here? You're sending your message unencrypted to this Web page, and it could be intercepted en route.

TIP **For a list of active anonymous remailers, see the Remailer list, located at www.cs.berkeley.edu/~raph/remailer-list.html.**

▶ **Level 5: Type-1 Anonymous Remailers**—The next level of anonymity is given by Type-1 anonymous remailers, which enable you to chain an encrypted message through a series of remailers (see Figure 16.3). This is the world of so-called *cypherpunk remailers*. Cypherpunks are computer

▶ **Do not cross-post excessively**—No message should ever be posted to a group that isn't concerned with the message's subject—in other words, all posts should be relevant to the newsgroup's mission. You may wish to cross-post to two or three groups that share a common interest area, but keep this to a minimum and follow the relevance rule.

▶ **Do not post binaries**—Anonymous remailers receive a great deal of traffic and cannot handle large binary files. Such files are generally pornographic, and there is no justification for using an anonymous remailer for the purposes of distributing this material.

▶ **Learn the policies of your anonymous remailer site, and respect them**—This site is being made available as a free service; somebody's putting their time and hardware into it, all for your benefit. Respect the site's rules.

▶ **Be aware that many Usenet users do not understand the need for anonymity**—Be prepared to see posts that call you a coward and try to goad you into revealing your identity.

▶ **Think twice before posting anonymously to the standard newsgroups (comp, misc, net, rec, sci, soc)**—In these newsgroups, there's a convention that you should back up your opinion with your name. However, anonymous posting to these newsgroups has become much more common in the past year. No one objects to anonymous posting to the alt newsgroups.

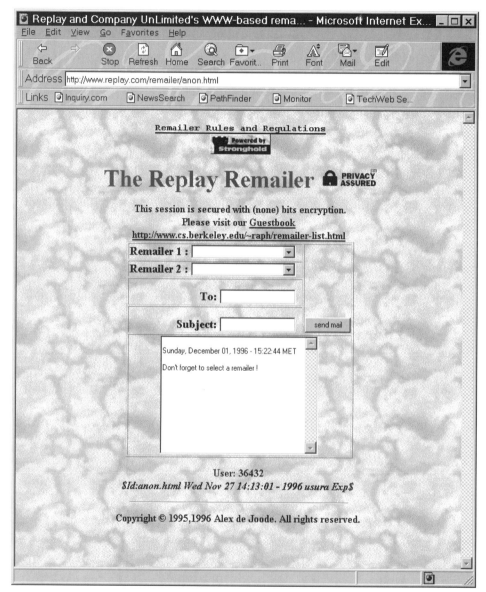

FIGURE 16.2   A Web-based anonymous remailer.

users who advocate strong personal privacy and use encrypted e-mail and other measures to guarantee their privacy while using the Internet.

One would think that these measures would produce perfect anonymity, but they do not. An investigator can gain important clues about a message's origin and destination by watching the timing of messages—if a message

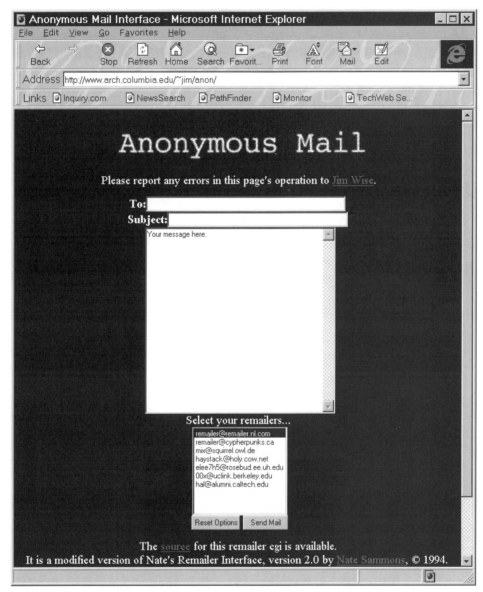

FIGURE 16.3   A Web-based anonymous remailer that enables chaining.

arrives, and then leaves an instant later, it's possible that the messages are one and the same. Through this and other stratagems, an investigator could follow a message's trail through a series of remailers. Even so, prodigious resources would be needed to do this. Still, cryptographic experts feel that Type-1 remailers leave something to be desired.

▶ **Level 6: Type-2 Anonymous Remailers**—Type-2 anonymous remailers, also called Mixmaster remailers, ensure total anonymity by eradicating the possibility of trail tracing. A message is scrambled into a number of separate packets with strongly encrypted headers so that each part of the message appears as if it is a single, independent message. Only the last remailer is able to tell that the various parts of the message are related.

Using WinVN to Post Anonymously

This book's CD-ROM includes a copy of WinVN, a public-domain program that enables you to directly edit the headers of Usenet posts. With WinVN, you can achieve a small measure of anonymity—enough to keep you off junk e-mail lists and to avoid casual harassment, but not enough to protect you should an investigator have a strong interest in tracing your message's origin.

WinVN's Requirements.   The copy of WinVN included on this book's CD-ROM is the 32-bit version of the program. It requires Windows 95 or Windows NT.

Installing WinVN.   To install WinVN, follow these directions carefully:

1. Create a new directory on your hard drive, called WinVN.
2. From the WinVN folder on the CD-ROM, copy the file wv32i998.zip to the new WinVN directory.
3. Use WinZip for Windows, or another decompression program, to unpack all the files in wv32i998.zip.

CAUTION   You are about to move a file, but *do not confirm the move* until you have read all the instructions in Chapter 11. Use Windows Explorer to move the file CTL3D32.DLL from the WinVN directory to the \WINDOWS\ SYSTEM directory (Windows 95) or the %SystemRoot%\SYSTEM32 directory (Windows NT).

If you see a message indicating that the file CTL3D32.DLL already exists (see Figure 16.4), *cancel* the move if the existing file in the Windows direc-

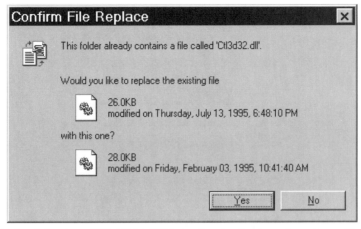

FIGURE 16.4 Moving CTL3D32.DLL to the \windows\system directory.

tory is *newer* than the one you are moving, and then *delete* the copy of
CTL3D32.DLL that is located in the WinVN directory. Approve the move only
if the CTL3D32.DLL file is *older* than the one you are moving.

Note that there should be only *one* copy of CTL3D32.DLL on your computer!

Configuring WinVN. The first time you run WinVN, you will see dialog boxes that guide you through program configuration. Follow these instructions carefully to set up your program for anonymous Usenet posting. To install WinVN for anonymous posting:

1. In the WinVN directory, double-click winvn.exe. You'll see a dialog box asking you to identify the location of winVN.ini.
2. Just click Open or press Enter. You'll see another dialog box asking you whether you would like to create this file.
3. Click Yes. Now you'll see a dialog box asking you to find newsrc. Click Open or press Enter. You'll see a dialog box asking you whether you would like to create this file.
4. Click Yes. WinVN starts, and you see the Communications Options dialog box, shown in Figure 16.5.

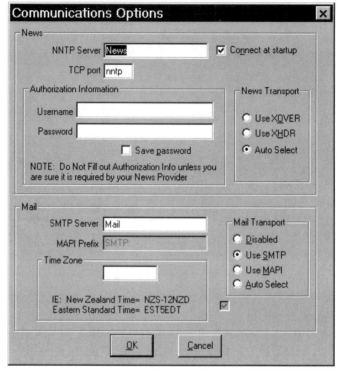

FIGURE 16.5   Use this dialog box to configure your WinVN communication options.

5. In the NNTP server box, type the name of your Usenet server. Important: Leave the Mail section blank.
6. Click OK. You'll see the Personal Information dialog box, shown in Figure 16.6.
7. In the Your Name Here box, type the pseudonym that you want to use for online posting.
8. In the e-mail address box, just type a space.
9. Erase the text in the Organization Name box.
10. Click OK. You'll see a dialog box asking whether you would like to download the latest group list from the server.
11. Click Yes to download the latest group list. This will take a few minutes. When downloading is finished, you see the newsgroup list—a very long list in alphabetical order (see Figure 16.7).

FIGURE **16.6**   Don't type your real name!

Reading the News with WinVN

In this chapter, I'm assuming that you've already used a newsreader and know the basics. Here's a quick summary of the techniques you use to read the news:

▶ **Subscribing to a newsgroup**—To subscribe to a newsgroup, highlight one or more newsgroup names, and choose Subscribe Selected Groups. After you've subscribed, WinVN automatically moves the subscribed newsgroup to the top of the list.

▶ **Viewing the article list**—To view the articles in a newsgroup, just double-click the newsgroup's name. You'll see a new window that lists the available articles (Figure 16.8). Note that WinVN is a *threaded* newsreader. Articles are organized to show the "thread" of a conversation, with replies positioned under an original post.

▶ **Reading an article**—To read one of the articles in the newsgroup, just double-click it. You'll see a new window that shows the full header information (see Figure 16.9), and then scrolls down to hide it. By scrolling up, you can bring this information back into view.

There's much more to WinVN from the newsreading point of view, including the ability to sort the article list in numerous ways, decode binaries, and filtering out unwanted messages. Here, we're concentrating on WinVN's anonymity features.

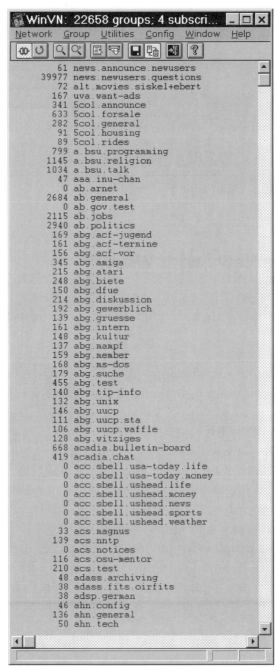

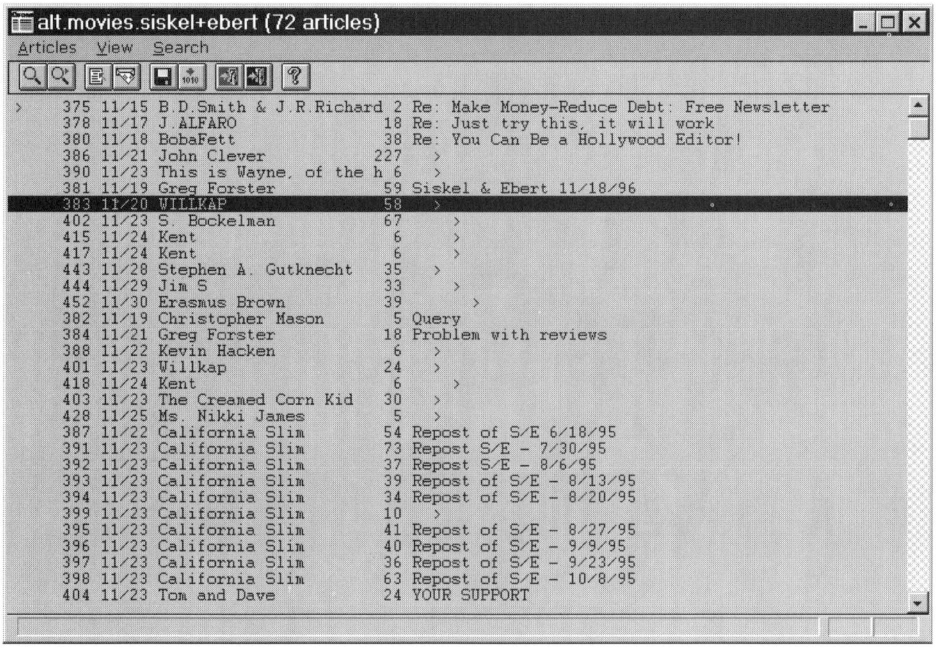

FIGURE **16.8** Viewing a newsgroup's article list.

Posting Anonymously with WinVN

With WinVN, you can hide your e-mail address and name from online harassers and junk e-mailers, but you can't shield yourself from a determined investigator. This level of anonymity is sufficient for someone who wishes to participate in an innocuous Usenet newsgroup.

NOTE I realize that there is a long tradition of discouraging anonymity in the standard newsgroups (com, misc, news, rec, sci, and soc). However, I defend my advice here—that is, to use a pseudonym and omit the poster's e-mail address—because junk-mail marketers have made Usenet participation impossible for anyone who wishes to avoid unsolicited e-mail. In addition, many Usenet participants—especially women—have valid reasons for wishing to disguise their identities out of fear of online harassment.

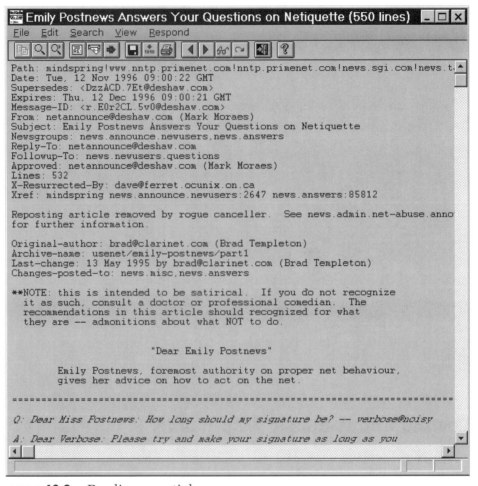

FIGURE 16.9   Reading an article.

Posting a New Message.   To post a new message anonymously with WinVN, do the following:

1. Switch to the newsgroup to which you would like to post.
2. Double-click the newsgroup name to open the article list.
3. Choose Articles New Article. You'll see the New Article dialog box, shown in Figure 16.10.
4. Choose Edit Header Part. You'll see the Edit header part dialog box, shown in Figure 16.11.

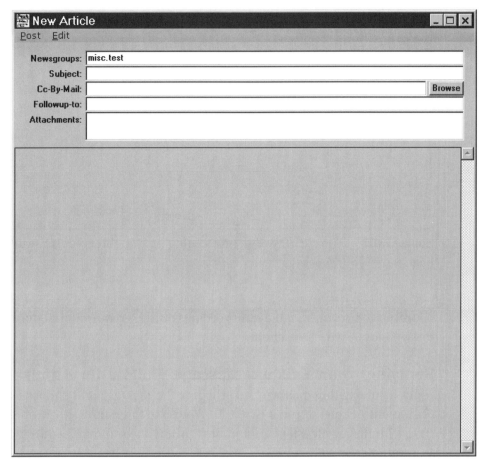

FIGURE 16.10 In the Articles New Article dialog box, you type a new message.

5. Carefully type X-no-archive: yes.
6. Click OK.
7. Type your message.
8. Choose Post Send, or just press Ctrl + S.
9. Try posting to misc.test. After a few minutes, your post will be available for scrutiny (see Figure 16.12). As you can see, this post does not contain the sender's true name or e-mail address. In addition, it contains the X-no-archive: yes setting in the header area. This message can still

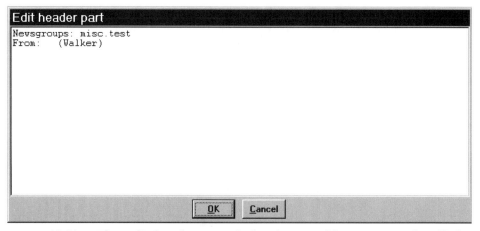

FIGURE 16.11   The Edit header part dialog box enables you to edit all the headers in your message.

be traced to its origin, but a court order would be required to determine the true identity of the sender.

Replying to an Existing Message (Follow–Up Articles).   To reply to an existing message, just display the message and choose Respond Follow-up Article, or press Ctrl + L. You'll see the Follow-up Article dialog box, with the article's text quoted. Just follow the same procedure you used to post an anonymous new message: Choose Edit header part and add the X-no-archive: yes setting, and follow the same steps to type and send the message.

Using Anonymous Remailers

If you would like to post something to Usenet and do a better job of covering your tracks, you should use an anonymous remailer. You can choose from pseudoanonymous remailers, Web-based anonymous remailers, or encrypted anonymous remailing with programs such as Private Idaho.

TIP   Because they are subject to so much abuse, anonymous remailers come and go. This section discusses some of the services available at this writ-

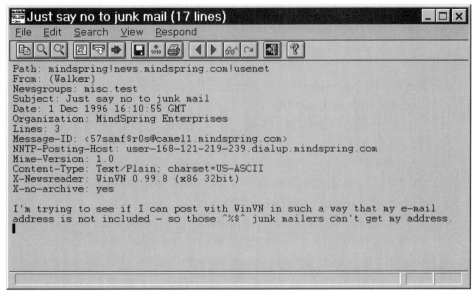

FIGURE 16.12   This anonymous message does not contain the sender's true name or e-mail address. It is nevertheless traceable to its origins.

ing, but it is very possible that they will have disappeared by the time you read this book.

Posting to Usenet via a Pseudoanonymous Remailer.   If you would like to post anonymously in such a way that people can respond to you privately via e-mail, the WinVN technique just described won't work. People can respond to your posts by posting a follow-up article, but they can't send you mail.

Posting via a pseudoanonymous remailer enables you to post with relative anonymity, while at the same time enabling people to respond to you via e-mail.

Currently, a Web-based pseudoanonymous remailer is available called Mailmasher (www.mailmasher.com). In order to use Mailmasher, you must register by providing your true e-mail address. You need not supply your real name, however. Still, you should bear in mind that Mailmasher's system administrator clearly states that he will not go to jail to protect your privacy should investigators produce a court order. Do not use Mailmasher if you are posting something that could put your job or security at risk.

To post to Usenet with Mailmasher:

1. Access www.mailmasher.com, and follow the on-screen instructions to register with this service.
2. Click the links that enable you to log on as a registered user.
3. When you see the page informing you how many messages are waiting for you, click Post to Usenet. You'll see a policy statement. Click the link at the bottom of the page to continue. You'll see the Post To Usenet page, shown in Figure 16.13.
4. In the Newsgroups area, type one or more newsgroup names, separated by commas. Avoid cross-posting unless you are certain that your message is relevant to all the groups you type here.
5. In the subject area, type a brief, descriptive subject for your message.
6. In the Message text area, type your message.
7. Click Post Anonymously if you do *not* want people to be able to reply to you by e-mail. If you leave this box blank, the message is still posted anonymously, but your Mailmasher e-mail address is included in the message.
8. Click Send.

More Web-Based Anonymous Remailing Services

▶ **Anonymous Mail** (www.arch.columbia.edu/~jim/anon/)—This service does not offer a high degree of privacy, because you must upload your text unencrypted to the server.

▶ **Anonymous remailer Java applet** (www.ozemail.com.au/~geoffk/anon.anon.html)—This applet encrypts your message so that it cannot be read en route, thus offering a higher degree of security than other Web-based remailing services. You can download the applet free for your own personal use.

▶ **Cyberpass** (www.cyberpass.net)—This is a fee-based service; you pay in advance for anonymous mail.

▶ **Free Anonymous Remailer** (interlink-bbs.com/anonremailers/anonform.html)—Like Anonymous Mail, this service does not provide a high degree of privacy, because you must upload your message to the server as plain text.

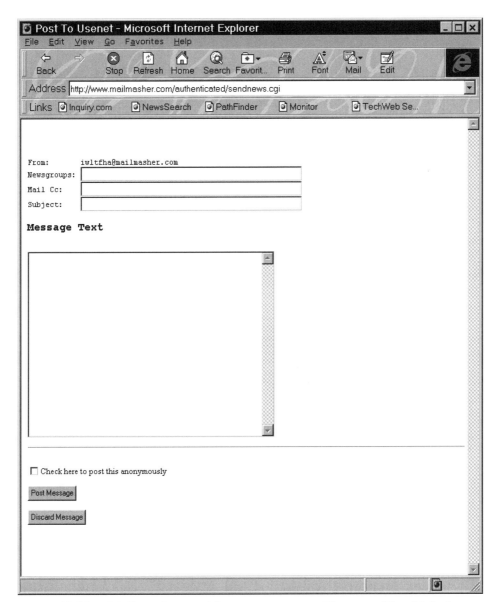

FIGURE 16.13 Mailmasher enables you to post to Usenet with a high degree of anonymity.

If you included your Mailmasher e-mail address in your post (that is, by leaving the Post Anonymously check box blank), you may receive replies to your messages. To see them, access www.mailmasher.com using your browser, and log on. You'll find out how many messages are waiting for you (Figure 16.14). To see the messages, click the message you want to see.

FIGURE 16.14   Mailmasher tells you when you have messages waiting.

Posting with True Anonymous Remailers.

To ensure a high degree of privacy with anonymous remailers, you need to post using an encrypted mail program (such as Pronto Secure, discussed in the next chapter). However, you can gain some measure of anonymity by posting via a Web-based remailer service. These services are very easy to use, but your message can be read by snoops while you're uploading it to the Web server.

Like pseudoanonymous remailers, you can expect Web-based remailer services to come and go. A service available at this writing is The Replay Remailer (www.replay.com/remailer/anon.html), shown in Figure 16.2. Although this service makes use of true anonymous remailers, it should be considered to have the security of a pseudoanonymous remailer. The server log shows the origin of every message this service receives, and the site administrator has made it very clear that he will cooperate with investigative agencies if the system is abused.

Horizons of Anonymity: Private Idaho. Should you fear that your post may lead to the loss of your job, physical injury, or worse, you may wish to consider combining military-strength encryption with Type-2 anonymous remailers. The software of choice for this purpose is Private Idaho, available for download from http://www. eskimo.com/~joelm/pi. html). You will also need a copy of Pretty Good Privacy (PGP), discussed in the next chapter. At this writing, there were several Type-2 remailers that enabled Private Idaho users to post to Usenet, but it is hard to say whether they will continue to operate.

From Here

Do your kids use your computer? You'd best be concerned about their privacy while they're online. In the next chapter, you learn how to use Cyber-Patrol, which offers excellent privacy-protection features for kids browsing the Net.

CHAPTER 17

Safeguard Your Children Online

The Internet just isn't safe for kids. I'm sure you've seen the news reports about pederasts and other online predators who prey on children's gullibility, encouraging them to reveal their names, addresses, school names, e-mail addresses, phone numbers, and more. Repulsive in another way are the commercial services that try to extract demographic information from children, in return for full access to a few stupid games and prizes. If you permit your children to use the Internet, you should closely supervise them. Make it a family affair—show them what's out there and what they should avoid.

Even if you do supervise your children's surfing closely, you can't look over their shoulders every minute your kids are online. And while you're not watching, your child could divulge his or her e-mail address, your telephone number, or other personal information to some total stranger—or to some marketing firm.

That's why you need to install Cyber Patrol on your computer. Cyber Patrol is best known as a sort of Internet nanny, restricting access to sex-related sites. Of very strong interest here, though, is Cyber Patrol's capability to block outgoing text, such as your child's personal information. Cyber Patrol blocks the uploading of prohibited text in *any* application while your computer is connected to the Internet: Internet Relay Chat (IRC), Gopher, the World Wide Web, FTP, and more. Once you've established a list of prohibited words, there's no way your child can divulge his name, e-mail address, school name, or any other sensitive personal information while he's surfing the Net.

This chapter isn't intended to cover all aspects of Cyber Patrol, just the ones that pertain to child privacy considerations. However, I am certain you will want to explore the program's capability to block access to sex-related sites on the Internet. In particular, Cyber Patrol can block access to all the sex-related Usenet newsgroups, which contain material that is not only unsuitable for children but also that very well may be illegal in some areas. I believe that Cyber Patrol should be installed on *any* computer that a child is likely to use!

Introducing Cyber Patrol

Cyber Patrol enables you to define a set of access restrictions for each individual that uses your computer. You can control access by the amount of time spent at the computer, by the type of Internet service accessed, and by the content of the material that's being downloaded or uploaded.

Cyber Patrol works at the level of Internet access, examining the byte stream coming into and out of your computer. It's impossible to circumvent, and any attempt to do so will shut down Internet access completely.

Controlling the Amount of Access. You can control the *amount* of Internet access by limiting the following:

► Time of day
► Total hours per day
► Total hours per week

By specifying time limits, you tell Cyber Patrol to allow Internet access only if the total hours per week have not been exceeded, the total number of hours per day have not been exceeded, and the current time is within the allowable periods for Internet access.

Controlling Access to Specific Internet Services. You can also block or selectively filter access to the following Internet services:

▶ **Internet Relay Chat (IRC) groups**—You can block IRC entirely (a good idea, in my opinion), or selectively block access to any IRC channel that contains a prohibited word in its name.

▶ **Web or FTP sites that distribute offending content**—Access is blocked on the basis of the CyberNOT list, an encrypted file containing the names of specific sites that distribute material you may wish to control. Because new sites are constantly appearing, you may wish to obtain updates of this list. You can also enable access to only those sites on the CyberYES list, a list of sites that contain material suitable for children.

▶ **Specific online service providers (by domain)**—You can block access to any site that contains a prohibited word or phrase in any part of its URL. If you wish, for example, you can exclude any COM site—a great way to make sure that your kids aren't pelted with unwanted advertising and marketing shenanigans.

▶ **Games or other applications**—You can restrict access to up to 16 Windows applications based on time of day and cumulative hours spent on the application. In addition, you can prohibit access to certain applications.

Filtering Content with the CyberNOT List.

This is an encrypted file containing the names of thousands of sites that contain prohibited material (see the sidebar, "What's Blocked in the CyberNOT List"). You can selectively enable access to any of these categories. For example, if you do not mind your child accessing sites that show partial nudity in art, you can deselect blocking by Partial nudity and art. To select blocking categories, choose Site Control Category Restrictions. This dialog box also enables you to download new CyberNOT lists from the Cyber Patrol server.

What happens if an adult site isn't on the CyberNOT list? This may happen, because new adult sites are appearing all the time. You can obtain updates of the CyberNOT list, but it's safe to assume that the site doesn't contain all the adult sites out there. To prevent your child from accessing adult sites that are not yet on the CyberNOT list, Cyber Patrol examines the URL that your child is trying to access, and automatically blocks any site that contains one of several prohibited words (such as "XXX," "adult," "sex," and the like).

Permitting Access to Child-Safe Sites (CyberYES List).

This list contains sites that have been judged child-safe by an advisory panel. If

What's Blocked in the CyberNOT List

The CyberNOT list is based on an advisory panel's consensus regarding content that a hypothetical 12-year-old should not access without parental supervision. The exclusion list consists of newsgroups or sites that contain the following categories of content:

► **Violence/profanity (graphics or text)**—The famous Carlin 7 Dirty Words, as well as additional violent or profane usages.

► **Partial nudity and art**—The nude female breast or nude buttocks (whether male or female).

► **Full nudity**—Pictures that include genitalia.

► **Sexual acts**—Pictures or text depicting sexual acts.

► **Gross depictions**—Pictures or descriptive text of anyone or anything that is vulgar, grossly deficient in civility, or scatalogical.

► **Intolerance**—Pictures or text advocating prejudice or discrimination of any type.

► **Satanic/Cult**—Pictures or text advocating Satanism or cult membership.

► **Drugs and drug culture**—Pictures or text advocating the illegal use of drugs.

► **Militant/extremist organizations**—Pictures or text advocating extreme aggression as a way of solving social or political problems.

► **Sex education**—Pictures or text advocating the use of contraceptives.

► **Gambling/questionable/illegal**—Pictures or text advocating any potentially illegal or dubious activity, including chain letters, copyright infringement, hacking, phone phreaking, software piracy, and gambling-related activities.

► **Alcohol, beer, wine, and tobacco**—Pictures or text advocating the sale or use of any of these.

Note that the CyberNOT list does not exclude sites that discuss any of these subjects in a historical or educational context. For example, CyberNOT does not block access to sites that discuss the role of marijuana in the politics of the Vietnam War era, or the oppression of Jews in Nazi Germany.

you select this list, your child can access *only* those sites that appear on the list.

Blocking Uploaded Text.   This feature, called ChatGard, is of particular interest to parent readers of this book. It prevents children from uploading any text that could be used to identify them, including their name, e-mail address, street address, phone number, city, and school name.

Customizing Cyber Patrol with Additions and Overrides.
Once you've set up restrictions, you can selectively override them by adding the URLs of permissible sites.

Registering Cyber Patrol

The demo copy of Cyber Patrol will run for seven days. To continue using the program, you must register it by doing one of the following: Choose Options On-Line Registration, and fill out the form. You'll need to supply your credit-card number. This information is encrypted before uploading. Or, call 800-828-2608 or 508-879-9000, and register the program with a credit card.

Currently, Cyber Patrol costs $29.95 with a free three-month list. An additional six-month list is $19.95 extra, while a year's list is $29.95 extra.

To install Cyber Patrol, do the following:

1. Insert this book's CD-ROM in the drive.
2. Use My Computer or Windows Explorer to locate and open the Cpatrol folder.
3. Double-click Cp-setup.exe.
4. Follow the on-screen instructions.

CAUTION   Do not delete the Cyber Patrol files. Cyber Patrol is designed to defeat attempts to circumvent it through deletion. If you try to delete some or all of the Cyber Patrol files, you will not be able to access the Internet.

Should you wish to stop using Cyber Patrol, you should uninstall the program by running the Uninstall utility, included in Cyber Patrol's folder.

Running Cyber Patrol

Cyber Patrol starts automatically after you install it. However, you will need to access the Cyber Patrol Headquarters in order to set up users.

To start Cyber Patrol, choose Start Programs Cyber Patrol, and click Cyber Patrol HQ from the pop-up menu. Alternatively, just click the Cyber Patrol icon on the taskbar. You'll see the Cyber Patrol Access Checkpoint dialog box, shown in Figure 17.1.

Since this is the first time you've accessed Cyber Patrol, you haven't set up your password yet. Just click Validate Password and you'll see the Cyber Patrol window, shown in Figure 17.2

You should do the following: Establish a Headquarters access password, set up default user access, and create user names for your kids.

Establishing a Headquarters Access Password.   Your first step in setting up Cyber Patrol is to establish a Headquarters password. To choose Cyber Patrol configurations and gain access to the control center, you must supply this password.

CAUTION   **Do not forget your password! Write it down somewhere, or store it in Password Book.**

To establish a Headquarters password:

1. Choose File Set HQ and Deputy Password. You'll see the Cyber Patrol Passwords dialog box, shown in Figure 17.3. As you can see, this

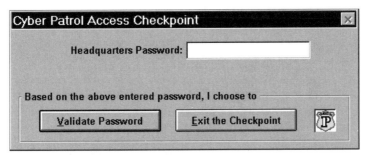

FIGURE 17.1   You must type a password here to gain access to the Cyber Patrol Headquarters.

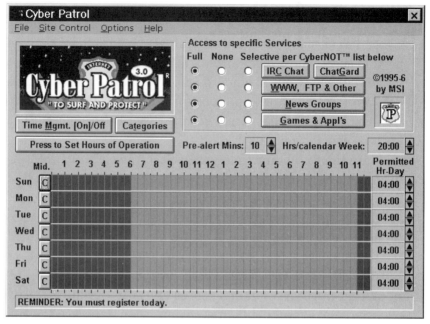

FIGURE 17.2   Here, you choose Cyber Patrol's options.

dialog box also enables you to set up a password for a "Deputy." Deputy access bypasses the headquarters, and enables full, unrestricted access to the Internet. You can use the same password for Administrator and Deputy.

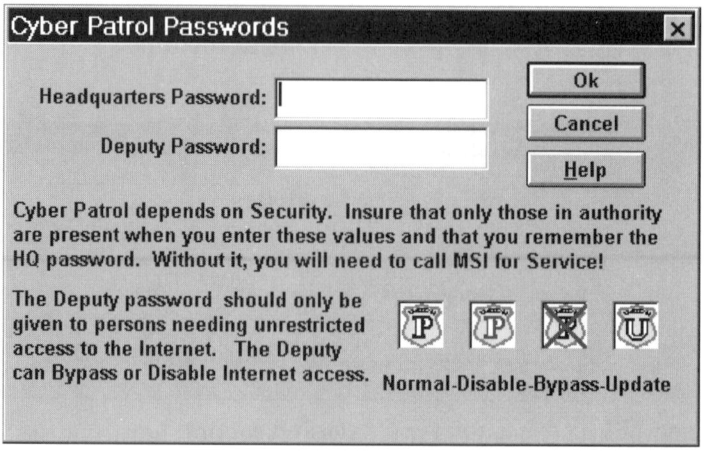

FIGURE 17.3   Create your headquarters password in this dialog box.

2. In the Administrator and Deputy areas, type the password you want to use, and click OK.

TIP **After you've established a Deputy password, you can quickly gain full Internet access. Right-click the Cyber Patrol icon on the Windows 95 taskbar, choose Deputy Bypass, type your password, and click OK.**

Defining a Default User. When you first access the Cyber Patrol Headquarters, you see the access settings for the Default user. These are the settings that are in effect automatically, unless you or another defined user supplies a password. These settings should be very restrictive.

TIP **In the Access to specific Services area, click Selective next to WWW, FTP & Other and News Groups. Click None next to IRC Chat. On the time chart, disable access during the hours you're not home by clicking the time slots so that they're red. Click the Save button to save your settings.**

Defining Users. Now that you've set up your password and chosen default settings, you can set up passwords for the kids who will be using the system. To define user names and passwords for your kids, do the following:

1. Choose File User (Default) to . . . , and choose Configure User(s) from the pop-up menu. You'll see the Configure User dialog box, shown in Figure 17.4.
2. To enter a user, type the user's name in the top edit portion of the list box, and press Enter.
3. To create a password for this user, select the user's name in the list box, and type the password in the Password box.
4. When you are finished setting up users, click Save Changes.

Defining Access for a User. Now that you've defined user names, you can configure each user's access rights.

This chapter focuses on Cyber Patrol's privacy-related features. What follows is a brief overview of the procedure you follow to set up access restrictions for a given user. The next section goes into the ChatGard feature in more detail.

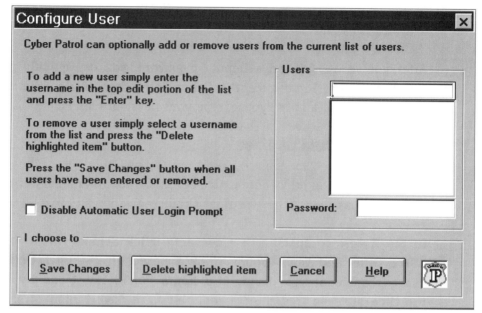

FIGURE 17.4   Define your kids' passwords here.

To configure a user's access rights:

1.   From the File menu, click User (Default) to . . . , and choose the user name you want to define. After you choose the user, you'll see the user's name next to Access to specific Services for (at the upper right corner of the Cyber Patrol window).

2.   Choose the services you want this user to access. For each, you can choose Full, None, or Selective. To choose more options for each service, click the button.

3.   Click Press to set hours of operation, and click or drag the mouse over the restricted times. Restricted times are shown in red.

4.   To enable access to some of the restricted categories, click Restricted, and deselect the categories to which you would like to grant access.

5.   To change the amount of time allotted per week, click the up or down arrows next to the Hrs/calendar Week box.

6.   To save your settings, click Save Settings.

Accessing the Internet after Defining Users.   After you define users, you see the dialog box shown in Figure 17.5 whenever you or someone launches an Internet application. To log on, choose your user name in the list box, type the password, and click Validate Password.

Safeguarding Your Child's Privacy with Cyber Patrol

To safeguard your child's privacy online, you should set up ChatGard for each child that's using your computer. If you're unhappy with the blatant and manipulative commercialism that's aimed at kids on the Web, you may also wish to restrict access to all commercial sites. The following sections discuss how to do these two tasks.

Using ChatGard.   If you're concerned about your children's privacy while they're online, you'll want to investigate the ChatGard feature, which prevents kids from uploading their names and other personal information. ChatGard works with any Internet application, including IRC clients, Web browsers, and e-mail programs. To configure a user's ChatGard setttings, do the following:

1. Display the Cyber Patrol Headquarters, if it isn't already on-screen.
2. Choose File User to choose the user whose ChatGard settings you wish to define.
3. Click the ChatGard button. You'll see the ChatGard–Chat Filtering Control dialog box, shown in Figure 17.6.

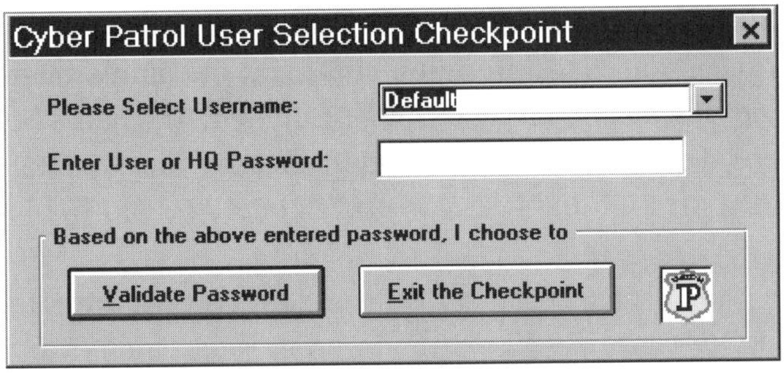

FIGURE 17.5   Select a user name and type a password to access the Net with a predefined access level.

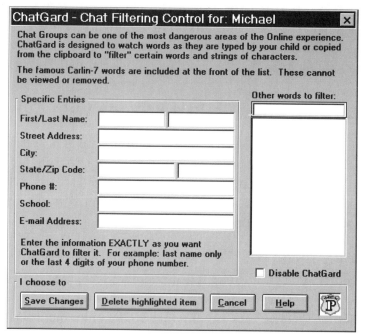

FIGURE 17.6   ChatGard enables you to prevent your kids from uploading personal information.

4.   Fill out the dialog box with all your child's personal information.
5.   If you would like to prevent your child from uploading any other text, type the word in the Other words to filter box, and press Enter.
6.   To save your settings, click Save Changes.

Restricting Access to All Commercial Sites.   If you would like to protect your child from the onslaught of commercialism on the Web, you can completely block access to any site with the name "com." To do this, you add *com* to the list of prohibited IRC words, and then tell Cyber Patrol to use the IRC list to prohibit access to Web or FTP sites. To block all com sites:

1.   Select the user whose access privileges you want to define.
2.   Click IRC Chat. You'll see the Internet Relay Chat–IRC Control dialog box, shown in Figure 17.7.
3.   In the "Reject" Wildcards box, type com, and press Enter.

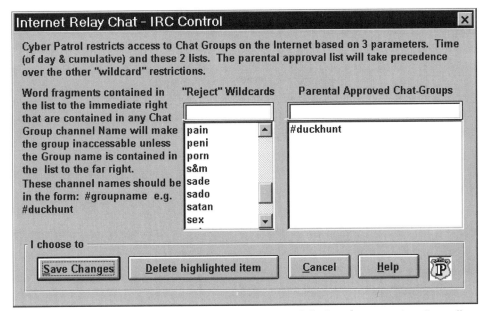

FIGURE 17.7   You can limit access to commercial sites by entering "com" as a prohibited domain name.

4. Click Save Changes.
5. In the Headquarters window again, click WWW, FTP, & Other. You'll see the WWW, FTP, & Other Site Control dialog box, shown in Figure 17.8.
6. Make sure Apply IRC WildCard filters to URL names is selected.
7. Click Save Changes.

TIP This measure is rather Draconian—for example, it will prohibit access to search engines such as Alta Vista (altavista.digital.*com*) as well as many other legitimate sites. To selectively enable search and other commercial sites that are okay for your kids to visit, you can enter the URLs of these sites in an approved sites list. To do this, click WWW, FTP, & Other, and add the names of approved sites in the Additional Parental Approved Services list box. Click Save Changes to confirm. If you would like to reenable access to COM sites, access the Internet Relay Chat–IRC Control list box (see Figure 17.7), and delete COM from the "Reject" Wildcards list. Click Save Changes.

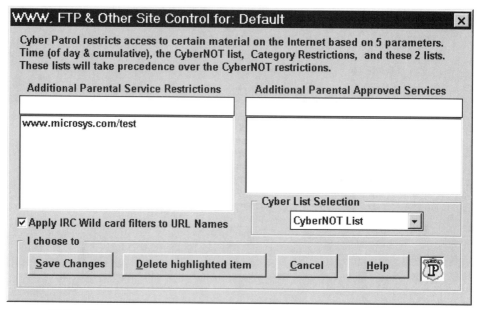

FIGURE 17.8   Be sure to apply IRC wildcards to URL names.

From Here

Now that you've protected your kids, it's time to protect yourself—namely, by getting into encrypted e-mail. As you'll see, you don't have to be a hacker or cypherpunk to use Pronto Secure, an e-mail program that enables anyone to prevent intruders from reading your mail.

CHAPTER 18

Use Encrypted E-Mail

To ensure your privacy while you use the Internet, you should routinely encrypt your electronic mail. This ensures that nobody can read your mail while it's en route without first seeking your permission.

To send and receive secure e-mail, some Internet users have been making their way with the DOS version of Pretty Good Privacy (PGP), the world standard in public-key encryption software.

However, PGP is notoriously difficult to use. Pronto Secure, created by CommTouch software, puts an end to the difficult part. Providing a virtually automatic interface to PGP, Pronto Secure enables you to send and receive electronic mail with impregnable privacy.

Pronto Secure is based on the e-mail interface of Pronto Mail, chosen by *PC Magazine* as Editor's Choice in a rundown of Internet e-mail programs. Coupled with the industrial-strength security that Pronto Secure offers, this program is a winner!

NOTE Because of U.S. export restrictions, it was not possible to include Pronto Secure on this book's CD-ROM. However, you will find a copy of Pronto96, named the best e-mail client of the year by *PC Magazine.* Pronto96 closely resembles Pronto Secure, so you can install it to explore Pronto Secure's e-mail features. To download an evaluation copy of Pronto Secure, access the Commtouch home page at www.commtouch.com, and follow the links to the download area.

Note also that Pronto Secure requires that you place a copy of Pretty Good Privacy (PGP) on your hard drive. Like Pronto Secure, PGP could not be included on this book's CD-ROM due to U.S. export restrictions. To obtain the most recent copy of PGP by downloading it from the Internet, see Appendix A. PGP is freeware and is widely available.

Understanding Public-Key Cryptography

This section introduces the fundamentals of public-key cryptography, the technology that is used to make secure e-mail possible. You'll learn the difference between symmetrical encryption and public-key encryption, and you'll also learn about Pretty Good Privacy, the DOS encryption software that Pronto Secure requires.

Symmetrical Encryption.   In this type of encryption, a message is encrypted with a key. You can't decrypt the message unless you have this key. This is the type of encryption that is used by Cryptext, the program discussed in Chapter 11. Symmetrical encryption gets its name from the fact that the same key is used to encrypt and decrypt the files. It offers the highest level of encryption, but it has one big disadvantage for e-mail purposes: You must communicate the key to the recipient. If somebody intercepts the key en route, your security is compromised.

Public-Key Encryption.   With public-key encryption, it is not necessary to communicate the key to the recipient of your message. That's because public-key encryption enables secure, encrypted communication between two people *who have never met and never before communicated.*

Here's how it works. Unlike symmetrical encryption, which uses one key, public-key encryption uses two keys, an encryption key and a decryption key. You start with an encryption key, which you make publicly available. This key is used to encrypt anything that's being sent to you, such as an e-mail message. While en route, nobody can read the encrypted message. Furthermore, the encrypted message cannot be decrypted using the encryption key.

To read the message, the decryption key is required. This is private; only you have it. By applying the decryption key to the message encrypted with your own encryption key, you can decode the message and read it.

What's the potential hole in public-key cryptography? It might be possible to derive the decryption key from an analysis of the encryption key. In practice, this is virtually impossible—it would require hundreds of thousands of years of computer time to do this.

How Secure E-Mail Works.   To use secure e-mail, you need a public-key encryption program that can generate a *key pair* for you. This pair consists of your public key, which you send to others, and a private key, which you keep on your computer.

Once the key pair has been generated, you can exchange secure e-mail with someone who has also generated a key pair. To send mail to this person, you need that person's public key. You use the public key to encrypt the message, and she decrypts it using her private key. When she sends a message to you, she encrypts it using *your* public key, and you decode it using your private key.

The Authentication Problem.   It's all very well to exchange e-mail securely with someone by means of public-key encryption. But there's one little problem. Suppose you want to send secure e-mail to Mary. But Maureen, a spy, sends you a message that you think has come from Mary. This message includes a public key—but it isn't Mary's.

This is called the *authentication problem,* the problem of not knowing whether somebody's public key is really that person's key or a fake.

To solve this problem, secure e-mail employs *digital signatures.* A digital signature is an encrypted version of the e-mail message's header and text. The signature is encrypted using the sender's private key. This signature can be decoded using the sender's public key. Since the message cannot be properly decoded if it has been altered en route, or encoded with anyone else's key, proper decryption means that the message actually came from the person who ostensibly sent it.

What Public-Key Encryption Software Must Do.   This brief discussion of public-key encryption has probably been enough to persuade you that secure e-mail is a lot more complicated than insecure e-mail. And that's true. Software is required to do the following:

▶ Generate a key pair
▶ Distribute your public key to others
▶ Receive others' public keys
▶ Create a digital signature for your outgoing messages
▶ Decrypt the digital signatures of incoming messages to make sure they are valid
▶ Encrypt an outgoing message with someone else's public key
▶ Decrypt an incoming message with your own private key

Until Pronto Secure came along, the best way to send and receive secure e-mail was to use a DOS package called Pretty Good Privacy (PGP), but it is horrendously inconvenient and difficult to use—you have to prepare your e-mail message in an e-mail program, and then switch to PGP (in DOS) to encrypt it. Along the way, you have to learn legions of hard-to-remember commands. It's a small wonder that so few people outside the computer hacking community have taken advantage of secure mail.

Basically, what Pronto Secure does is to provide an easy-to-use interface to Pretty Good Privacy. This ensures not only that secure mail is easy to use, but also that you can exchange secure e-mail with anyone who's using PGP, whether or not they're using it with Pronto Secure.

Let's take a closer look at PGP.

Pretty Good Privacy (PGP)

Pronto Secure makes use of what is generally considered to be the best public-key encryption software around, Pretty Good Privacy.

Pretty Good Privacy (PGP) is a DOS public-key encryption program created by Phil Zimmerman, now CEO of PGP, Inc. Zimmerman wishes to keep the DOS version of PGP in the public domain, and you can easily download it from the Internet. This book's CD-ROM does not include a copy of PGP due to U.S. export restrictions. You'll need to obtain a copy of PGP. For more information, see Appendix A.

Relationship between PGP and Pronto Secure. You can think of Pronto Secure as a user-friendly front end for PGP, and an all-around useful e-mail program. Pronto Secure has all the features you've come to expect from a quality e-mail program, such as attachments and filtering rules. (You'll learn more about these features later in this chapter.)

Pronto Secure makes the use of PGP virtually automatic. You don't have to run PGP from the DOS prompt or memorize any of its difficult commands. In fact, you won't even have to unzip or install PGP. Pronto Secure takes care of everything for you.

Obtaining and Installing Pronto Secure

Pronto Secure is an e-mail program that uses PGP to add security to your electronic mail. In this section, you'll learn how to obtain and install Pronto Secure.

Obtaining Pronto Secure. To get your copy of Pronto Secure, access www.commtouch.com, and follow the links to the download area. The 30-day evaluation version of the program is fully functional, enabling you to explore all the security features discussed in this chapter.

Download Pronto Secure to a temporary directory on your hard drive, such as c:\temp.

Installing PGP. To run Pronto Secure, you must have a copy of PGP on your hard drive. For information on obtaining PGP, see Appendix A.

CAUTION   **After you have downloaded the PGP software, *do not install it or decompress it*. Simply place the compressed file in a directory called c:\pgp.**

To install Pronto Secure, do the following:

1. Use My Computer or Windows Explorer to open the temporary directory, to which you downloaded Pronto Secure from the Internet.
2. Double-click the Pronto Secure self-extracting archive. The latest version at this writing is called psecv113.exe.

3. Follow the on-screen instructions. If the installation program is unable to locate the PGP file, you may need to type PGP's directory.

Registering Pronto Secure.   Pronto Secure is distributed as a 30-day evaluation program. You will not be able to continue using the program past the 30-day limit unless you register the program. Currently, the program registration fee is $99.

   To register Pronto Secure, do the following: Call 408-245-8682 and order a copy of Pronto Secure with your credit card. You'll be given a registration number that enables you to unlock the software.

Running Pronto Secure for the First Time

To start Pronto Secure for the first time, choose Start Programs Pronto Secure, and choose Pronto Secure from the pop-up menu. Because this is the first time you are running Pronto Secure, you'll see the Mailbox Settings dialog box, which asks you to provide information that the program needs (see Figure 18.1).

Using the Mailbox Settings Dialog Box.   To provide the information required by the Mailbox Settings dialog box, do the following:

1. In the Host Login box, type your e-mail user name. Normally, this is the first part of your e-mail address (the part before the @ sign).
2. In the Password box, type your e-mail password, or leave this blank so that Pronto Secure will prompt you for your password.
3. In the Mail Server box, type the Internet address of your POP3 mail server. If you're not sure what this is, give your Internet service provider a buzz.
4. In the Name and Title box, type your name and optionally your job title.
5. In the SMTP server box, type the Internet address of the computer that's used to send your mail, if this differs from the computer that houses your POP3 server. Leave this box blank if the address is the same as the POP3 server's—which is usually the case.
6. In the Return Address box, type your e-mail address, but only if your POP3 and SMTP server are different. Normally, they aren't.
7. Click OK to continue setting up Pronto Secure.

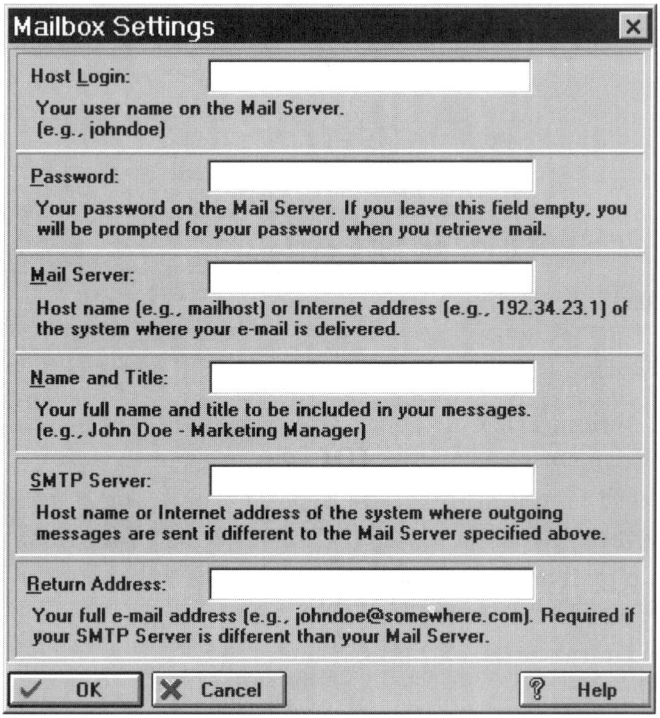

FIGURE 18.1   The Mailbox Settings dialog box asks for information needed to connect Pronto Secure to your mail server.

Creating Your Private Key.   After you finish filling out the Mailbox Settings dialog box, Pronto Secure searches PGP's directory to see whether you have used the program to create a private key. If you have followed this chapter's instructions, you haven't, so the program prompts you to create one in the Setup Private Key dialog box (see Figure 18.2). To set up your private key, follow these instructions:

1.   Choose Generate New Private Key, and click OK. Pronto Secure runs PGP, and you'll see a DOS dialog box, shown in Figure 18.3. In the DOS dialog box, you'll choose the length of the private key you want to use. The longer the key, the better the security. The first option, 412 bits, gives low, commercial-grade security, which is fast but less secure than the other options. The second grade, 768, gives medium speed and good security. The

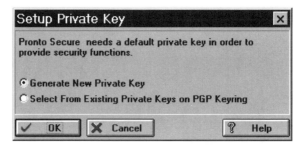

FIGURE 18.2   Pronto Secure prompts you to set up a new private key.

final option, 1,024 bits, gives military-grade security, but it's slow. I chose
the second grade.

2. To select your security grade, type 1, 2, or 3, and press Enter.
3. Now you must enter a user ID. This should be your name followed by
   your e-mail address in angle brackets, such as the following:
   Mary North <mnorth@mendocino.net>
   Type your user ID, and press Enter.

FIGURE 18.3   Generating your keys.

4. Now you must enter a password phrase. You can use the random password generation software discussed in Chapter 9 to do this. Just be sure to create a password with at least ten characters. For maximum security, create a *passphrase*, a series of two or more randomly generated passwords that is at least 30 characters in length. Please be sure to write this down somewhere so you don't forget it!

5. After entering your password and pressing Enter, you'll be asked to type some text. PGP uses the space between your keystrokes to generate random numbers. After the program has gotten enough input from you, it generates the private key, and you see the Private Key Management dialog box in Pronto Secure (shown in Figure 18.4). In this dialog box, you see your public key's fingerprint (which you can use to verify that your public key is indeed yours and valid) and your User ID.

6. Click OK to continue. You'll see the Passphrase dialog box. I hope you wrote down your password!

7. Type your password or passphrase and click OK.

8. After checking your password, Pronto Secure displays handy tips concerning e-mail security. This is all probably quite meaningless at the moment, so just click OK.

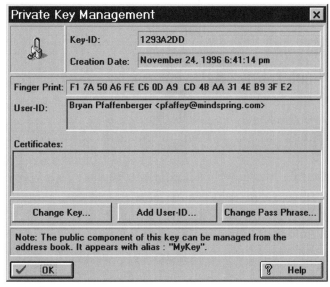

FIGURE **18.4** Looking at your fingerprint.

9. Now you'll see a registration form. Type your name and optionally your company, and click OK. That's that! Now you'll see the Pronto Secure window.

You're ready to begin your adventure in secure e-mail! In the next section, you learn how to use Pronto Secure.

Learning Pronto Secure's Interface

In this section, you'll learn the basics of Pronto Secure's interface, which I'll run through pretty fast. I'm assuming you've used an e-mail program before, and you just need to learn how to use Pronto Secure's special features.

The Toolbar.   Pronto Secure gets a lot of criticism due to the fact that its default window doesn't show all the tools on the toolbar—including the all-important Send and Receive button. The first thing you should do, therefore, is enlarge the window so that you can see most of what Pronto Secure has to offer.

Here's a quick rundown of what you'll see on the toolbar:

▶ **Compose**—Displays a window that enables you to create a new message.
▶ **Reply**—Replies to the sender of the selected message.
▶ **Reply all**—Replies to all of the senders of the selected message.
▶ **Forward**—Forwards the selected message to someone.
▶ **Address Book**—Opens the address book.
▶ **Security Errors Log**—Opens the Security Log dialog box, which records security-related events. If there's something here that needs your attention, this button flashes with a cute, little, red skull-and-crossbones icon.
▶ **Copy**—Copies the selected message to another folder.
▶ **Move**—Moves the selected message to another folder.
▶ **Open Folder**—Opens the selected folder.
▶ **Delete Message**—Deletes the selected message by moving it to the Wastebasket.

- ▶ **American Speller**—Checks spelling using the default dictionary (American English).
- ▶ **Print Message**—Prints the selected message.
- ▶ **Send & Receive Mail**—Sends any messages you've created, and checks to see whether any new messages have arrived at the server.
- ▶ **Cut**—Cuts the selected text to the Clipboard.
- ▶ **Copy**—Copies the selected text to the Clipboard.
- ▶ **Paste**—Pastes the selection from the Clipboard to the cursor's location.

TIP You can configure the toolbar to work as you please. To do so, choose Setup Toolbar. To add a button to the current toolbar, scroll through the available buttons, and click on the desired button. Click on the Add arrows to add the selected button to the current toolbar.

Understanding the Inbox. Pronto Secure displays your mail in folders. The default folder, Inbox, shows your incoming mail (see Figure 18.5). You see the text of the selected message in the bottom pane. To see whether you have any mail, log on to the Internet, and click the Send and Receive button.

The Inbox displays mail using the following columns, from left to right:

- ▶ **Status**—The icons tell you whether you've read (opened) the message.
- ▶ **Priority**— If someone has sent you an urgent message, you see three exclamation marks (!!!) in this column. A low-priority message has a dash in the priority column. Normal priority messages don't have an icon in this column.
- ▶ **Sender**—The sender's name. You may also see the sender's e-mail address if the sender didn't define a name in his or her e-mail program.
- ▶ **Date**—The date and time the message was sent.
- ▶ **Size**—The message's size, in kilobytes (K).
- ▶ **Security status**—Icons tell you whether a message has been encrypted (a lock icon) or digitally signed (a signature icon). A key denotes a message that contains a public key.
- ▶ **Subject**—The message's subject, if there is one.

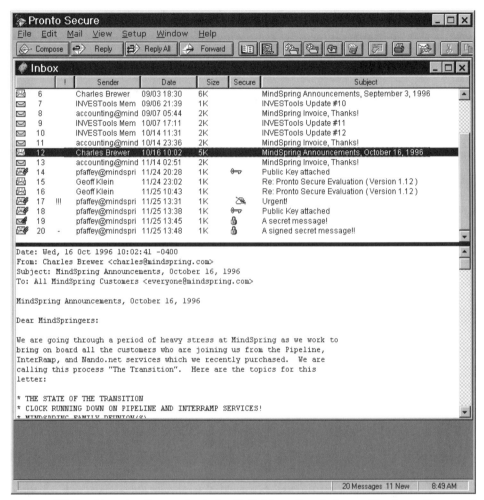

FIGURE 18.5 Pronto Secure's default folder, the Inbox, displays the mail you have received.

TIP You can quickly sort your messages just by clicking the header buttons. To sort your messages by priority, for example, just click the Priority header (the exclamation point).

Understanding Pronto Secure's Folders.

The Inbox is just one of several folders that come with Pronto Secure by default, and you can create additional ones. These folders fall into two categories:

▶ **System Folders**—These are folders that Pronto Secure requires in order to function: Inbox (receives your incoming messages), Outbox (temporarily stores your outgoing messages until they are sent), Sent Log (permanently stores your sent messages), and Wastebasket (stores your deleted messages).

▶ **Custom Folders**—These are folders that you create and name. You can copy or move messages to these folders. You can also write *rules* that automatically move certain messages to these folders, instead of placing them in the Inbox.

Displaying Folders.   To display folders, click Open Folder on the toolbar, or choose File Open Folder. You'll see the Open Folder dialog box, shown in Figure 18.6. To open a folder, just double-click its name.

Once you have opened more than one folder, you can use the Window menu commands to arrange them. You can cascade the windows on-screen, as shown in Figure 18.7, or tile them, as shown in Figure 18.8.

TIP **To help you work with folders, you may wish to display the Folder Manager, which always stays on top of other windows. To display the Folder Manager, choose File Folders. The Folder Manager window looks just like**

FIGURE 18.6   Use this dialog box to open folders.

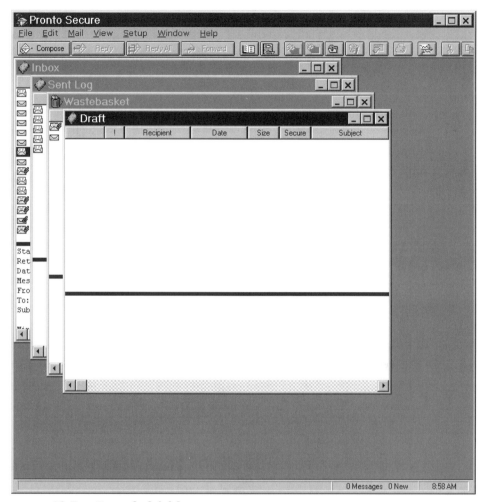

FIGURE **18.7**   Cascaded folders.

the Open Folders dialog box. To open any folder, just double-click its name.

Viewing a Message.   To view a message, just double-click it. You'll see the View window, which displays the message you've just clicked (Figure 18.9).

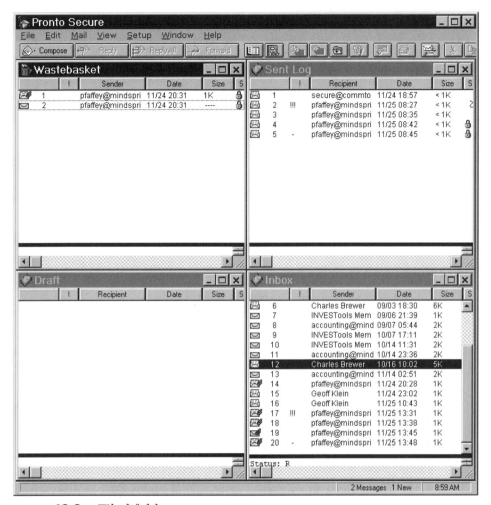

FIGURE 18.8   Tiled folders.

Sending and Replying to Ordinary E-Mail

This section briefly reviews the steps you take to send and receive ordinary (unencrypted) messages with Pronto Secure.

Creating a Signature.   Experienced e-mail users like to add *signatures* to their messages. These differ from the digital signatures discussed earlier in this chapter. A signature includes a few lines of text that includes

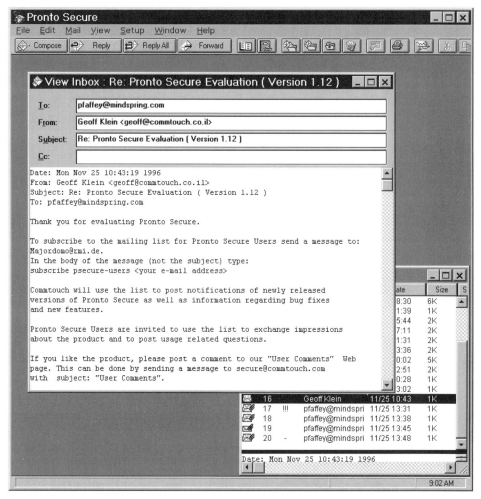

FIGURE 18.9 The View window enables you to read a message, but not to edit it.

the sender's name, e-mail address, organizational affiliation, additional contact information, and perhaps a witty quotation.

To define your signature, choose Setup Signature. You'll see the Signatures dialog box, which enables you to create multiple signatures for different types of messsages. To create a new signature, click New Signature, and type the signature text in the Edit Signature area. In the Current box, give the signature a name. To set the signature as your default signature, click Set as Default. Click OK to exit this dialog box.

Composing a New Message.   To compose a new message, do the following:

1. Click the Compose button. You'll see the Compose window, shown in Figure 18.10.
2. Click the To button to display the Address Book. If your correspondent's name and e-mail adress aren't listed, click Add, type an alias (short nickname) and the e-mail address, and click OK. To add a name to the To, CC

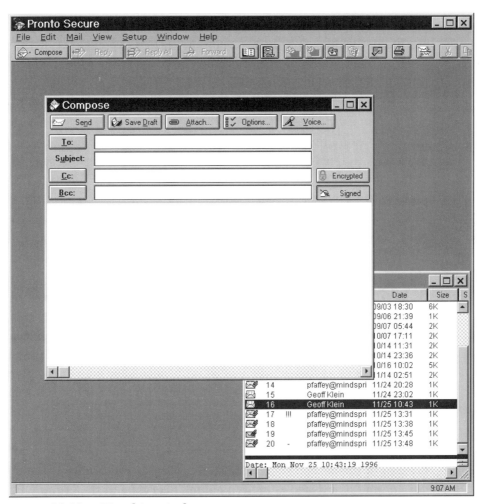

FIGURE **18.10**   Use this window to compose a message.

(carbon copy), or BCC (blind carbon copy) boxes, double-click the name. When you are finished selecting names, click OK to exit the Address Book.

3. In the Subject box, type a subject.

4. In the message area, type your message.

5. Note that Pronto Secure has selected the Signature button by default. This means that every message you send will contain a digital signature, giving the recipient the opportunity to discern whether the message is actually from you.

6. To change the text signature, adjust the message priority, or request receipt confirmation, then click Options. Choose the message options you want in the Options dialog box, and click OK.

7. If you would like to attach a file to this message, click Attach, and select the file in the Select a File to Attach dialog box. After selecting the file, you'll see the Attachment Type dialog box. Select the MIME type for this file (for example, if you're sending a GIF file, type image in the Type box and gif in the subtype box). This will ensure that the recipient will be able to launch the attached files, as long as he or she is using a MIME-compliant e-mail program.

8. If you would like to add a WAV voice recording to your message, click Voice, and start recording. You'll need a sound card and microphone to make use of this feature.

9. To save a draft of this message that you can continue to work on later, click Save Draft.

10. Click Send to send the message.

Replying to Messages.   To reply to a message you have received, select the message and click Reply (to reply to just the sender) or Reply to All (to reply to everyone, including carbon-copy recipients). You'll see a Reply window, like the one shown in Figure 18.11. This is just like the Compose window, and has the same options, with one exception: If you would like to quote the original text, click Original. Pronto Secure adds an angle bracket (>) before each line of quoted text.

CAUTION   Be careful when you choose Reply to All. If one of the addresses in the carbon-copy field is a group alias (an address that enables you to send a message to many people), everyone in the group will receive

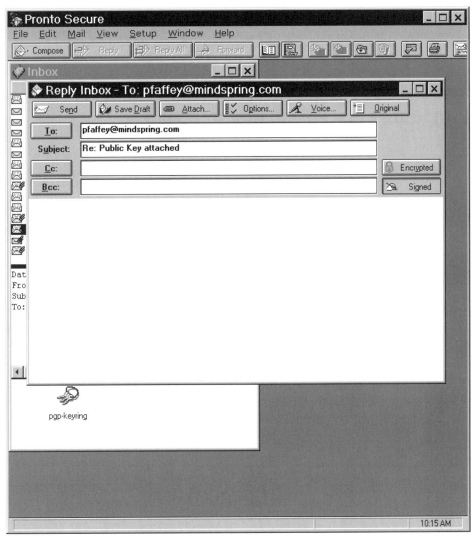

FIGURE **18.11**   Replying to a message.

a copy of your message. If the message matters only to the sender, the other recipients might get angry at you for cluttering their mailboxes. You might also say something of a personal nature that would be inappropriate for the whole group to hear. People have really harmed their reputations this way, so watch out!

Forwarding a Message.   To forward a message to someone, select the message and click Forward. In the To box, select the recipient's address from the Address Book, or type it directly. You can add your own message text if you wish. Click Send to forward the message.

Providing Your Public Key to Others

To get into secure e-mail, you must first distribute your public key to others. Without your public key, they cannot encrypt messages to you.

Distributing Your Public Key to Non-Pronto Secure Users.   If you're corresponding with somebody who isn't using Pronto Secure, you can mail this person your public key. To do so, follow these steps:

1.   Click the Address Book icon to open the Address Book.
2.   In the Address Book, select My Key.
3.   Click Security. You'll see the Public Key Management dialog box, shown in Figure 18.12.
4.   Click Send. You'll see a Compose window.
5.   Choose the recipient's address from the Address Book. If there's no entry for this recipient, create one.
6.   Click Send.

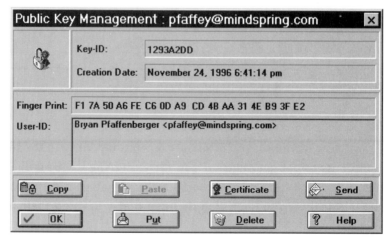

FIGURE 18.12   You can use this dialog box to mail someone your public key.

Publishing Your Public Key on a Public-Key Server.   Another way to make your public key available is to publish this key on a public-key server. A public-key server is a publicly accessible computer service that enables people to search for a person's public key. By default, Pronto Secure publishes your key to pgp-public-keys@pgp.mit.edu. To change this setting, click Setup Security Policy, enter your passphrase, and type a new server name in the PGP Key Server box.

To publish your public key:

1. Click the Address Book icon to open the Address Book.
2. In the Address Book, select My Key.
3. Click Security. You'll see the Public Key Management dialog box, shown in Figure 18.12.
4. Click Put. This sends a message to the server and makes your public key available for searching.

Exchanging Public Keys with Other Pronto Secure Users. The easiest way to send and receive secure e-mail is to correspond with other Pronto Secure users. Pronto Secure enables you to automatically exchange public keys with other Pronto Secure users. To exchange keys with another Pronto Secure user:

1. Click the Address Book icon to open the Address Book.
2. In the Address Book, select the Pronto Secure user's name.
3. Click Security. You'll see the Add Public Key dialog box, shown in Figure 18.13.
4. Click Exchange. You'll see a dialog box informing you that the exchange is about to begin (see Figure 18.14).
5. Click OK.

FIGURE **18.13**   This dialog box gives you several options for public key management.

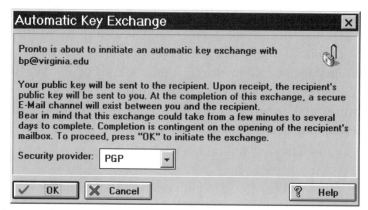

FIGURE **18.14** This dialog box enables you to initiate an automatic key exchange.

After you return to the Address Book, you see an open lock next to this correspondent's name in the Address Book. Once your copy of Pronto Secure has received the reply, a secure channel exists between the two of you, and the lock closes.

TIP Don't expect the lock to close immediately—it all depends on when the recipient opens his or her mail. At that point, the recipient's copy of Pronto Secure responds automatically to your exchange request. When you receive this reply, the transaction is complete. But this may take anywhere from a few minutes to several days, depending on how often you and your recipient check e-mail.

After exchanging public keys with another Pronto Secure user, you can view this individual's public key. Open the Address Book, select this correspondent's name, and click Security. You'll see the Public Key Management dialog box, which gives details about this person's public key.

Getting Keys from Others

If your correspondent is using Pronto Secure, it's easy to get his or her public key: Just initiate a public key exchange, as explained in the previous section. Here, you learn how to obtain a public key from a PGP user who isn't using Pronto Secure.

To obtain a public key from someone who isn't using Pronto Secure:

1. Ask that person to mail his or her public key to you.
2. When the message arrives, double-click the message to display it in a View window. You'll see a PGP keyring icon.
3. Double-click this icon. You'll see the PGP Key Ring Management dialog box, shown in Figure 18.15. In the left panel, click the key you just received, and click the right arrow to add it to your Address Book. If no e-mail address or name is associated with this keyring, you'll see an Add dialog box that prompts you to enter this correspondent's information.
4. Click OK to close the dialog boxes.

After you have added this person's public key to the Address Book entry, you see a lock icon in the Address Book next to this person's name. This indicates that a secure channel has been created.

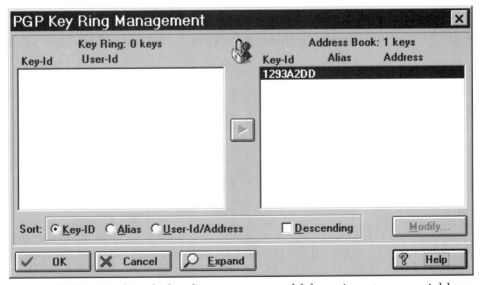

FIGURE 18.15   In this dialog box, you can add key rings to your Address Book.

Sending and Receiving Encrypted Messages

Once you have exchanged public keys with an e-mail recipient, you can send and receive encrypted mail.

Sending Encrypted E-Mail.   Sending encrypted e-mail is just like sending ordinary e-mail; you click the Compose button, choose a recipient from the Address Book, and compose your letter. But there are two changes:

▶ You must select the recipient from the Address Book, and this recipient's entry must have a closed lock icon (indicating that you have his or her public key).
▶ Before you send the message, click the Encrypt button.

That's all you have to do to send encrypted e-mail!

Receiving Encrypted E-Mail.   You'll know when you've received encrypted e-mail, thanks to the lock icon that appears in the Inbox folder. To read the message, just double-click it, and Pronto Secure will decrypt it automatically.

TIP When you receive a message with a digital signature, the signature appears at the bottom of the message, as shown in Figure 18.16.

Ensuring Maximum Security through Certification

Digital certificates and encryption provide excellent protection against intrusions and forgeries, but this protection is not perfect. To make absolutely sure that the public key you have received is the correct one and really originated from the sender, you should call the sender by telephone, or meet with the sender personally, and verify the sender's *fingerprint*. You can then *certify* this public key by attaching your digital signature to it.

Checking Someone's Fingerprint.   A fingerprint is a string of 16 hexadecimal numbers that are generated when somebody creates his or her

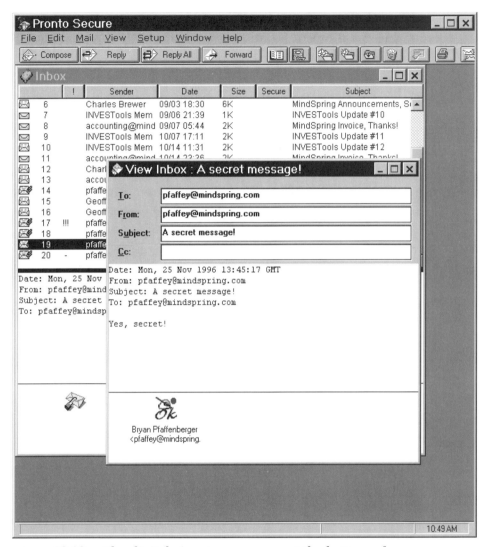

FIGURE 18.16   The digital signature appears at the bottom of a message.

public key. To verify somebody's fingerprint, highlight this person's entry in your Address Book, and click Security. You'll see the Public Key Management dialog box, shown in Figure 18.12. You see the fingerprint in the Finger Print area. Over the phone or in person, read this aloud for verification.

Locating Your Own Fingerprint.   If someone calls you to verify your fingerprint, open the Address Book, click My Key, and click Security. You'll see your fingerprint in the Finger Print area.

Certifying a Public Key.   If you have validated somebody's fingerprint, you can attach a certificate to that person's public key. In effect, this is a public attestation that this public key is valid and in fact comes from the public key's rightful owner.

CAUTION   Do not do this unless you have actually gone through the process of verifying someone's public key by contacting them and making certain that their fingerprint is valid.

To certify a public key, do the following:

1. Select the key owner's name in the Address Book, and click Security. You'll see the Public Key Management dialog box.
2. Click Certificate. You'll see the Certificates dialog box. This dialog box shows the certificates, if any, that have been attached to this key.
3. To certify this key yourself, click Certify. You'll see the Certificate of Authenticity, shown in Figure 18.17.
4. Click Sign to complete the certification. You'll see a DOS PGP window. After adding your certification, you see the certificate in the Certificates dialog box (see Figure 18.18).
5. Click OK to close the Certificates dialog box.

Pronto Secure Horizons

This chapter is intended to get you going with Pronto Secure, and to cover its main features for secure e-mail. There's much more to this program, though. Here's a quick rundown of some features you should explore.

▶ **Preferences**—To choose preferences for handling your mail, displaying windows, and other operating options, choose Setup Preferences.
▶ **Security Policy**—To choose security options, choose Setup Security Policy. You can choose whether to store your messages in encrypted form,

FIGURE 18.17   A certificate enables you to attest to a key's authenticity.

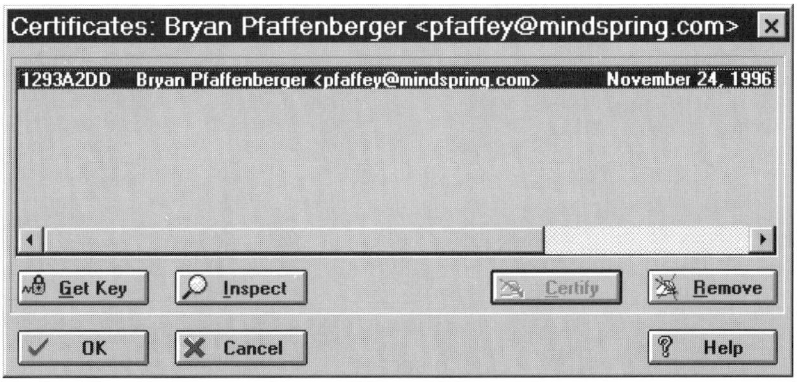

FIGURE 18.18   This dialog box enables you to manage certificates.

when to demand the passphrase, whether to sign messages by default, and whether to enforce certification. The default options are fine for most users.

▶ **Rules**—If you've joined one or more mailing lists, you will certainly want to create custom folders for the messages you receive from these lists. You can also write filtering rules that automatically route these messages to these folders, so they don't clutter up your Inbox. To create rules, choose Setup Rules. Click the Add button to create your first rule. Basically, you tell Pronto Secure to look for text in one or more of the incoming message's fields. Then you specify what should be done with this message.

From Here

With this chapter, you come to the end of *Protect Your Privacy on the Internet*. I hope this book has helped you lower your online profile.

Now that you've learned what's at stake, and what to do about it, won't you please share your knowledge with others? For example, if you know parents who let their kids access the Net, show them the chapters on children's privacy issues. Tell your co-workers that their e-mail isn't as private as they think.

Also, please get involved with one or more of the organizations that are working hard to safeguard our privacy rights in cyberspace. You'll find a guide to these organizations in Appendix B.

APPENDIX A

Locating and Downloading Pretty Good Privacy

Pretty Good Privacy (PGP) is the world standard for encrypted computer communications. The program's author, Phil Zimmerman, is committed to making the DOS version of the software available for free. Although it's difficult to use, several Windows-based interfaces have been developed, including Pronto Secure, the encryption-based e-mail program discusssed in this book. In order to use Pronto Secure, you will need to obtain a copy of the DOS version of PGP. The program could not be included on this book's CD-ROM due to U.S. export restriction laws.

Obtaining PGP on the World Wide Web

You can obtain PGP from the following Web sites:

▶ **http://web.mit.edu/network/pgp-form.html (U.S. PGP primary distribution site)**—You must be a U.S. citizen to download PGP from this site.
▶ **http://www.ifi.uio.no/~staalesc/PGP/home.html (International PGP primary distribution site)**—If you are accessing the Internet from outside the U.S., download PGP from this site.

Obtaining PGP with FTP

Dozens of sites worldwide make PGP available via FTP. For a current list, see "Where to Get PGP" (http://ariel.cs.trinity.edu/Other_Attractions/Getting_PGP.html).

Privacy-Related Organizations and Resources on the Internet

Now that you've read this book, I hope you'll get involved in the efforts underway to safeguard our privacy in cyberspace. Fire up your browser; you'll find that several privacy-related organizations have established Web presence, where you can learn more about these organizations and how to get involved. To learn more about privacy resources on the Web, you can make use of several excellent privacy *trailblazer* pages (Web pages that provide high-quality links pertaining to a specific subject). To keep informed, you can read privacy-related Usenet newsgroups, and subscribe to privacy-related mailing lists.

Privacy-Related Organizations

American Civil Liberties Union (ACLU)

American Civil Liberties Union (ACLU)
132 West 43rd Street
New York, NY 10036
URL: http://www.aclu.org

The American Civil Liberties Union (ACLU), founded in 1920, is the oldest organization devoted to safeguarding the Bill of Rights of the U.S. Constitution. The ACLU has recently turned its attention to cyberspace; check out the Cyberspace Initiative page at http://www.aclu.org/issues/cyber/hmcl.html. Also worth reading regularly is the Cyber-Liberties e-zine

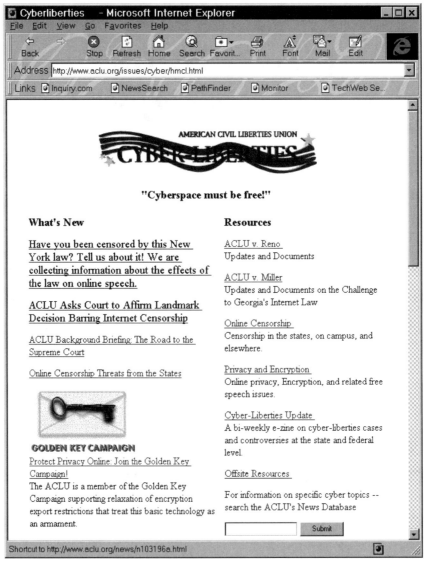

FIGURE B.1   Cyberspace Initiative page (American Civil Liberties Union).

(http://www.aclu.org/issues/cyber/updates.html), which contains weekly bulletins concerning civil liberties in cyberspace (see Figure B.1).

Center for Democracy and Technology

Center for Democracy and Technology
1634 I St. N.W. #1100
Washington, DC 20006
Voice: 202-637-9800
Fax: 202-637-0968
E-mail: info@cdt.org
URL: http://www.cdt.org

Founded in December 1994, the Center for Democracy and Technology (CDT) focuses on developing public policies that preserve and advance democratic values and constitutional civil liberties on the Internet and other interactive communications media. This nonprofit, public-interest organization is supported by a broad spectrum of industrial sponsors, foundations, and individuals.

CDT maintains a Privacy Issues page (Figure B.2), located at http://www.cdt.org/privacy/index.html, that will prove of great interest to this book's readers.

Computer Professionals for Social Responsibility

Computer Professionals for Social Responsibility
P.O Box 717
Palo Alto, CA 94302
Voice: 415-322-3778
Fax: 415-322-4748
E-mail: cpsr@cpsr.org
URL: http://www.cpsr.org

CPSR is an alliance of computer professionals and industrial sponsors who are concerned about the impact of computers on society, including privacy-related issues. Of particular concern to CPSR is the impact of computers on the workplace. The organization offers a draft e-mail and

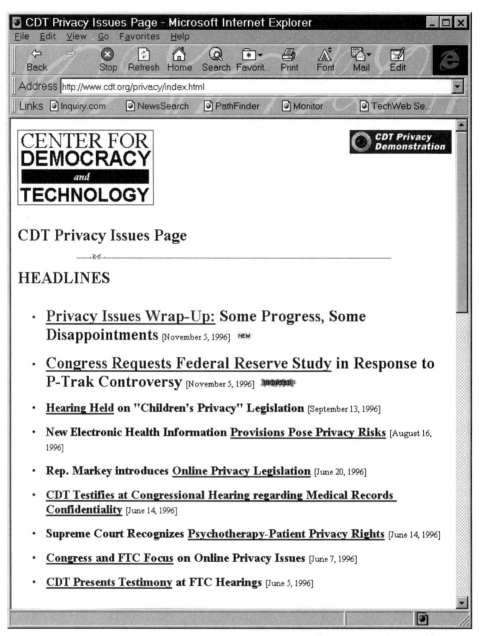

FIGURE B.2 CDT's Privacy Issues page contains information that will prove of interest to this book's readers.

voice-mail policy for employers (http://www.cpsr.org/dox/program/emailpolicy.html).

Electronic Frontier Foundation

Electronic Frontier Foundation
1550 Bryant Street #725
San Francisco, CA 94103
Voice: 415-436-9333
Fax: 415-436-9993
E-mail: eff@eff.org
URL: http://www.eff.org

The Electronic Frontier Foundation is a nonprofit, civil-liberties organization devoted to protecting public freedom in cyberspace. Currently, EFF is focusing on privacy, free expression, and access to public resources and information online. Be sure to visit EFF's What's HOT in Privacy and Surveillance page (http://www.eff.org/pub/Privacy/HTML/hot.html), shown in Figure B.3.

Electronic Privacy Information Center

Electronic Privacy Information Center
666 Pennsylvania Ave. SE #301
Washington, DC 20003
Voice: 202-544-9240
E-mail: info@epic.org
URL: http://www.epic.org

Founded in 1994, EPIC is a public-interest research center in Washington, DC. The organization focuses on emerging civil liberties issues and privacy protection in cyberspace. EPIC works in association with Privacy International, an international human-rights group based in London, UK. EPIC's home page (see Figure B.4) offers fast-breaking news summaries, an online bookstore, and other information resources of interest to this book's readers.

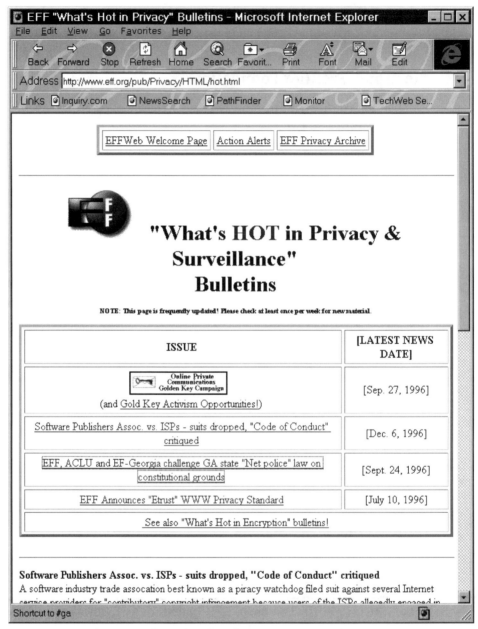

FIGURE B.3 This page lists fast-breaking news stories concerning Internet privacy.

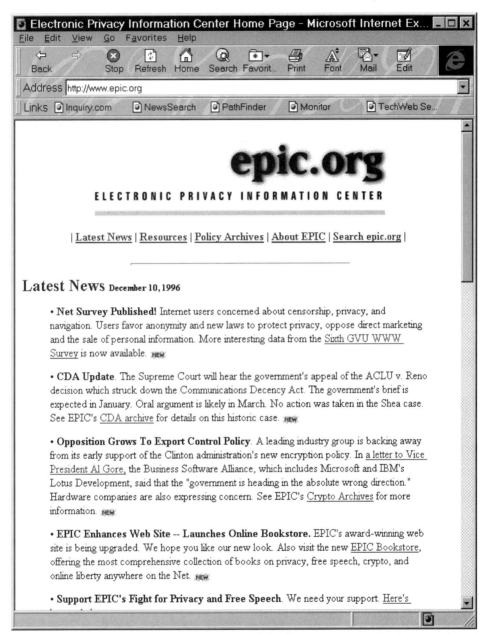

FIGURE B.4 EPIC's home page is one of the best sources of privacy-related information on the Internet.

Internet Privacy Coalition

E-mail: ipc@privacy.org
http://www.privacy.org/ipc/

The mission of the Internet Privacy Coalition is to promote privacy and security on the Internet through widespread public availability of strong encryption, and the relaxation of export controls on cryptography. Founded by a group of leading cryptographers, the organization is sponsored by a number of industry associations, including the American Banking Association, the ACLU, and the American Library Association.

Currently, IPC is sponsoring the Golden Key campaign, an effort to raise public awareness of the need to preserve the right to communicate privately as communications move to electronic media.

National Coalition for Patient Rights

National Coalition for Patient Rights
Suite 218
Lexington, MA 02173
Phone: (617) 433-0114
Fax: (617) 861-0635
URL: http://www.tiac.net/users/gls/cprne.html

The National Coalition for Patient Rights (NCPR) is an organization of health care practitioners and professional health care associations that are concerned with protecting confidentiality in the doctor-patient relationship. The organization's home page has a link to privacy-related issues raised by medical databases.

Privacy Rights Clearinghouse

Privacy Rights Clearinghouse
5998 Alcala Park
San Diego, CA 92110-2492
Telephone: 619-260-4160
Fax: 619-298-5681
Hotline: 619-298-3396

E-mail: prc@acusd.edu
URL: http://pwa.acusd.edu/~prc/

The Privacy Rights Clearinghouse is a San Diego-based consumer rights organization that focuses on general privacy rights. Of interest to beginning Internet users are the Fact Sheets (in both English and Spanish) concerning privacy in cyberspace. Note: This organization is no longer affiliated with the University of California, San Diego, and the site will have moved by the time you attempt to access the above URL. There should be a page that links to the new location.

Privacy Trailblazer Pages

Bacard's Privacy Page

URL: http://www.well.com/user/abacard/

Andre Bacard, author of *Computer Privacy Handbook* (Peachpit Press, 1995), maintains a useful privacy page with links to privacy resources and organizations on the Internet. There's also a copy of his interesting interview in *Playboy*.

Cryptography, PGP, and Your Privacy

URL: http://world.std.com/~franl/crypto.html

Maintained by Francis Litterio, this excellent Virtual Library page (Figure B.5) focuses on advanced cryptography, Phil Zimmerman's PGP software, and related privacy issues in cyberspace.

HotWired Privacy Archive

URL: http://www.hotwired.com/Lib/Privacy/

This is a don't-miss site. You'll find links to full text articles pertaining to computer privacy and related issues in *Wired* magazine, as well as news reports and press releases.

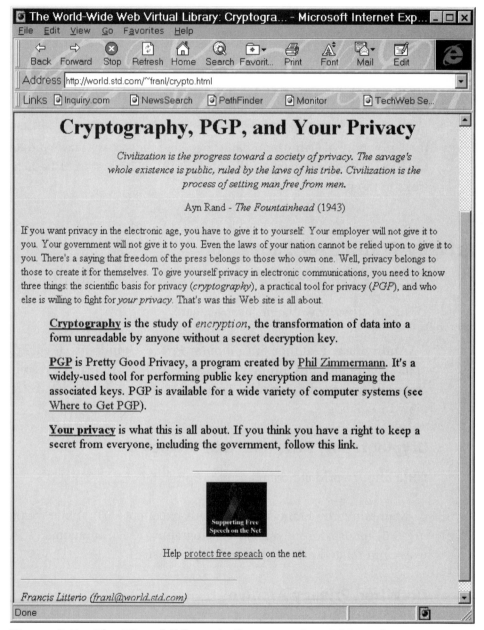

Figure B.5 The Virtual Library's Cryptography, PGP, and Your Privacy page is the place to start if you're interested in encrypted mail.

The Privacy Pages

URL: http://www.2020tech.com/maildrop/privacy.html

A good compilation of links concerning Usenet, Pretty Good Privacy (PGP), encryption, computer security, PGP-related software, hackers, phreakers, software piracy, anonymous remailers, privacy invasions, and privacy organizations.

Privacy-Related Newsgroups

Usenet newsgroups are of two kinds, *moderated* and *unmoderated.* In moderated newgroups, a human moderater screens the messages to make sure they conform to the newsgroup's mission. Unmoderated newsgroups can make for interesting reading, but they're filled with off-topic posts, inappropriate advertising, pranks, and pathetic pleas for help from new Internet users.

alt.privacy.   This newsgroup focuses on privacy issues in cyberspace. It's an unmoderated newsgroup; you'll find some interesting discussion mixed with posts from the lunatic/paranoid fringe.

alt.privacy.anon-server.   Focusing on anonymous remailers, this newsgroup contains discussion and news about anonymous remailer services. If you're having trouble finding an anonymous remailer, this is a good place to look.

alt.privacy.clipper.   This newsgroup focuses on the Clinton Administration's repeated proposals to insert a chip into digital communication devices. The chip, dubbed the Clipper chip, would enable investigators to decode encrypted communications. An earlier Clipper proposal was discredited when it was found to be easily circumvented, but a new proposal (Clipper II) has been made.

alt.privacy.private-investigator.   This newsgroup is well worth reading if you'd like to know more about the mindset, technologies, and strategies of private investigators, who are increasingly using the Internet as a low-cost means of tracking people down.

comp.org.cpsr.announce.   This moderated newsgroup is used for bulletins and newsletters from Computer Professionals for Social Responsibility (CPSR).

comp.org.cpsr.talk.   This newsgroup contains unmoderated discussion of issues related to the Computer Professionals for Social Responsibility. Topics include privacy, the National Information Infrastructure (NII), telecommunications reform, and social implications of technology.

comp.org.eff.news.   This moderated newsgroup contains news from the Electronic Frontier Foundation (EFF).

comp.org.eff.talk.   This newsgroup includes unmoderated discussion concerning the EFF's goals, strategies, and issues.

comp.risks.   This is the newsgroup version of the RISKS Digest, a moderated mailing list concerned with the risks of computer use (including privacy risks). High-quality and interesting discussion is the rule.

comp.society.privacy.   One of the few privacy-related Usenet newsgroups worth reading on a regular basis, comp.society.privacy is a moderated newsgroup focusing on the effects of technology on privacy. This newsgroup contains the same content as the Computer Privacy Digest mailing list, described later in this appendix.

Privacy-Related Mailing Lists

Numerous mailing lists concerning privacy can be found on the Internet. To subscribe to one of these mailing lists, send e-mail to the list's administrative address. (This address differs from the address to which you address contributions to the list itself.) After you subscribe, you will receive an information mailing, which includes instructions on unsubscribing. *Please save this information.* Never send subscribe or unsubscribe requests to the list address!

Note that mailing lists are managed and distributed in different ways. In *moderated* mailing lists, a human moderator scrutinizes each submission to ensure that it conforms to the list's topic areas and mission. Moderated mailing lists contain less extraneous material than unmoderated ones. Some moderated mailing lists do not accept public submissions; they are used to distribute news bulletins. Whether moderated or not, some mailing lists are distributed as *digests* (a compilation of messages distributed as a single message). Digests reduce clutter in your mailbox.

ACLU Cyber-Liberties Update. The American Civil Liberties Union (ACLU) publishes the ACLU Cyber-Liberties Update, a biweekly newsletter. To subscribe to the ACLU Cyber-Liberties Update, send a message to majordomo@aclu.org. Type subscribe Cyber-Liberties in the body of the message.

Computer Privacy Digest. This moderated mailing list focuses on privacy issues connected with computing. To subscribe, send e-mail to comp-privacy-request@uwm.edu. In the body of the message, type subscribe. Back issues are available at gopher://gopher.cs.uwm.edu, as well as ftp://ftp.cs.uwm.edu/pub/comp-privacy/.

Computer Underground Digest. This weekly moderated digest focuses on the underworld of computing, including rebel crytographers (cypherpunks), hackers, and phone phreaks. To subscribe, send e-mail to cu-digest-request@weber.ucsd.ede. In the subject header, type subscribe cu-digest. You'll find back issues at http://www.soci.niu.edu/~cudigest.

CPSR Announce. CPSR (Computer Professionals for Social Responsibility) publishes a moderated mailing list that includes Telecom Report and other CPSR newsletters and releases. To subscribe, send e-mail to list-serv@cpsr.org. In the body of the message, type subscribe cpsr-announce.

Cypherpunks. This unmoderated mailing list features discussion of cryptography and technical protections of privacy. It is not distributed in a digest form, and has high volume. Don't subscribe unless you're very interested in this subject and prepared to handle as many as 100 messages per day. To subscribe, send e-mail to majordomo@toad.com. In the body of the message, type subscribe cypherpunks.

EPIC Alert.   The Electronic Privacy Information Center publishes a bi-weekly news bulletin called EPIC Alert. To subscribe, send e-mail to epic-news@epic.org. In the *subject header* of your message, type subscribe. You can read back issues at http://www.epic.org/alert/.

eTRUST Mailing List.   eTRUST is an organization dedicated to promoting public confidence in the Web by certifying the privacy level of Web sites. To join the eTRUST mailing list, access http://www.etrust.org/06talk.html and fill out the form.

IPC Alert.   The International Privacy Council's IPC Alert mailing list distributes information and news bulletins concerning cryptographic policy and the Golden Key campaign. To subscribe, send e-mail to ipc-announce@privacy.org. Include the phrase, subscribe ipc-announce, in the message body. Note that traffic will be light—this is for IPC Alerts and special posts. If you would like to unsubscribe at any time, send e-mail to ipc-announce@privacy.org with the phrase, unsubscribe ipc-announce.

PRIVACY Forum.   The PRIVACY Forum, probably the best mailing list concerning general privacy issues, is published by means of a moderated digest (a single mailing every few days). To subscribe, send a message to privacy-request@vortex.com or listserv@vortex.com, with a line in the body of the message of the form, subscribe privacy <your full name>, where <your full name> is your actual name, not your e-mail address (your e-mail address is determined automatically by listserv). Also please note that the subscribe command must be in the body of your message, not in the "Subject:" field; the "Subject:" field of all messages to listserv is ignored. To unsubscribe from the PRIVACY Forum mailing list, follow the same procedure as given previously for individual subscriptions, but send the command, unsubscribe privacy, in the body of your message instead of the subscribe command.

Pronto Secure.   If you would like to get the most out of Pronto Secure, the secure e-mail program discussed in this book, subscribe to the Pronto Secure Users mailing list by sending e-mail to majordomo@rmi.de. In the body of the message (not the subject) type subscribe psecure-users <your e-mail address>. Commtouch will use the list to post notifications of newly released versions of Pronto Secure, as well as information regarding bug fixes and new features.

RISKS Digest.   This moderated mailing list, distributed as a digest, focuses on the risks of using computers, including privacy risks. To subscribe, send e-mail to risks-request@csl.sri.com. In the body of the message, type subscribe. Back issues are available at unix.sri.com /risks/.

APPENDIX C

What's on the CD-ROM

In Part II of this book, you learn how to get technology on your side—specifically, how to use advanced Windows software to secure your computer against unauthorized snooping and safeguard your privacy online. These programs are easy to install and use, and you'll find full instructions for their use in the Part II chapters.

NOTE Although some of these programs run on Windows 3.1 or Windows NT, this software collection is designed for Windows 95 users.

Programs Included on the CD-ROM

The following programs are included on this book's CD-ROM and fully discussed in Part II.

AMSD Ariadna. This freeware browser has many of the features of Netscape and Internet Explorer, including tables, bookmarks, and Java. What it doesn't have is the ability to receive, store, and upload cookies, which can compromise your privacy. If you're concerned about the privacy implications of cookies, you can use Ariadna as your default browser. Ariadna requires Windows 95.

Cyber Patrol.   This is one of several programs that protect kids from adult content while they're using the Internet. Unlike the others, it contains a utility that protects kids' privacy online. Called CyberChat, it prevents them from uploading personal information about themselves. This is an indispensable program if you let your kids access the Internet. On the disk is a fully functional evaluation version of the program; registration is $29.95. Cyber Patrol requires Windows 95.

IEClean.   Included is a demonstration version of this indispensable utility, which cleans up Internet Explorer's trails on your computer so that snoops can't tell what you've been doing online. IEClean requires Windows 95.

IE-KILL.BAT.   This freeware batch file (for Windows 3.1 and Windows 95 systems) automatically deletes your Internet Explorer cookies at the beginning of each operating session. This effectively prevents sites from setting up long-term tracking, while enabling certain legitimate cookie uses during the current operating session.

Mutilate.   This Windows 95 shareware utility provides an easy-to-use interface to DOS file wiping programs (including ZAPFILE and PGP). This program can be used to ensure that deleted files cannot be recovered through "undelete" techniques. Included on the disk is a fully functional evaluation version of the program; registration is $15.

NSClean.   Included is a demonstration version of this indispensable shareware utility, which cleans up Netscape's trails on your computer so that snoops can't tell what you've been doing online. NSClean requires Windows 95.

NS-KILL.BAT.   Like IE-KILL.BAT, this public domain batch file (for Windows 3.1 and Windows 95) automatically deletes your Netscape cookies at the beginning of each operating session.

Password Book.   This convenient application gives you a way to store the passwords you use for private computer and Internet usage. It's shareware (registration is $15). Password Book will run on Windows 3.1 and Windows 95 systems.

Random Password Generator. This shareware program can generate up to 1,000,000 random passwords, which help protect you against unauthorized access to your Internet account. Random Password Generator runs on Windows 3.1 and Windows 95 systems. The registration fee is $15.

TSS PGPWord. A free evaluation version of TSS PGPWord, which enhances Microsoft Word for Windows 95 (version 7) so that you can automatically encrypt or decrypt documents when you close and open them. The evaluation version will encrypt documents up to one page in length, and it can decrypt documents of any size. You can upgrade to the full version of TSS PGPWord for $19.95.

Pronto96. This book discusses Pronto Secure, which couldn't be included on the CD-ROM due to U.S. export restrictions. However, you'll find a fully functional evaluation version of the same company's Pronto96, an award-winning e-mail program that shares much of Pronto Secure's interface. Pronto96 requires Windows 95.

Win–Secure–It. This excellent Windows 95 shareware utility enables you to secure your system against unauthorized use, which could compromise your privacy. A "stealth mode" gives you a way to tell whether someone is accessing your system while you're away from your desk. A fully functional evaluation version is included; registration is $27.

WinVN. This public domain newsreader is packed with features — and what's more, it gives you the ability to post semi-anonymously and to modify message headers so that Usenet search engines don't archive your posts. Included is the Windows 95 version of WinVN.

WinZip v6.2. This wonderful utility developed by Nico Mak Computing, Inc. runs on Windows 95 and Windows NT, providing compression and decompression of zip file formats. An evaluation version is included.

ZAPFILE. This suite of freeware DOS utilities provides secure file-wiping capabilities for Windows 3.1 and Windows 95 systems. Mutiliate provides a Windows interface to ZAPFILE.

Additional Programs Discussed in This Book

Due to U.S. export restrictions (which define encryption-enabled programs as "munitions"), this book's CD-ROM does not include several of the discussed programs. However, you can easily download these programs from the Internet.

Cryptext.   This freeware utility modifies Windows 95 so that file encryption and decryption commands appear on Windows 95's pop-up menus (in My Computer and Windows Explorer). You can obtain Cryptext from many online sources, such as Shareware.com (www.shareware.com), Tucows (www.tucows.com), or the program's home page (www.pcug.org. au/~njpayne/).

Pretty Good Privacy (PGP).   This freeware DOS utility provides public-key encryption capabilities for Mutilate, TSS PGPWord, and Pronto Secure. You don't have to run PGP from DOS or learn any of its commands; these programs provide a Windows "front end" for PGP's amazing capabilities. However, you do need to download and install PGP on your computer. PGP is widely available and won't cost you a cent. For more information on obtaining PGP, see Appendix A.

Pronto Secure.   This excellent e-mail program enables you to send and receive encrypted e-mail without getting into all the mysteries of PGP. A Windows 95 program, it makes use of PGP, which runs in the background, invisibly. To download your free evaluation copy of Pronto Secure, access Commtouch Software's home page (www.commtouch.com), and follow the links to the download area.

Understanding Public Domain Software, Freeware, and Shareware

Public domain software has been made available for public use with no restrictions whatsoever. You may do anything you like with a public domain program, including modifying it or giving it to others.

Freeware is software that is freely distributed by disk, through BBS systems, and the Internet. There is no charge for using it, and can be distributed freely as long as the use it is put to follows the license agreement included with it. Note that most freeware authors expressly prohibit the resale of their programs for commercial purposes.

Shareware (also known as user supported software) is a revolutionary means of distributing software created by individuals or companies too small to make inroads into the more conventional retail distribution networks. The authors of Shareware retain all rights to the software under the copyright laws while still allowing free distribution. This gives the user the chance to freely obtain and try out software to see if it fits his needs. Shareware should not be confused with Public Domain software even though they are often obtained from the same sources.

If you continue to use Shareware after trying it out, you are expected to register your use with the author and pay a registration fee. What you get in return depends on the author, but may include a printed manual, free updates, telephone support, etc.

Hardware Requirements

This book's software collection is designed for users of Windows 95, although some of the programs will run on Windows NT or Windows 3.1 systems. In general, your system should be equipped with a minimum of 8 MB of RAM, and you will need approximately 75MB of hard disk space to install all the software contained on the CD-ROM.

Installing the Software

The enclosed CD-ROM contains several folders, within which are stored the setup utilities for the various programs included with this book. For specific instructions on installing the software, please see the relevant chapter. For example, Chapter 10 shows you how to install Win-Secure-It.

NOTE There's no SETUP program for the entire CD-ROM. If you insert the CD-ROM into your CD-ROM drive and type SETUP, you'll get an error message. You must install each program individually, following the instructions given in the relevant chapter.

Using the Software

The chapters in Part II, "Get technology on your side," explain how to use all the software included on the CD-ROM.

User Assistance and Information

Please note that the author does not have the resources to provide technical support for the software included with this book. To receive technical support for the shareware programs on this book's CD-ROM, please register your software. This entitles you to technical support from the software's author.

The software accompanying this book is being provided as is without warranty or support of any kind. Should you require basic installation assistance, or if your media is defective, please call our product support number at (212) 850-6194 weekdays between 9 A.M. and 4 P.M. Eastern Standard Time. Or, we can be reached via e-mail at: **wprtusw@jwiley.com**.

To place additional orders or to request information about other Wiley products, please call (800) 879-4539.

Index

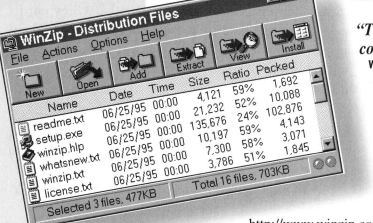

Using the Software

This software contains files to help you utilize the models described in the accompanying book. By opening the package, you are agreeing to be bound by the following agreement:

WILEY